Letter to My Father

A Memoir

G. Thomas Couser

Hamilton Books

Lanham • Boulder • New York • Toronto • Plymouth, UK

Copyright © 2017 by Hamilton Books
4501 Forbes Boulevard, Suite 200, Lanham, Maryland 20706
Hamilton Books Acquisitions Department (301) 459-3366

Unit A, Whitacre Mews, 26-34 Stannary Street,
London SE11 4AB, United Kingdom

Library of Congress Control Number: 2017944076
ISBN: 978-0-7618-6958-0 (pbk : alk. paper)—ISBN: 978-0-7618-6959-7 (electronic)

To my mother, Ann Van Stelten Couser (1909-1974),
who made it all possible

Death ends a life . . . but it does not end a relationship,
which struggles on in the survivor's mind . . .
toward some resolution, which it never finds.
—Robert Anderson, *I Never Sang for My Father*

Contents

List of Figures

Acknowledgments

This personal project has taken far longer to research and write than any of my academic books; moreover, it has taken a different kind of commitment and emotional investment.

In the process I have been very lucky to have had encouragement, assistance, and advice from a large number of friends, relatives, colleagues, and students. Over the years, the following have read parts (or even all) of the manuscript (my prized "first responders") or otherwise encouraged me: Rachel Adams, William Andrews, John Barbour, Sergio Barcellos, Maria Barton, Nick Barton, Kenneth Bleeth, Lynda Bogel, John Bryant, Ginny Bryant, Leonard Cassuto, Holly Chase, Richard Cohen, Judy Conley, Kay Cook, Bill Couser, Grif Couser, Ken Couser, Shirley Couser, Christine Crosby, Linda Davidson, Lennard Davis, Carol DeBoer-Langworthy, Beth Donaldson, Paul John Eakin, Judy Ford, Richard Freadman, Margaret Gibson, Vesna Goldsworthy, Robert Hasserjian, Russ Harrison, Marcel Herbst, Emily Hipchen, Patti Horvath, Craig Howes, Margaret Jackson, Meg Jensen, Margaretta Jolly, Irene Kacandes, Georgina Kleege, Taki Koudsi, Nathaniel Lachenmeyer, Thomas Larson, Christopher Leise, Joanne Limburg, Stephen Mansfield, Lance Mayer, Maureen McCabe, John Mergendoller, Janis Mink, Susannah Mintz, Chris Morehouse, Nelly Murstein, Gay Myers, Jill Nash, Sharon O'Brien, Brendan O'Neill, the late David Parker, James Payne, Maureen Perkins, Roger Porter, Julie Rivkin, Connie Roberts, Julian Ross, the late Keith Ross, Lauren Ross, Ralph Savarese, Ellen Seale, Barbara Sherman, John Sherman, Rachel Simon, Monica Soeting, Willard Spiegelman, Tom Smith, Carol Steen, Leslie Swartz, Kristen Thomas, Linda Visscher, Pieter Visscher, Julia Watson, Mel B. Yoken, Grace Zabel, and Lee Zimmerman. Many more encouraged me by listening and responding to talks I've given over the years the manuscript was in process.

Special thanks to Kristen Thomas and her sisters for permission to quote the letters of their grandmother, Rosalind Parker; to my cousins Jay Couser, Libby Collins, and Susan Farkas for permission to quote their father's letters to their mother; my cousin Judy (Neubert) Conley for permission to quote her email; and Dr. Robert Parseghian for the photo of his father's class at Aleppo Boys High School.

My sister Jane Griffith has been an engaged audience from the beginning of the process. We share a father—William Griffith Couser was her father before he was mine—but her story is her own.

Finally, I owe most to Barbara Zabel, who has given me a home (and a family of in-laws) that has helped to make up for the loss of my parents before she and I met. I regret, as she does, that they never knew each other.

In addition I am grateful to the following for assistance with research: the staffs of the Manchester (NH) Public Library, the Manchester Historic Association, the Concord (NH) Public Library, and the cemetery registrar of Concord.

An earlier version of chapter 8, "In Aleppo Once," appeared in *Life Writing Annual* (2008) published by AMS Press.

And grateful acknowledgment for permission to reprint the following:

Excerpt from *I Never Sang for My Father* by Robert Anderson, copyright ©1968. Used by permission of Samuel French.

Excerpt(s) from *Death of a Salesman,* by Arthur Miller, copyright 1949, renewed © 1977 by Arthur Miller. Used by permission of Viking Books, an imprint of Penguin Publishing Group, a division of Penguin Random House LLC. All rights reserved.

Excerpt from *All That Is,* by James Salter, copyright © 2013 by James Salter. Used by permission of Alfred A. Knopf, an imprint of the Knopf Doubleday Publishing Group, a division of Penguin Random House LLC. All rights reserved.

Excerpt from *A Backward Glance,* by Edith Wharton, copyright © 1934, used by permission of Watkins Loomis Agency.

Prologue

In My Father's Closet: Life, Death, and Letters

When I was 23, I killed my father—with a letter.

Not literally, of course. This is not a confession—at least not of a criminal act.

In the summer of 1969, I returned to my home in Melrose, Massachusetts, from Oxford, England, where I'd spent the year doing graduate work in English. I was stunned to learn one day, quite by accident, that my hitherto well-behaved father, a respected high school English teacher, had begun to drink secretly, to a degree that imperiled his job, his marriage, and his health. That fall, from a New Hampshire prep school where I was teaching, I sent him a long letter confronting him about his drinking and reflecting on our relationship, which had been severely damaged by this revelation. I intended it as a kind of long-distance intervention—an attempt to get him to acknowledge the seriousness of his situation and to change his ways. I felt I could express on paper things I would have difficulty saying face to face. I hoped my letter might initiate a healing dialogue between us.

Whatever my intentions, the letter proved counterproductive. Dad was devastated by it. Or so my mother told me; he declined to discuss it with me. So instead of initiating dialogue, I foreclosed it. Worse than that, I further damaged our relationship. I came to regret writing it.

～

Five years later, in November of 1974, my mother died from ovarian cancer at the age of sixty-five. Eight months after that, Dad died of drink and depression at the age of sixty-nine. At that time, I feared my letter might have accelerated his decline by undermining his self-esteem. I regarded it as toxic, if not fatal.

That summer I gradually emptied the house in which I had grown up and prepared it for sale. Doing so compounded my grief. Having lost both parents in quick succession, I had to purge our home of the material traces of our family life, leaving it an empty, echoing shell. The only consolation in this dispiriting process was my discovery of a trove of personal documents in a closet behind Dad's bed. From a quick perusal I learned things I hadn't known, or even suspected, about him:

- In his thirties he had earned a private pilot's license.
- Before he met my mother, he had had a decade-long romantic relationship with a woman named Rody.
- At the same time, he was in love with his best friend's sister, who was married and the mother of a small boy.
- That best friend—and sometime roommate—was probably gay.
- His two other closest male friends in his twenties and early thirties were also evidently gay.
- In the summer of 1941, only months before he married, he had looked into joining the Royal Canadian Air Force.
- Immediately after his discharge from the Navy at the end of World War II, he had applied to join the FBI.
- In the early 1950s, he had applied for a job with the CIA.

His archive, as I came to think of it, disclosed much more than these discrete facts about him. The quantity and quality of the personal correspondence revealed that he had lived a good deal of his early life in, or through, letters. An adventurous three-year stint teaching English in Aleppo, Syria, generated letters to various parties—his family, his close friends, and his church. His military service in the South Pacific at the end of World War II produced letters to my mother. He was a fine writer, and he cultivated friends who took pleasure and care in writing. It was no accident that he saved so many letters: he and his friends, male and female, took correspondence very seriously. He may have been most intensely alive when he wrote his letters; he certainly is most alive to me when I read them.

~

Not all of the letters in the archive were new to me, however. Among them was that lethal letter I had written him six years earlier. I recognized it right away; though yellowed with age, the Eaton's Corrasable Bond™ paper retained its crinkly feel and glossy surface. But I was shocked to find it. Given his inability, or refusal, to respond to it in any way, I presumed Dad had long since disposed of it. His retaining it suggested that he may have valued the impulse behind it, even if he found my words painful. Nevertheless, when I discovered it, I was unable to read it, fearful of the guilt it might trigger, a kind of toxic blowback.

After sorting the documents, I placed them in a carton and sealed it. That carton accompanied me through several moves. When I settled in the house I still occupy, I stored it in the attic, where it would be out of sight and, hopefully, out of mind.

I did not touch that box for more than thirty years.

~

As I approached the age of sixty, however, I was keenly aware that I was nearing the age at which my father had fallen into a deep, lasting, and ultimately fatal depression. Fearing the same fate, I had always dreaded turning sixty. There was a strong family history of depression: my sister's suicidal depression in periods of great stress, an acute depression of my own in my twenties, and my recent diagnosis of chronic mild depression.

In addition to my biological clock, I heard my *biographical* clock ticking. I felt the need to come to terms, at last, with the sad ending of Dad's life. I felt ready—sort of—to confront the documents I'd been avoiding for so long. So I retrieved the box from the attic and, with moist palms, opened it.

With thirty years' perspective, I was able to read through the letters calmly and appreciatively. I found myself transported to the past, eavesdropping on intimate conversations. Doing this initiated a long-deferred process of reckoning with Dad's complexity and my very conflicted feelings about him. Unbeknownst to me, he'd had a rich and gratifying life before he married in his late thirties. The contents of the archive have given me extraordinary access to his complicated emotional life during his early adulthood. It shed light on some mysteries, too. Excavating his past in this way also led me finally to a compassionate sense of why he succumbed to depression in his prime.

~

All parents elude their children's complete comprehension, of course, but compared to my mother, my father was quite opaque to me. He always felt a bit remote; we were certainly never friends. I am therefore all the more grateful for his archive, my true patrimony. Purposely or not, he left behind a trove of personal documents, some quite intimate, which have enabled me to know him differently than I had when he was alive—even, perhaps, to forge a posthumous rapport with him.

I have come to think of this memoir, then, not as a mere record of my father's life, which was quite extraordinary in some ways, but as a letter to him—a letter that might make up for my letter of 1969, which so damaged our relationship. (In order to write this letter, of course, I had to reread that one. But I put that off as long as I could.) I consider this memoir an expression of love and affiliation. That is not to say that my father would have wanted to read it: there is much unpleasant truth in it. But as his letters have spoken to me, I have at long last written back to him, in the spirit of recognition and reconciliation.

I

The Father I (Thought I) Knew

Chapter One

After the War

Manchester, New Hampshire 1947–1954

I have wondered since [his death] what stifled cravings had once germinated in him, and what manner of man he was really meant to be. That he was a lonely one, haunted by something always unexpressed and unattained, I am sure.
—Edith Wharton, *A Backward Glance*

My full name connects me closely with my father. Our signatures—W. Griffith Couser and G. Thomas Couser—are parallel in form. Similarly, Dad went by his middle name shortened: Grif; likewise, I go by mine, Tom. Moreover, my first initial stands for Griffith.

I shadow him in my name—and much else.

I have often wished my name didn't lead off with the Welsh Griffith (my father's mother's maiden name). Officialdom insists on addressing me by it. Reportedly, in my first days of kindergarten, I failed to answer the roll call; after a couple of days, the principal called home to find out why "Griffith" hadn't been attending. Had I sat there silently, wondering who "Griffith Couser" was? Or did I refuse to respond to that unfamiliar moniker?

Much later, as an adolescent, I reversed my two given names, becoming "Thomas G. Couser"—a mild act of rebellion that destroyed the father-son parallel.

Both gestures can be seen as anticipating the later distance between us.

~

Dad and Mum married not long before the World War II in Manchester, New Hampshire, where they had met as colleagues in the Central High School English Department. Dad enlisted in the Navy soon after Pearl Har-

3

bor but served near home in the early years of the war. He not only survived the war; he seemed to thrive in the Navy, and growing up I came to realize that he had found his military service immensely gratifying. He enjoyed the male camaraderie and relished having an active role in a just and world-shaping war. Its end was no doubt a relief for him, in obvious ways. But turning his attention from a world war to his family must have required a big adjustment—in both the import of his labor and his daily routine. Although children often assume their primacy in their parents' lives, I'm not sure that parenting was the highlight of Dad's life. Indeed, I fear that it may have registered as an anticlimax.

~

After his discharge in February 1946, Dad worked for the Veterans Administration—a way of extending his involvement in the cause. He, Mum, and my older sister Jane, who was born in 1944, lived in Melrose, Massachusetts, a northern Boston suburb, where Dad and Mum had lived while he was in training at the Charlestown Navy Yard. I was born in September of 1946—part of the post-war baby boom. Nearly all of my parents' siblings also had children in the next few years.

About a year later, Dad was hired by the V.A. in Manchester. So in November of 1947, we moved to Manchester. In their first six years of marriage, Dad and Mum had lived at half a dozen addresses in two states, and Dad had served halfway around the world in the Pacific. After the war, then, both of them were truly "demobilized." In this, too, they were in step with their siblings, the progenitors of my generation. It was a time of consolidation, stability, fertility, and relative tranquility.

Dad and Mum bought a modest two-story house on Roy Avenue, a short, dead-end street lined with small frame houses on small lots. Our neighbors were lower-middle or working class, white but of mixed ethnicity—many French Canadians, some Poles, a few Greeks. Many worked at a nearby shoe factory and worshipped at a Catholic church in the neighborhood.

On a nostalgic return to Roy Avenue in early 2011, Jane and I found ourselves underwhelmed. Predictably, everything seemed smaller than we remembered it. Our house and garage were unchanged, but the neighborhood seemed shabby; properties were not as neat and well-kept as they had been when we were small. It was hard to conjure up how pleasant it seemed to us as children—much less to imagine how homey it must have seemed to our parents after their nomadic years.

Intimate and self-contained, the neighborhood was child-friendly; we could identify and greet every resident who drove in or out. We could play ball in the street or in driveways, hide-and-seek up and down the one long block. And there were enough children to provide us with playmates without our having to cross a through street.

We Cousers had no television—by parental fiat—but most of the neighbors had sets. Jane and I would watch as much as we could while "playing" at their houses, surreptitiously consuming forbidden mass culture in the form of game shows, crime shows (like *Boston Blackie*), Westerns (starring Gene Autry, the "singing cowboy," and Roy Rogers, who also sang), and comedies (*The Life of Riley*). To watch a few approved shows, like *Mama*—a family saga of a Norwegian immigrant family in San Francisco around 1910—we were permitted to don our pajamas after dinner and go across the street to our friend Claudette's. When confined to the house, we listened to radio dramas, especially Westerns, like *The Lone Ranger,* and *Our Miss Brooks*—a favorite because of it was set in a high school not so different from the one at which our parents worked.

~

I have a relatively poor autobiographical memory; still, it seems odd that I have so few memories of time alone with Dad. Occasionally he took me fishing. The memory that sticks is of a trip with him and other men that lasted until after dark and involved slogging through buggy swamps to some remote fishing-hole. I remember being miserable but not wanting to complain for fear of embarrassing him in front of the other men. I certainly do not remember these excursions as fun for me, much less "quality time" with my father. In situations like this, to seem like one of the guys, Dad would act and talk differently than he did at home—indulging in mild profanity and off-color jokes. Such conduct seemed disingenuous or somehow alien to me—not my real Dad. I didn't know quite what to make of it. I had difficulty negotiating among his different personas in different circumstances. But this didn't become a serious matter until high school, when I was his student.

My memories of this period consist primarily of typical family activities. When Dad was older, I remember seeing him dandle small children on his knees, holding their hands in his. He'd chant: "Trot, trot to Boston; Trot, trot to Lynn; Trot, trot home again; And don't fall *in!*" On "in," he'd spread his knees and pretend to drop the child, eliciting squeals of delight. I have no memory of this kind of play with me. In contrast, I do have memories of sitting in Mum's lap, snuggling against her breast. I offer this as testimony to the very different relations I had with each of my parents—or so my memory suggests.

So although I remember Dad as having a gentle way with children, I don't have much memory of physical intimacy with him. Our family archive, however, contains photographic evidence of exactly such intimacy—e.g., a snapshot of me hanging on Dad's shoulders while Jane kneels between his legs in a park. Discovering this, I found it hard to credit. What has happened, I'm afraid, is that the later disintegration of our relationship has obscured my memories of such uncomplicated times.

Dad and I must have played catch—as all American fathers and sons are supposed to do—but I have no memory that, either. To the extent that he and I bonded in my early childhood, it was not through sports, either as players or fans, but through books; his reading to us children was a precious nightly ritual. I manifested a very early interest in words and learned to read quite young. Even after I could read on my own, he would lie down with me and read to me in bed. It's hard to imagine now, but this continued into a phase when we read quite lengthy adventure stories, like *The Scarlet Pimpernel* and exotic novels by John Buchan, not to mention more literary fiction like *Great Expectations*. As I think of this now, I wonder whether these were books he had read as a boy. Was he transfusing me with his own romantic sense of adventure? Perhaps he was just making up for time lost in his own life; I'm

Figure 1.1. Dad, Jane, and Me.

sure his no-nonsense father did not read fiction with him. Either way, this activity served us both well. In my case, it stimulated my historical and geographical imaginations; I learned to visualize distant places and times. And of course, I learned to value reading, which became my profession as an English professor.

Most of my memories from these years have to do with things we did as a family rather than with one parent or the other. Some of the most pleasant accrue from our many summer camping trips to scenic areas of New Hampshire, Maine, and even the Maritime provinces of Canada—state parks with good swimming beaches, whether on lakes or the ocean. Neither parent had grown up camping; both were the children of immigrants—Dad's parents from Northern Ireland, Mum's from Holland. Few of their friends or relatives camped, either, but for Mum and Dad, it was the vacation mode of choice; it was economical and it allowed them to explore during their generous vacations.

We loved being in the woods, sitting around a campfire at night, and being near the water. Our campsites were homes away from home. But although life in a small tent involved physical proximity and lack of privacy, I don't remember it—or our family life in general—as emotionally intimate. Though sensitive and attentive, he and Mum were not physically affectionate with each other or with us children—in public or at home.

~

On the whole, our life in Manchester was peaceful, happy, and uneventful in a good way—a proper respite after a half a decade of wartime separation and uncertainty. There was, however, one major exception. Like my mother, her younger sister Mina married just before the War and had a baby girl during it. During the last years of the war, with their husbands away—both in the Navy—the sisters and their daughters lived with their mother in Manchester. Snapshots show the two girls, Jane and Judy, sharing a huge pram.

After the war, life seemed to be going well for both sisters, who were living mere miles apart. But Mina was diabetic. And on April 18th, 1949, while Al was at work and Judy was at kindergarten, Mina lapsed into insulin shock. When Judy came home, she thought her mother was merely napping, so she crawled into bed with her. When Al came home and found Mina unconscious, he recognized her condition and called the doctor.

When I reached this point in reconstructing this period, I got in touch with Judy—after a long lapse—to see if she could fill in the details. She responded generously by email: "I remember sitting in a chair outside my parents' bedroom while the doctor worked on my mother trying to revive her. When that failed, your father carried me out of my house and brought me to yours. What a terrible night that was." (April 1, 2012) In the aftermath of his wife's death, Al could not work full-time and properly care for Judy. So she came to live with us. Suddenly, our family of four had an additional member. I was two-and-a-half; Jane not quite five.

Judy's recollection of her time with us in the aftermath of a traumatizing episode is surprisingly positive. I credit Dad and Mum for making her feel welcome and comforting her when Mum, too, must have been grieving. Mina's death was a huge blow to her, especially since her father had died in his forties when Mum was a mere teenager.

I have vague recollections of the three of us children playing happily in our basement, where we built structures—houses or stagecoaches—out of large wooden crates, the legacy of the wartime moves. As it turned out, however, the arrangement was short-lived. Jane was less than delighted with the new ménage. She enjoyed the company of another girl, but not the competition. No longer the oldest child in the household, she made it clear that this new addition was not entirely welcome. It was decided that the home of Al's sister in Concord, New Hampshire, was a better placement. And there Judy thrived.

From my parents' perspective, then, this immediate post-war period was not as serene and tranquil as it seemed to us children. In 1949, Mum lost her only sister, leaving only her long-widowed mother and younger brother. Four years later, Dad lost his closest friend, Bob Riedel, to a brain tumor. (Only after Dad died and I read Bob's letters did I realize how close they'd been.) Oddly, Bob's death registered with Jane and me in a way that Mina's had not. Jane remembers waiting in the car while Dad visited Bob at his sister's house in his final illness. We both remember Dad coming home distressed on the night of Bob's death and breaking the news to Mum in the kitchen, after which they embraced tearfully. As far as I can remember, this was the first time I saw my father cry—and one of the last. Just as we were not physically affectionate, we were not emotionally demonstrative. We children were never taken to funerals—not Mina's, not Bob's, not even, much later, our grandparents'. Jane and I learned to repress, rather than to express, our feelings.

There was one more significant post-war death, that of Dad's father. Isaac was not young when he died in 1951, and Dad was in his mid-forties, well established in life. But, as I well know, a father's death is always a significant event for a son. I'd always wondered what this event had been like for him. So when, in his archive, I came across a eulogy Dad wrote for Isaac's funeral, I hoped it would shed light on their relationship.

At the beginning of Dad's handwritten text, the minister jotted, "What finer tribute could be paid a father by a son!" It *is* a fine tribute, in a way, and it may illuminate their relationship. But not in the way I had hoped. Although it is eloquent, it is also disappointingly formulaic:

[My father] has been in complete attendance upon my mother for many years with never the slightest word of complaint though it has meant the sacrifice of many other interests which meant much to him.

My father was a man who always effaced himself in behalf of the interests of his family. In coming to this country from the country of his birth, he thought of the greater opportunity for his children here. He became a citizen at the earliest possible moment and always had a remarkably fine conception of democratic values and the principles of freedom upon which this land was founded.

And so on. Isaac comes across as a paragon of the hardworking, patriotic American immigrant and a benevolent patriarch, and Dad comes across as a dutiful son. But there is no sense of intimacy between them nor of Isaac's personality, much less idiosyncrasies. The effect is to characterize him as somewhat distant from Dad, unapproachable as well as irreproachable. If that reflects their actual relationship, perhaps that is part of his legacy as a father, and mine as his son.

Dad noted, finally, that "as a deeply religious man . . . he believed strongly in immortality . . . [and] was never afraid to die." It's interesting that Dad knew these things about his father's beliefs. I have no idea what Dad actually believed as a Christian—certainly not whether he believed in immortality. Whether he did or not—and I suspect he did not—Dad was apparently not afraid of dying. Rather, well before he reached the age at which his father died, he became afraid of living—or at least no longer interested in doing so. Was that because he was not sure he'd lived up to his own father's example, because he was not as content as Isaac to be the self-sacrificing father and husband—because he had had a life before his marriage that married life could never equal? Writing his life using his personal documents, especially his correspondence, has made me suspect that my father found his father's example both intimidating (in its self-effacement) and somewhat suffocating (in its bland self-satisfaction).

~

In any case, having survived the War without losing any relatives or close friends, Dad and Mum suddenly lost several important ones in the next half dozen years. Older parents with young children, they must have sensed their own mortality quite keenly. Having begun a family after a late start, he and Mum may have felt, too, that they had some catching up to do. In any case, he was not content with the status quo. And in 1954, not long after these deaths and the failed experiment in taking in Judy, we left Manchester for good, returning to Melrose.

This was a significant move. It must have taken strength for him and Mum to pull up stakes and move away from their families. Dad's three brothers lived in New Hampshire or Maine, within easy visiting distance even before the interstate highways. (His sister, whom we seldom saw, lived in New Jersey.) And his mother, who was beginning to be affected by Parkinson's disease, remained in the family homestead in Dover, New Hampshire. My mother's family members were concentrated even more closely: her mother, brother, nieces and nephew, all lived in or near Manchester. So did their many friends, colleagues, and fellow church-members.

Moreover, Manchester had been home to both of them—for Mum nearly all of her life, for Dad during his formative years. So they remained attached to the city, returning regularly to visit family and friends. (For years we continued to have our teeth cared for by our Manchester dentist, Dr. Frost, on Saturday mornings.) I don't think Dad and Mum ever had—or could have had—the same deep connection to Melrose, which they came to in mid-life, that they had to Manchester.

But the advantages of Melrose trumped their sentimental ties to Manchester. As an inner suburb of Boston, Melrose provided ready access to its many cultural institutions. Melrose was also a move up socially, a more homogeneous, middle-class town than Manchester, which was industrial—indeed, post-industrial and economically depressed. Reflecting its socioeconomic status, Melrose schools were superior. And the town was already familiar to them, as they had lived there briefly during the War.

At that time, Dad had made a favorable impression on Harold Poole, the husband of Mum's good friend Dorothy and, conveniently, the principal of Melrose High School. When, in the early 1950s, Melrose High needed a new English Department head, Harold recruited Dad—despite Dad's not having taught since the War—and he held this post for the rest of his life. For him it was clearly a career move. And Mum soon found work in neighboring towns, eventually settling into the job which she held for the rest of her life, teaching English at nearby Arlington High School.

The move was not only better for them; a strong impetus must have been the sense that Melrose would offer Jane and me social, cultural, and academic resources that Manchester could not. So we moved to the suburbs. And in Melrose, we lived the life of a fairly typical post-war suburban family in the era of *Ozzie and Harriet*. We matched the template of a father, mother, son, and daughter. We were white, Protestant, and middle-class.

But our lives, and especially Dad's, might have taken a very different direction. I know this only because of a document I found in my father's closet. Dated June 1952 and headed "Personal History Statement," it contains a trove of personal data—such as Dad's addresses for the previous ten years. But more important than its documentation of his past is its hint of a different future: it is part of an application to the CIA. Until I came across this document a quarter of a century after he filled it out, I had no idea that Dad had ever sought to join "the Company." Not only that, it was only by perusing the form that I learned that at the end of the War he had applied for jobs with the FBI and Naval Intelligence.

I have no idea whether Dad was offered a job with the CIA. I would think that, as a decorated veteran, a man of obvious intelligence and good work habits with a squeaky clean record, he would have seemed an attractive candidate. This impulse seems utterly inconsistent with the man I knew as a high school teacher. At the same time, I regard these successive applications for intelligence work as consistent with what I now know of his adventurous life in Aleppo and his seeking to join the Royal Canadian Air Force before the United States entered World War II. Before getting married, then, he was evidently attracted to a life of risk and adventure, eager to take part in the great historical conflict of his times. Resuming his first career as a teacher was not likely to satisfy these impulses. Nor was teaching middle-class sub-urban American students likely to provide the deep gratification of teaching Armenian refugees, as he had in Aleppo. His impulse to join the FBI, Naval Intelligence, or the CIA was probably driven more by the aura of intrigue than by Cold-War ideology or politics. At least I hope so. Part of him seems to have resisted the letdown of peacetime life on the home front.

In his application he did his best to seem worldly and well-traveled. He noted his sojourn in Syria and travels in Western Europe, Russia, and Fin-land. He claimed adequate command of French and, thanks to his time in Aleppo, some familiarity with Turkish and Arabic. Though a father of two young children, he expressed a willingness to travel. In response to a query as where he would be willing to accept appointment, he checked all three options: "in Washington, DC; anywhere in the United States; and outside the United States." In short, anywhere in the world.

Instead of becoming a spy, however, in 1954 he moved to Melrose and resumed high school teaching in a homogeneous suburb. I sometimes wonder what that choice cost him. As much as he evidently found being a father, teacher, and husband gratifying, I suspect that life in Melrose left some deep needs unmet.

Chapter Two

Suburban Life

Melrose 1954–1968

I rarely visit Melrose, but it remains an important mental landscape. I travel there often in memory, sometimes using Google Street View to visit my old neighborhood, which is surprisingly little changed. It's an eerie experience, floating through it with the click of a mouse—seeing but unseen, like a revenant.

The decade following our move to Melrose was a formative one for me, taking me through high school and into college, and those years defined Dad for me. But some parents, like my father, had lives that were far different from what their children knew or imagined. That's the thrust of my (or our) story—the extent to which I did not know the father I grew up with.

∾

Not long after we settled in Melrose, Dad and Mum finally relented and we got a television. *Got*, not bought: we inherited our first TV, a small black-and-white set, from Mum's Dutch mother, Leida van Stelten, when she died in 1956. We were by far the last of our peers to have a TV; if our book-loving, English-teacher parents had had to pay hard-earned cash, we might never have got one.

Of course our viewing options were severely limited. One show we were allowed to watch, for obvious reasons, was *Navy Log*, which I loved. That provided me with a sense of what shipboard life might have been for Dad during the War. As a result, I still visualize his wartime experience in black-and-white. The sole sitcom I remember is *Sergeant Bilko*, with Phil Silvers as the conniving noncom. Dad found it uproarious. His military past was our ticket to popular culture.

We could also watch *I Led Three Lives,* based on the memoir of a former Melrose resident, Herbert Philbrick, who had overlapping lives as a citizen, a "Communist," and a counterspy. An advertising executive, Baptist youth leader, and pacifist, Philbrick joined the Cambridge Youth Council in the early War years only to discover that it was a Communist front. After informing the FBI, he was paid to infiltrate the Party. During his career as a counter-espionage agent, he lived in Melrose and joined cells in neighboring towns. His charade was convincing, and he rose rapidly in the hierarchy of the New England chapter. In 1949, however, he gave up his cover to testify publicly against Party members. In 1952, he published his memoir, and the serial aired from 1953 to 1956. Although the show featured very little action—no matter how sinister their intentions, cell meetings just weren't very exciting—it sustained my interest, at least in part because of its local resonance. I relished its suggestion that my environs might not be as secure and bland as they seemed.

I wonder now what Dad thought as his children were entertained by a narrative of the life he never led. Did he wish his life had additional, secret dimensions? This show may have stirred his desire for a more adventurous post-war life, one more in keeping with the life he'd led to date.

❧

In the manner of the day, my recreation was unscheduled and unsupervised—benign parental neglect. After school, I was on my own and played outdoors, weather permitting. In the fifties cold winters provided natural ice for skating and snow for sledding. It was common for young boys to throw snowballs at passing cars or even cling to their bumpers for a short "sleigh ride" on slippery streets. One of my rare flashbulb memories of my youth in Melrose arises from these circumstances. A friend and I were playing in the snow when Dad approached our house on his way home from school. (At the time, we had only one car, which Mum drove to work, so Dad walked to work regardless of weather.) He strode along the opposite sidewalk, fedora on his head and briefcase in hand, oblivious to us. From cover behind a neighbor's garage I lobbed a snowball in his direction. I intended it to splat on the sidewalk in front of him, startling him and announcing my presence. It startled him, all right: I failed to lead him enough and watched in horror as its trajectory approached his path. My missile didn't hit him, but it passed within inches of his nose. He wheeled, his face contorted. Recognizing me, he softened, said only "Hey, call your shots!" and continued home.

I wasn't afraid I'd injure him; rather, that I would incur his wrath. Perhaps I felt I deserved it, that some repressed hostility had been behind that throw. But he did not explode. Perhaps it would have been better if he'd grabbed some snow and retaliated, but he was too dignified for that. The moment passed, but I have not forgotten it. It still has an Oedipal feel.

In 1963, when Jane was a high school junior and I was a freshman, our family took a summer camping tour of Europe. We loaded our gear and baggage into our blue and white 1957 Ford station wagon and drove to Montreal, where a crane lifted it onto an ocean liner; we spent the next week in transit to Europe the old-fashioned way. In Southampton, England, the car and gear were offloaded, and we began our European itinerary.

I had been tasked with laying out the route and locating camp grounds, and I helped to navigate once we were there. We traveled north to Edinburgh, south to London, across the channel to France, east into Holland, down the Rhine through Germany, across the Swiss Alps to the Italian lakes, on to the French Riviera (where I saw my first bikinis—a very big deal for a hormonal American teenager), north to Paris, and finally le Havre, where we boarded another liner for the return trip. During the entire trip we indulged only once or twice in the luxury of a hotel. I still remember my first duvet—for its novelty as much as its welcome comfort.

Having spent summers in Europe during his three years teaching in Aleppo in the 1930s, Dad was familiar with much of the territory we traversed, and it was a nostalgic journey for him. At last, he had a chance to share what had been such an important part of his early life, and he gloried in it. It was Mum's initiation into foreign travel, and she loved it all, even though for six weeks she had to buy food in foreign languages and prepare meals for us on a Coleman three-burner camp stove.

For Jane and me, the trip expanded our horizons and whetted our appetites for international travel. It also set us off a bit from our peers. None of our friends or classmates had traveled to Europe. Indeed, most of my college friends didn't go to Europe until or unless they studied abroad. So in that sense, we acquired sophistication beyond our years. But for Dad, it may have been a bittersweet experience, a reminder of the road he hadn't traveled—that of an expatriate. I remember him talking animatedly with some younger men who were going to Pamplona to run with the bulls—the first I heard of this custom. I sensed even then that they were Dad's alter egos. They reminded him of footloose days in his twenties when he had roamed Europe with friends.

In addition to my memory and Jane's, I have two significant sets of documents to rely on in reconstructing these years. The first one consists of Christmas letters sent to friends and family from 1956 to 1971. These were produced in purple ink—first at home on a hectograph, later on a mimeograph at one or the other parent's school. True to their genre, these record the years' highlights, and their tone is consistently—one might say relentlessly—upbeat. As a family member, I can detect when the tone becomes a little strained or when the public narrative is incongruent with the private reality. But their usefulness to me as a memoirist is limited by their having been intended for public consumption.

My other source consists of Mum's spiral engagement calendars for what proved the last two decades of her life—1955 to 1974. Bound on plastic or metal spines, these volumes display the days of a week on a single page opposite a picture. Each page is only about 5 x 8 inches, and the space allocated to each day is a mere 3 or 4 square inches. Whether they were intended primarily to plan or to record events, they provide kind of collective diary, chronicling our life as a family. A couple of years are missing, and some have gaps of a couple of months; otherwise, Mum made a short note about nearly every day of our lives for twenty years. Each Christmas one of us would give her a blank calendar; in return—the far greater gift—she documented our lives in considerable detail. A biographer from outside the family would have difficulty deciphering them, but I can pretty much trace our individual whereabouts and activities on a daily basis over a twenty-year period. These documents were kept on her desk, and they were for her use, not public consumption. In her final years, they served her private needs, recording in code some difficult aspects of her life.

This memoir focuses on Dad because I found him rather remote; he was always a bit of a mystery to me, and writing the memoir is a way of trying to understand him in long retrospect. (It is typically the less available parent who becomes the subject of filial memoir; in a patriarchal society, this is usually the father.) But the memoir focuses on Dad also because his premarital life was extraordinary—and I know that only because he left an extensive archive of documents, many in his own voice. Mum's documentary legacy is very different from Dad's in ways that reflect her gender and her character. To begin with, it contains little from her pre-marital life, other than documents like yearbooks, birth certificates, and family photos. And whereas Dad's archive is intensive and lyrical—letters written over relatively short periods of time—the bulk of hers is extensive and prosaic—diaries written over decades. Even these do not offer her "voice" as such, however. The small spaces didn't accommodate many words, and entries rarely contain complete sentences. Mostly they consist of phrases noting social and cultural events, doctors' appointments, trips, and snow days (teachers' delights, as well as students').

Despite their seeming mundaneness, they express Mum's distinctive point of view and temperament. Her journals reveal her devotion to Jane and me, but also her centrality to our lives. On ample display here are her tact in juggling our sometimes conflicting demands and needs; her ability to organize our lives as a family unit; her generosity as a hostess to countless dinner parties and overnight guests. On a Friday, she might conclude a week's teaching, go "marketing" (i.e., food shopping) straight from work, and then prepare dinner for out-of-town guests. All of this on top of domestic chores. Very occasionally, she would note, almost guiltily, "lazy day" or "slept late."

Her diaries also document an extensive relational life beyond our nuclear family: she noted not only every visit but seemingly every long distance phone conversation with friends and relatives (my many uncles and aunts). She kept in touch with a large circle of female friends and colleagues as well, playing bridge at their houses, or having them over for tea, or, if they lived at a distance, writing them letters. I am amazed at how many evenings she spent writing letters or notes. (I wish I had access to them, as I do for much of Dad's correspondence.)

~

Overall, I think this period was happy for both of my parents—up to a point. For one thing, they seemed to genuinely enjoy being parents, and it is clear that their lives revolved around their children—even more than was the case for many of our friends. At this time, Jane and I were old enough not to require constant supervision or support. We were quite independent emotionally, and we did well in school. These documents impress me with how busy we were as a family. We took regular camping trips in the summer. We skied together in winter. We traveled to visit friends and museums and foreign movies year round.

They had got a late start as parents, and Mum had been told she might not be able to bear children, so they were grateful to have us. In addition to liking what we now refer to as parenting, Dad and Mum both loved teaching. Being in English departments put them in contact with compatible people, lovers of literature. And it allowed them time on their own, what Thoreau called having a large margin to one's life. Hence Dad's gardening and bee-keeping, my mother's sewing (she and Jane made some of Jane's clothes from patterns) and baking.

Dad and Mum never fought, argued, or even criticized each other in front of us. I never heard either of them say a sharp word to, or about, the other until the last few years of their lives—which was why it was so disturbing when that happened. They seemed like a harmonious, well-matched couple, if not soul-mates. Even—or especially—with Mum's family-oriented diaries, it's not easy for me to delineate Dad's life as an individual in these years. Ironically, I have far less insight into his emotional life during the years we lived in the same house than I do for his premarital years. In any case, during this period, I related to him more as the head of the family than as my Dad. Given his status as a faithful husband (as far as I know) and dedicated father, he had less private life than he'd had as a bachelor, and his emotional life was both less complicated and less rich than it had been. He seems to have thrown himself into his roles as husband, father, and teacher. But documents from his earlier life offer the nagging sense that he might have wanted—or at least imagined—a different, more exotic existence than his secure, rather staid, life in suburbia.

Although I think Dad and Mum truly loved each other, they were not physically affectionate with one another or with us. Like a lot of couples of that era, Dad and Mum slept in twin beds. In fact, because of the odd layout of their bedroom, their beds were at right angles to one another. Dad always rose first to make breakfast; one morning when he was late to do so, I went upstairs and into their bedroom to rouse him. Finding his bed empty, I turned to my mother's, and was startled to find him in bed with her, grinning sheepishly—the only time I ever saw them in bed together. Presumably, they made love occasionally, but their love life was totally opaque to us.

∼

When I review Dad's life, I inevitably find myself looking for signs of trouble, precursors of its later tragic turn—hints that might presage, and thus explain, his mental collapse in late middle age, when he was still otherwise healthy and vigorous. Even as I do so, I realize that this is not entirely fair. Had he died suddenly in his early sixties, I'd be writing a very different memoir. Or, more likely, I wouldn't be writing one at all. His death would not have been an anomaly, a mystery to solve. I might have been able to explore his archive much sooner had I not come to it so distressed by the time and manner of his death. One careful read-through might have sufficed; I might have organized the documents and never reexamined them. I wouldn't have been driven to investigate his past in such a forensic way. But unfortunately, and unfairly, our perceptions of people are affected by the circumstances of their deaths.

In any case, I cannot overlook Dad's disintegration in his last few years. I lived through it, too; doing so was extremely painful. And I have some residual sense of guilt from not having been able to arrest or reverse his deterioration, which I felt my letter of 1969 might have accelerated.

In part his disintegration was so challenging for the rest of us because it was so surprising, so seemingly out of character. In my reexamination of his life so far, I seek foreshadowing mostly in vain. There were a few signs of restlessness or discontent on Dad's part. As the head of the English Department, he could advance professionally only by going into administration. For a department head, the next rung of the ladder was assistant principal—a job that was largely devoted to disciplinary matters. (Transgressors were summoned to his office daily on the school's public address system.) Dad was evidently a capable administrator, and he got along well with his subordinates. But, to his credit, he was ambivalent about getting into administration. He sometimes chafed at the narrow-minded policies of higher-ups and may have been reluctant to have been drawn into their culture. Melrose High was a sports power, with attendant emphasis on athletics, which he resented and resisted. In any case, I think he languished a bit, hiding his resentment from Jane and me as much as possible.

One sign of professional frustration may have been his projection of ambition onto me. Although I think he was proud of my being in graduate school when he died, he never encouraged me to go into teaching. His idea of a good career for me was "international law." I put the phrase in quotation marks because I never knew quite what he meant by it. I'm not sure he did either. An admired former student had become an international lawyer, and somehow Dad thought this would suit my talents. He may have been right about my aptitude—I'm good at analysis and argument and languages—but not about my interests. The field may have appealed to him as an alternative to the life he had defaulted into after the war; it would have been more lucrative than teaching and more glamorous, as it involved multilingualism and travel. It would have fulfilled some of the same impulses that led to his sojourn in Aleppo and his application to the FBI and the CIA.

In retrospect, his taste in music may offer a hint of latent depression. One of my strong recollections of Melrose is that when Dad got home from work—usually well before Mum—he would retire to his bedroom to nap or listen to music. And he often chose to play a piece that always seemed to me quite lugubrious, Schubert's "Unfinished Symphony." I've never been able to hear the first movement of that piece without visualizing Dad lying on his back in his bed in the waning light of a winter afternoon. He didn't "sound" happy.

~

When Jane and I were both in high school, our relations with him—more mine than hers—became complicated in ways that went beyond the tensions that came with puberty. Our teachers were often people we'd see outside of school—at our house or theirs. Managing these relationships was sometimes a challenge—on both sides. I was a better student than Jane, and during my sophomore year, he and Mum suggested that I apply to a prestigious boarding school. There was family precedent for this: Dad's brother Tom's sons had gone to New England prep schools and then on to Ivy League colleges. But they lived in rural Lebanon, New Hampshire, where the schools didn't challenge them.

My situation was different. Melrose schools were rigorous, and I had plenty of extracurricular stimulation from my parents. In any case, I was not keen on the idea. I didn't see the advantage of private school, and of course I was not eager to leave my classmates and friends behind. I preferred the familiar. But I went along with the application process. I took the requisite aptitude test and visited the campus for the obligatory interview. When asked why I wanted to attend the school, however, I replied candidly that it was my parents' idea, not mine. That didn't end the interview, but it probably ended my candidacy. Dad was not pleased with my candor, interpreting it as a kind of self-sabotage. He was probably right.

At Melrose High I excelled academically, edited the school newspaper, and was accepted at Dartmouth on early decision. Once there, I realized that my academic preparation had been adequate. A different advantage of prep schools, lost on me, was more subtle: I'd have had a better class of class-mates—quite literally. I wouldn't describe Dad and Mum as social climbers, but they evidently thought I would benefit from having more sophisticated friends. Our home was on the edge of a working-class neighborhood. Most of my primary school classmates had stay-at-home mothers and fathers who worked in factories in places like nearby Lynn, where General Electric had a big plant. Many of these parents hadn't gone to college. They didn't travel. Or go to museums. My circle of friends changed somewhat as I entered middle and high school and mingled with kids from more affluent neighbor-hoods. But my parents felt I would benefit from having friends from more cosmopolitan backgrounds—the kind I eventually had in college. They had a point.

What might have been the most positive result of my going away to school for my junior and senior years, however, was probably something none of us could have foreseen: I would have avoided having my father as my senior English teacher. As the head of the department, he reserved the top section of senior English for himself. It was his prerogative, and he no doubt deserved it. Jane had taken senior English with him two years before me, without ill effect. I am envious of her experience because my relationship with him was irretrievably damaged by my year in his class.

I don't fault him. As Kafka wrote in *Dearest Father* (but with irony I don't intend here), "I believe [him] to be entirely blameless for our estrange-ment."[1] "Estrangement" is too strong a term for what happened to us; it was more a matter of distancing on my part. My pulling away had nothing to do with the kind of teacher he was. He was both popular and respected. Remark-ably, no one mocked him in front of me or teased me about being his son. At high school reunions decades later, classmates tell me they still value his teaching. So he did what all teachers aspire to: he made a lasting, positive impact on many students. But not on me.

I'm always pleased to hear their praise, but I can only envy their admira-tion, not share it.

Perhaps one reason I didn't appreciate his classroom teaching as much as my peers is that I had the advantage of his example—his reading habits, his large vocabulary, and his command of English—all the time. I was immersed in a household where books (novels, mostly) were read for enjoyment but also taken seriously.

More important, at school—especially in Dad's class—I found it awkward to act as if my father were just another teacher. What I found difficult, I suppose, was negotiating between being his student during the school day and being his son the rest of the time. At home, he and I refrained from discussing the homework. But it was downright weird to be writing my papers in my room, then taking them to school and handing them to Dad, only to have him take them home, grade them in his study, then take them to school and return them to me in class. Aside from the inefficient logistics, it was odd having him as my grader. How could he evaluate me fairly?

It must have been strange for him, too. What tone should he strike in his comments? How personal should he be? "Nice work, son"? "See me after dinner"? It was all very awkward. Being his student involved a kind of charade, a denial of identity on both our parts. And I was not good at pretending.

We had never been close. I don't remember confiding in him or seeking his advice—not because we were so different but because we were so similar: I knew what he'd advise. My being his student put more distance between us—or perhaps, to be fair, I should say it caused me to withdraw from him. One period each day, my seat in study hall afforded me a long view down the hall. It was a pleasant diversion to watch whoever walked by. Dad's routine took him down that hallway regularly during that period. My quandary was whether to acknowledge him, and if so, how—with a smile, a wave, a nod, a wink? Mostly, I resolved this dilemma by pretending to study intently when I detected his approach, quelling the natural impulse to look up at any passerby. (I could identify his distinctive footfall in the empty corridor as he approached.) But one day, I looked up and right through him—as if he was some stranger, some teacher I didn't know. That evening, at home, he took me to task for it. Rightly so. I'd snubbed him, though no one else noticed.

My high school years were full of subtle tensions between being his son and being his student. After all, for four crucial years, I was perceived and related to largely as his son by many people, including classmates; that involved an unwelcome degree of scrutiny. In response to this, rather than act out, I quietly withdrew into myself. Overt rebellion was not my style, and it would have gotten me—and him—unwelcome attention. My refusal to recognize him was not personal but rather an enactment of my desire to be just some anonymous student whom he didn't know and who didn't know him. I meant no harm, but it hurt him, nevertheless.

It wasn't that I didn't *like* Dad's classroom persona. My classmates seemed to, and I might have, had I not been his son; rather, I didn't recognize it. As an adolescent—struggling to differentiate myself from others—I had an inordinate investment in some notion of individual uniqueness and authenticity, and I had difficulty reconciling the public teacher with the private

Figure 2.1.   Dad in hall of Melrose High School 1964 (His inscription: "It makes me happy, too.")

father. At home I had a similar problem whenever he would turn on the charm for guests. That made me uncomfortable because it didn't seem entirely genuine. I never quite trusted his charm, even though I envied his social facility.

In any case, I found this situation inhibiting, alienating even, at a time when I might have benefitted from a closer relation with him. To be fair, this dilemma was far from unique. In those days parents weren't best friends with their children the way some are today. My friends were not much closer to their fathers than I was to mine. But neither did they see them at school every day. For me, every day was "bring your child to work" day. I knew all too much about Dad's workplace.

If puzzled about what Dad was thinking or feeling, I would ask Mum in private. I see now how naïve I was to think she would always know and, if she knew, tell me. This put her in an unfair position, as well. But it indicates my distinct relations with each of them, that I approached him through her on important matters. Never close, my relationship with him never recovered from this distancing at a crucial time for both of us.

~

An incident at my Dartmouth graduation in 1968 may suggest how the tension between us could manifest itself. Like Dad, I had joined a fraternity. But whereas he belonged to a notorious party house, DKE, at Wesleyan, I had joined a nontraditional house. This was quite an extraordinary fraternity—especially for Dartmouth, the site of the original "Animal House." We thought of ourselves, somewhat pretentiously but also accurately, as an "unfraternity." We sought out sympathetic faculty as advisors. And we had some outstanding members—mature and thoughtful men. One, Angus King, went on to be the governor of Maine and later one of its U.S. Senators. In my year we had two Rhodes Scholars, one of whom, Robert Reich, served as Bill Clinton's first Labor Secretary.

One evening in the run-up to Commencement, there was a gathering for parents of seniors at the house. One member liked to amuse us with a send-up of the College president, John Sloan Dickey, whom we regarded as a pompous windbag. During cocktails, he performed this act for the assembled parents. They may not have been an ideal audience, since they were not able fully to appreciate the mimicry. But most of them seemed to enjoy it.

Not Dad. During the act his face darkened into a scowl. And afterward he sought out the student to tell him he found it inappropriate. I was quite taken aback by this, embarrassed at Dad's scolding him for what I thought was innocent fun. I felt I too had been judged, along with my fraternity brother, for disrespectful behavior. In any case, this scene was very upsetting to me. It may seem trivial, but it cast a pall over what should have been a thoroughly celebratory occasion.

The Rhodes Scholarship may also be relevant here. I had been encouraged to apply for one, and I had. But after the practice interview on campus, I withdrew from the competition. I had sized up my competitors at Dartmouth. Although I was an excellent student, I was not a "big man on campus." I lacked their impressive résumés, their poise, their oral facility, and, crucially, their self-confidence.

From my perspective, things turned out well. I was awarded a Dartmouth fellowship equal in benefit, though not prestige, to the Rhodes. And the following September I sailed to Europe on the *SS United States*, along with many Rhodes winners, including Bill Clinton. But my decision to withdraw from the competition rankled Dad and Mum. Usually mild-mannered, my mother confronted me angrily about this. I'm certain that I would not have won a Rhodes. But the two were right to fault me for selling myself short; I should not have eliminated myself. Still, I think part of the anger, especially on mother's part, had to do with my not fulfilling her ambitions for *Dad*.

He was such a bright and articulate man, so intent on my academic success, that I assumed that he had been a good student himself—until he died and I discovered his college transcript; his grades were mixed at best, mediocre at worst. He (and Mum) evidently expected me to parlay my academic excellence into a kind of professional achievement and recognition that had eluded Dad. Or so I came to believe. In any case, my academic success was something which he may have found threatening even as he took pride in it. As always, his responses were difficult to read.

But there were other things putting stress on Dad at the time. More than my mother, he had trouble adapting to life after we children left for college. At the same time, our absence prevented us from fully appreciating that he was struggling to maintain his mental equilibrium. It was only after I returned from my year at Oxford that I began to realize, in painful retrospect, how troubled he had become, how much what appeared the harmonious relation of my parents was a façade, how desperately unhappy my "home" had become.

Chapter Three

The Empty Nest

1964 to 1973

"Attention must be paid."
—Arthur Miller, *Death of a Salesman*

I suppose Jane and I imagined that after we left home for college—she in 1962, I in 1964—our parents' lives would continue as usual, but of course they didn't. They couldn't; Mum and Dad had organized their married life around us.

When we were at college, it was difficult for Dad and Mum to get in touch with us, let alone stalk us electronically. Dormitory students didn't have private phones. Incoming calls to a hall phone would be fielded by someone on duty, who would summon the intended recipient, if present, to converse without much privacy. I did not communicate often, or even regularly, with my parents. A weekly phone call or even rarer letter would suffice. Although Jane and I did visit home during the term, Dad and Mum must have keenly felt the loss of our company. Wrapped up in my own life, I certainly did not consider the vacuum I'd left behind. I had lots of new stimulation and company; Mum and Dad had much less, having lost not just us but our visiting friends.

So in retrospect it isn't surprising that our annual holiday newsletters from the late 1960s give the impression that Mum and Dad were trying to compensate with a flurry of activity. The 1967 edition acknowledges this pretty directly: "With Tom away in Hanover, and Jane married, Ann and Grif, with more time to themselves, have filled the calendar with various events." I suspect that Dad suffered more from our absence, but Mum seems to have initiated most of this activity. (Later revelations suggest why she wanted to get Dad out of the house in the evening.) Among other new activities, they took up furniture refinishing; from my current vantage, this appears more a metaphorical than a literal necessity. They refurbished our home after half of its inhabitants departed.

∼

The emptying of the nest may have been particularly trying for them because they had had little time together as a couple before they had children. Their first years of marriage were the early War years, during which they moved frequently; then Dad went to sea for the duration. They had their first child, Jane, in 1944 and the second, me, in 1946. So they never got to settle into a comfortable married life on their own. Living without their children may have been a particular challenge because it came as a novelty in middle age.

Dad had always been prone to "black moods," as my parents called them. I suppose, then, that I grew up knowing he was susceptible to depression, without ever thinking of his gloominess in medical terms, much less as a mental illness. After all, he had always been able to function. But in reread-ing Mum's diaries, I inevitably seek early signs of the depression that took over—and eventually took away—his life. The first explicit indication is on May 7, 1963, when I was still in high school: "Grif low these days." This may seem unremarkable—everyone is low sometime—but it stands out here: it is the first mention of anyone's mood in what is otherwise an objective recording of our family life. The more I reflect on it, the more remarkable I find it that Dad's state of mind found its way onto the page in this way; it was not Mum's style to attend to moods, certainly not to register them in this semi-official way. It seems an ominous sign. And it suggests a suppressed backstory.

The next such notation comes nearly two years later, during my freshman year in college. On February 7, 1965, Mum wrote: "Grif cross all day!" A few weeks later, on March 2, she noted: "Grif & I quarrel *again*" (my empha-sis). I do not ever recall a quarrel—hard feelings or cruel words—much less raised voices, when I lived at home. Perhaps they repressed conflicts all too well. In any case, I grew up thinking of them as a pair who lived together in easy rapport, if not emotional intimacy.

A couple of years later, more evidence of discord: "Another fight with Grif" (July 17, 1968). Perhaps not surprisingly, the first mention of Dad's drinking comes that fall (when I was studying at Oxford)—in fact, right after Thanksgiving: "Grif drunk all day again!" The strike-through is Mum's, and it attests to her ambivalence about noting this in her journal. After all, this was apparently not the first transgression, and it wasn't minor. He was not merely tipsy but "drunk"; not for the first time, but "again"; and not briefly, but "all day." How many episodes had gone unrecorded before this, I wonder? Just when did this drinking start? It would have been very hard to conceal while Jane and I were young, except during our absences at summer camp. So it seems unlikely that he had begun tippling much before Mum took note of it.

Evidently she feared that Dad or one of us children might come upon this evidence. At the time, of course, I had no interest in reading her diaries, nor, as far as I knew, any need to. And while she wanted to record this transgression, she did not want to share it. Not yet. Thereafter, she resorted to a (rather transparent) code: a red D marked a day on which Dad was drunk. In some calendars she circled these dates at the front where the whole year was displayed on a single page, which charted his drinking. In the winter of 1968-1969 (my year at Oxford), the frequency of Dad's inebriation rose from four days in January through six in February to nine in March, then subsided. Half of these were weekdays, which meant that he did not get to work.

For a time I was puzzled by more frequent codes—LTT, LTJ, LFT, LFJ—thinking they might also be related to Dad's functioning. If so, what else did Mum want to record in code? Dad's being Late To or Late For something? For what? Eventually, I tumbled: this was just her space-saving way of noting when she got a Letter From, or sent a Letter To, either of her children, Tom or Jane. She had similar codes for telephone calls. A mystery solved, and a touching memento of her frequent communication with us.

~

At that time, of course, mental illness was far more stigmatized than it is today. As far as I know, Dad never saw a physician about, or was medicated for, depression until his drinking began to interfere with his work in his early sixties. There seemed to be a seasonal pattern to his drinking—more in the darker, colder months, less in the lighter, warmer ones. And he had a great deal more trouble with depression once Jane and I were out of the house. In addition to making him lonely, our absence probably lowered his inhibition against drinking. His disintegration eventually became an issue between him and Mum—indeed, the issue that dominated their relationship; at the same time, though, they were very reluctant to share it with Jane or me. As they both had shielded us from deaths in the family when we were young, they covered up his depression even as it undermined their marriage. Their protectiveness was understandable but entirely counterproductive.

My father's life was inflected by many world-historical events. The first was the Armenian diaspora in the aftermath of the genocide during World War I; most of his students in Aleppo in the early 1930s were Armenian refugees. The next was World War II, in which his involvement was direct. If the end of that war marked the beginning of our family life, the Viet Nam War marked its end. Unlike WWII, the Viet Nam War was controversial and divisive, a major factor in the "generation gap." And for a time it put a great strain on our family, adding to whatever demons Dad was privately grappling with.

As my college graduation approached, I was fixated on how the war would affect me. As much as I admired conscientious objectors for their courage—and envied them their moral certitude—I could not count myself among them. I was not a pacifist; I valued Dad's service in World War II and did not object to all wars. But like many of my classmates, I was opposed to the Viet Nam War and sought to avoid military service. The alternatives were the Peace Corps, Vista (a kind of domestic Peace Corps), and teaching, all of which exempted you from the draft. My career plan was to get a doctorate and teach in college, but I wouldn't have minded postponing graduate school to teach at the secondary level on a draft deferment. My opportunity to go to Oxford, however, seemed quite extraordinary. As it happened, Dad knew someone on our local draft board; in response to Dad's inquiry, he told Dad I'd almost certainly be safe for at least my first year out of college. So in the fall of 1968, I began my studies at Oxford.

When I was summoned to London for a draft physical within months of my arrival in England, I began to worry. As the war was extremely unpopular among my generation, there were lots of schemes for evading the draft. Some men sought psychiatric deferments from sympathetic psychiatrists; still others self-inflicted minor injuries, like broken eardrums. I was familiar with these ruses. Even so, when one of the men taking the exam with me in London—a grad student at the London School of Economics, no less—tried to fail the intelligence portion of the exam, I was incredulous. So was the Southern officer who administered it. I thought he showed remarkable patience as he reviewed each simple math problem, "Now, Ah know you can do this: how much is twenty-seven divahded by three?" I rather doubt that this student got his exemption.

Aside from being severely myopic, which didn't disqualify me, I was physically sound, and I was duly certified 1-A. In January 1969—memorably, on Nixon's Inauguration Day—I received the dreaded letter that began "Greetings and Salutations." I was to report for induction less than a month later, on Valentine's Day.

I panicked. I felt betrayed. If I had not been assured I'd be safe from the draft for a year, I'd never have gone to Oxford in the first place.

But there I was in England, and I had received my draft notice.

So I called Dad. Doing so was no simple matter. I lived in college, and there were no phones in students' rooms or even the halls. A transatlantic trunk call had to be booked in advance through the college porter and taken in his office just inside the main gate of the college.

When we talked, Dad shared my alarm and said he'd look into it. Then he did me an enormous favor: he somehow got my induction deferred until the end of the academic year. This opened a window in which to seek a teaching deferment. Dad and Mum investigated opportunities for me at private schools, which did not require certification, and circulated my credentials. Remarkably, miraculously, they got me an offer without an interview; I accepted it, sight unseen, to my enormous relief.

It's not likely that the deferment literally saved my life. As far as I know, not a single member of my high school class died in that war, and the only fatality in my college class was a pilot, not a draftee. But someone served in my place. And I don't know how legitimate my escape was, for although my teaching deferment was bona fide, having my induction deferred may not have been strictly kosher. In a sense, I was not different from many of my middle-class peers. By virtue of attending college, we avoided induction until our early twenties; such were the undeserved protections of social class. That I may have benefitted from Dad's connection is a source of some guilt to me, even now. (And I feel a little ashamed of my passivity in my rescue.)

What troubles me more is the fear that Dad compromised his integrity to spare me military service. I was disturbed to learn later that his drinking accelerated sharply during this period. By assuming responsibility for me, he may have suffered more than I did during this crisis. I am sure he hated to ask for a favor on my behalf. But he swallowed any reservations and did it. For that, I will always be grateful.

In the event, I returned to the United States in June, and in the fall I joined a cadre of new faculty members at a New Hampshire prep school, most of whom were teaching primarily to avoid the draft. This did not endear us to older, more conservative teachers, some of them veterans. (One had flown a bomber over Germany during WWII.) Meanwhile, Jane and her husband David had moved to Washington, DC. As the War dragged on, Jane and I became more and more outspoken in our opposition to it. Politics had never been much talked about in our household. Growing up, I was aware that like most of the Melrose population, Dad and Mum were Republicans. (In those days, it was possible to be a moderate Republican.) Eventually, the Viet Nam War converted first Mum, then Dad, to antiwar Democrats, but this was a long and difficult process.

When Jane and I participated in protests against the War in the late 1960s and early 1970s, Dad was not supportive—far from it. One weekend, I drove with colleagues all the way from New Hampshire to an antiwar march in Washington, where I got my first acrid whiff of tear gas—distinctive and unforgettable. Dad was displeased to learn this. In fact, he once said to me angrily that he hadn't helped get me deferred so that I could protest the War. He played the draft card, so to speak, suggesting that that I owed it to him not to join the "hippies and radicals," whom he considered ill-informed and unpatriotic.

A further irony—and a hard one for him to bear—was that it was his daughter, not his son, who eventually went to Viet Nam—as a volunteer.

Jane and David were far more committed to the antiwar movement than I. Acting on their convictions, they served a three-year stint in Quang Ngai, where they directed an American Friends Service Committee humanitarian program that built and fitted prosthetic legs to victims of American land-mines.

Neither Dad nor Mum was pleased at the prospect of their daughter being in harm's way during the War. But Dad was particularly incensed—openly hostile to the plan, for which he held David responsible. At one point, he remarked that he didn't want his daughter off risking her life taking care of "derelicts" in some distant country.

We tried to make the parallel—obvious to us—with what he had done at a similar juncture in his life, in traveling to Syria to teach Armenian refugees. But he refused to concede the similarity. One of his concerns, of course, was Jane's physical safety. This was not unreasonable: the clinic was in a heavily contested area. But an underlying concern had to do with her politics. Al-though the Friends were officially pacifistic and neutral and their facility served civilians, they were undeniably sympathetic to the "enemy" cause.

Disappointed by his opposition, but undaunted, Jane went to Viet Nam in the spring of 1971 and stayed until the spring of 1974 (almost exactly 40 years after Dad's stint in Aleppo). Remarkably, by the end of her time there, he and Mum had come around to supporting her mission and opposing the War. It helped that progressive Protestant clergymen like William Sloane Coffin spoke out in opposition to the War. But I credit Jane's commitment with changing their attitude, to the extent that eventually they would attend Friends' meetings in Cambridge and even meetings of the AFSC.

⁓

In June of 1969, safe from the draft, I came home from Oxford. There I reconnected with friends and prepared to begin teaching in the fall. Soon after I settled into my old bedroom, I began to suspect *something* was wrong. Dad would often sleep late. That was unusual—both he and Mum were quite early risers—but it didn't seem such a big deal. It was summer. School was out. Dad didn't have much that required his attention, aside from yard work. What raised my suspicion was not that he lingered in bed, but that Mum seemed so worked up about it. It didn't seem like her. The tenor of the household had somehow changed during my absence.

One evening, we three were in the kitchen as Mum prepared dinner. No one, as far as I knew, had consumed any alcohol. But I thought I smelled gin, and said so. Dad and Mum glanced at each other and shrugged. I dismissed my sensation as an olfactory hallucination. *That's* how naïve I was. Or that's how much Dad's drinking caught me by surprise.

Ours was not a drinking family. Dad and Mum did not routinely drink beer or wine, much less hard liquor, before, with, or after dinner. We kept a modest supply of liquor in a dining room cupboard, but it was served mostly to dinner guests. For overnight guests, perhaps a nightcap.

In the summer of 1969, it seemed unlikely that I had actually smelled gin. But one day—a day that changed my life suddenly and dramatically—I heard Mum yelling at Dad in their upstairs bedroom. For her to yell at him was unprecedented. But it was what she said that stunned me: "Damn it, Grif. I'm sick and tired of your being drunk all the time!"

This "flashbulb memory" haunts me still.

My father—a man I had never seen even mildly intoxicated—drunk?

All the time?

My mind reeled.

I went to the bottom of the stairs and looked up. Mum came to the head of the stairs and apologized tearfully to me. But the genie was out of the bottle, so to speak. She could not unsay what she'd said. Although she behaved as though this was a spontaneous outburst, it may have been her way of "accidentally" letting me in on a secret she could no longer bear to keep to herself.

This was a crucial moment for all of us. As alcoholic husbands often do, Dad had made his wife his enabler, having her cover for him. She told me later that he had sworn her to secrecy, telling her that my finding out would "destroy" him. That constituted both emotional blackmail—putting an entirely unfair burden on her—and a self-fulfilling prophecy: once I knew, it did destroy him in my eyes. It has taken me decades—and the labor of writing this memoir—to rehabilitate his image. Of course, ironically, exposure also removed one final disincentive for his drinking—his fear of my finding him out. It was a disaster all around.

Or maybe not. If anyone benefited, it was Mum. Now she had me to share her burden. I did not immediately tell Jane, however.

Later that summer, Mum, Dad, and I attended a production of *Death of a Salesman* at the Harvard Summer Repertory Theater. We had all watched the TV version (1966) with Lee J. Cobb, and found it affecting. But things were different then. A mere three years later, I found the parallels between Dad and Willy excruciating. As far as I know Dad was faithful to Mum, but in my eyes the betrayal of his drinking was far more serious than any sexual indiscretion. It made me terribly angry at the time, and I still have trouble accepting it. The result was that, although he was not a failure like Willy, I found Dad pitiable.

Linda's loyal plea, "Attention must be paid," still makes my eyes fill up.

When I did pass the terrible news on to Jane she too had difficulty assimilating it. It was one of those revelations that make you wonder, have we all been living a lie? For how long? How could I not have known what was going on in my own home? How could I have been so wrong about my parents' lives? Who was this man, the father I thought I knew?

◟∿◞

Late that summer, I accompanied Dad and Mum on a camping trip to Nova Scotia and Cape Breton Island. At 22, I found it somewhat awkward to be camping with my parents—rather than with a friend or girlfriend. But I had no other plans, and no girlfriend, and the uncertainty of my draft status had prevented me from lining up a summer job. So I went along.

I was glad I did. Dad often rebounded in natural surroundings, especially in proximity to the sea; cold as the water was, in he went. Swimming—indoors or out, in fresh water or salt, smooth or rough—was his preferred form of exercise all his life. Dad must have learned to swim at the YMCA in Manchester as a boy, and it was a form of recreation (in the etymological sense) that gave him lifelong gratification. He had the most graceful, effortless crawl I have ever seen. His body seemed to move through the water faster than his slow, rhythmic arm strokes could possibly propel it. I remember his venturing into post-hurricane surf at a beach in Maine, unable to resist the challenge, as my mother beseeched him to stay on shore. I watched with a mixture of admiration, excitement, and fear as he was tossed about by the waves. When he came ashore, he was reprimanded for ignoring signs that the beach was closed. On this trip his frequent immersion was, or seemed to be, a sign of recovery.

The three of us got along well, and he and Mum behaved as affectionately as I'd ever seen them—even, uncharacteristically, occasionally holding hands. Perhaps, I thought, I'd overreacted to the discovery of his secret drinking. Perhaps he'd just had a particularly stressful year, with his children away and my draft problems. The two weeks were a pleasant, and reassuring, interlude, like a second honeymoon, albeit with an adult child in tow.

But as soon as we got home, he relapsed; the post-vacation letdown triggered a binge.

Within weeks, I moved to New Hampshire to assume my teaching duties, leaving him and Mum without me as a buffer. From my new vantage, I attempted to put his drinking and my relationship with him in perspective. Not surprisingly, very much his son, I did this in the form of a long letter. I put a good deal of care into composing it. I suppose I naively expected that I might receive a candid letter in return, that my letter might begin a fruitful dialogue.

Unfortunately, our next communication took the form of a phone call from me, during which I inquired—just to be sure it had arrived—whether he'd received my letter. At this point, he lost his composure, and he handed off the phone to Mum. In a later conversation, she reported to me that he described the letter as "devastating" and refused to share it with her. He and I never mentioned it again, and I assumed he'd destroyed it.

So I was stunned when I came across it in his personal archive after he died. To my utter surprise, Dad had added it to his trove of significant correspondence.

I can't recall exactly what I did with it when I found it. I didn't dare to read it, afraid of what he found so hurtful. Even decades later, in the early 2000s, as I mined the archive in composing this memoir, I kept putting this letter aside in its original envelope—unopened, unread. I approached the narrative chronologically, with that letter always waiting for me to read it at the appropriate time. I knew that I would have to read it eventually; it would be hypocritical—cowardly, even—to cite so many letters by others, without at least reading my own. Yet I hesitated, delayed, deferred, and procrastinated. Frankly, I was afraid that the letter that had once devastated Dad would devastate me; I was the same age Dad had been when he received it, and I'd been coping with my own depression. I carried enough guilt about the deterioration of our relationship; I was reluctant to shoulder any more.

Finally, I asked a visiting friend—a responsive reader of early chapters of this memoir and a student of psychoanalysis—if he would serve as my surrogate. He took the letter to another room. After an excruciatingly long interval, he reported to me: although he could see why my father might have had trouble assimilating it, given that it arose out of anger and disappointment on my part, he found it ultimately loving and felt that Dad must have perceived that, too. With that reassurance, I summoned the courage to read it myself.

Rather than paraphrase it and gloss it for readers, it seems only fair to insert it here and let readers form their own impressions of what it says—and otherwise reveals—about the relationship between me and him at this critical juncture in our lives—as he approached retirement and I began my career in his field, if not his footsteps.

Always eager to make short excursions to visit me, he and Mum had recently driven to New Hampshire to visit me on the Kimball Union Academy campus. I was pleased at first to see him, but I sensed right away that he was recovering from a binge. After long being oblivious, I had become quite skilled at detecting the signs of drink and its aftermath. I was furious that he had arrived in this condition and could hardly contain my anger in his presence. The visit did not go well. It was in the aftermath of that visit that I composed my missive.

> September 16 [1969]
> Dear Dad,
> This letter has been a long time coming, and I hope it will be good, that is, I hope it will be an accurate and complete expression of my feelings and that it will help us to understand each other better. Who knows, this may be the most important thing I have ever written.
> You must have known what was bothering me on Sunday, and I can hardly believe that mother didn't. Sometimes I think she sees only what she wants to

see, and I suppose her present circumstances justify that, to some extent. At any rate, you mustn't think I am unhappy here. In many ways it is more satisfying than anything I have previously done, and I only wish you could share in some of the luxuries I have come by so easily: pleasant and peaceful surroundings, genial colleagues, good students in small classes.

Disregarding the matter of your bad manners in arriving in the wretched state you did (not drunk but too obviously recuperating) and of my bad manners in receiving you so coolly, there is still the question of what you had hoped to gain from the visit. Couldn't you foresee that the consciousness in both our minds of what we were pretending so desperately to ignore would make it impossible for us to relax and enjoy each other, as we have in the past? Given your condition, the only possible outcome was for us to hurt each other's feelings, as we did.

The possibility of my being embarrassed at having to introduce you to someone is really minor; I could survive that, though it would be unpleasant. My inability to look you in the eye has deeper causes. You really do look ghastly in your post-drunken state; at least to the concerned eye you are a spectre of your former self. That in itself is painful to see, particularly since the damage is self-inflicted. (Incidentally, I wonder just how many people you are fooling. To someone familiar with the symptoms you must be a giveaway. I only wonder how I was ignorant as long as I was. My realization of your habit suddenly brought the details of the shaking hand and the sweetish breath into sudden relief.) More than this, however, in that condition you are a living reproach to me, a reproach for years of neglect .This neglect I think is partly fostered, but certainly not excused, by a home atmosphere in which none of us is particularly demonstrative or communicative.

I think the history of this condition can be profitably traced. For the power-ful message of that desolate Saturday following our trip was not "My father is an alcoholic" but that my father must be desperately unhappy. Not only that, but he must have been so for a long time. The encouraging two weeks of the trip and indeed whole years of the past which I had blithely considered satis-factory were suddenly revealed as sham. Mother had told me many times while I was away (at various places) how much you missed me. Only now, (and perhaps not even now), do I realize the urgency of that statement.

So we must examine the past a little. It must be obvious to you and probably also painful, that I enjoy a much better rapport with mother than I do with you. This is deceptive, however. for I think that that rapport depends on the fact that I sense that I am temperamentally essentially much more like you than like her. I enjoy Mom, I think, for precisely the same reasons you must have been attracted to her originally; we shared psychological needs which her ebullience, her resilience, her capacity to enjoy seem to fulfill. I don't know how far back my recognition of our essential affinity goes. Certainly I think it crystallized the year I had you in high school. In retrospect, your impulse to send me off to private school seems an intelligent one, though if followed I doubt that it would have solved the problem. Probably you refrained partly from fear of what in fact happened anyway, we became estranged from each other. Suffice it to say that I became hyper-conscious in classroom exposure of the fact that our minds and emotions worked in astonishingly similar fashion. For petty examples, Peter Berg once asked me how to rearrange a clumsy sentence only to have me give precisely the same answer you had given him earlier; I am sure that my success in composition and in vocabulary analogies was at least partly due to the fact of this mental kinship. You had supervised my mental development, my reading and writing for years, and only now am I beginning to realize how closely there too are related and how profoundly they influence one's whole personality and outlook if one enjoys and cultivates these activities.

In short, my reaction to this situation was quite immature. I began to disown you in subtle ways, not because there was anything in you I didn't admire, but because we were so frighteningly alike. Now, there is something scary in the mere similarity; in order to be sure of his identity an adolescent must be convinced of its absolute uniqueness. This being threatened in my own personality, I began to hide things; our relationship, already objectified by our new pupil-teacher confrontation, became more distant. Aside from the naked similarity, there must have been something frightening in what I was similar to; I must have realized that you were essentially a melancholy, lonely man, though I never thought about it consciously. Our estrangement became such that you complained that I did not "recognize" you when you passed my study hall. I was guilty, and this is no excuse, but the nearest I can some to an explanation. (And much of this I am understanding only as I submit to the discipline of a written exploration of it.)

My college years, I am afraid, extended this trend. I led, as I imagined all students did, something of a double life. I talked much of my work and little of my pleasure, or of my emotions. (It is ironic to realize now how you have led a double life and what a strain that has been on both you and mother.) As I suggested earlier, I felt that in order to have anything of my own, to be anything on my own, I would have to hide it from you. This is not to say that I did anything terrible, but simply that I shared little of my experience with you or with mother, though she obviously has suffered less from the deprivation. At any rate I always felt a little more at ease with her; I always feared your disapproval more. . . .

In short, to bring things to the present, after my realization in adolescence that you had, consciously or not, formed me very much in your own image, I have cultivated enough privacy so that we are now at least superficially very different. . . . The differences are still, I think, deceptive. At present, the lack of conversation between us is as often due to consciousness of our unspoken agreement on something as to my fear of disagreement. Given your present condition, however, these similarities, which are basic, take on a new aspect. Your condition frightens and depresses me particularly because I see in it a vision of my future. Can you see how this fundamental affinity between us gets in the way, how it makes it difficult for to respond? My own fear of reaching retirement age lonely and depressed compels me to disown my similarities with you. In your vulnerability and discontent I see my own, and I must dissemble in order to maintain my equilibrium.

This much in explanation of my role in the development of our relationship, which is all I can furnish. I cannot see into your mind, nor have we given each other much evidence of our knowledge of the changes along the way. I am quite sure I do not understand your present predicament. I think your depression is due to a combination of things: partly perhaps to the physiology of ageing, more to the psychology of ageing, largely but not solely to problems at school, partly simply to a melancholy temperament and a natural dissatisfaction with life. These factors are all involved, I think but I have no idea in what proportions or whether they account for the whole problem. And there is now, of course, the problem of our dependence on alcohol to get you through a life you no longer find satisfactory. Presumably, this problem originally arose as a result of depression caused by other things, but now undoubtedly it is as much cause as effect: you drink because you are depressed and you are depressed and ashamed because you drink. And the trouble is complicated by the apparent fact that your psychological dependence on the alcohol has become a physiological one as well. Here is the real difficulty for the rest of us. We have no way of measuring the compulsion, psychological or physiological, for you to drink. We are willing to excuse your drinking, to an extent, if, as an addict, you are in the control of the drug. Otherwise, your continual drinking seems merely cowardice.

Several points may help to put your problem in perspective. First, although it will undoubtedly be of little consolation, your discontent is usual, to some extent, at your age. Retirement age is a notoriously bothersome one for many people. Children have left home more or less permanently, and one finds himself with neither offspring nor a job to occupy him. In your case because of your special devotion to both children and job, the deprivation is particularly acute. This will be an important and difficult transition in your life; it is like a second adolescence without youth. You will have to rediscover yourself and Mother; you will have to find new activities (which involve relatively little responsibility) to engage your interest. You will have to discover new people.

Jane and I are particularly concerned about you; so is Mother. But as I realized with anguish this summer, we can't lick this problem for you. We may be able to do it with you, but still, essentially it is up to you to learn to like living again.

To turn to the problems at school specifically, let me oversimplify the problem to indicate the course it seems, to me, to be taking. You are and have been all your life a man too complex and too sensitive to be fully content either with your jobs or your colleagues. You feel more and more alienated from the creeping mediocrity at MHS (and as I tried to suggest to you, this fact of the success of mediocrity is generally accepted). Here I think you have affinities with the discontented young of today, though you seem unconscious of the fact. Unlike them, of course, you are not politically radical. You fail to generalize on your experience as facilely as they do. For this I admire you, but I wish you did not so wholly internalize the problem. The young blame and excoriate the Establishment; you seem only to blame and pity yourself. Some men would take pleasure and satisfaction from such martyrdom (and many of your students must know what you are up against and what it costs you; you are admired by them); you seem to derive none. Again, I would probably not enjoy you in the role of the self-righteous martyr; it is not your style. But your cornered reaction is, I think one of gradual self-destruction and I cannot bear to witness that. You are making yourself and your family pay for something that is primarily beyond your control, neither our fault nor yours.

I can no longer drink gin since I have seen you poisoning yourself with it. To put things schematically and simply, you have found yourself too sensitive, and your response has been, finally, to dull your senses and your sensitivity with drink. You have been too responsible, and your response is to become, with drink, irresponsible to yourself and family. You are losing, surrendering even, the battle against mediocrity by the weakness of your response. You are letting them destroy you; you are letting them make you more like them. With each bout of drunkenness, the difference between you and those you despise diminishes. This is perhaps cruel to say, but I have deliberately oversimplified to show you the terrible irony of the situation.

The question of understanding the problem is for the moment done with. Solution of the problem is much more difficult. Without being informed at all of the real nature and depth of the problem, I sensed, even though I was deferred in June, that I ought to return home for the summer, that I was needed there. I don't mean to congratulate myself on this, for I soon learned that my powers of perception were far inferior to what I thought they had been, and was shocked at my naivety. But I do want to say that I saw little evidence on your part this summer to do anything but conceal the problem from me. I realize that you were in a sense trying to protect me as well as yourself, but that was silly and immature, and symptomatic of the whole tradition of individual secrecy in our family that got us into this whole mess. I saw little desire on your part to face and beat the problem, little evidence of any initiative on your part of change your ways or to engage yourself, even though Mother said you were "much better." Under those circumstances, I could hardly imagine how she got through last year, and of course by requiring that she hide the problem from Jane and me, you put her in the intolerable position of having to suffer it alone. I could not fathom her resentment of your staying be in bed until I realized what you were doing there.

You were probably right in wanting to hide your problem from me in the sense that my discovery of it does to some extent diminish my respect at least for your courage, while it increases my compassion for you. I was put in the position this summer, as Mother must have been numerous times before, of having to discipline you as I would a child. This is hardly conducive to a mature relationship between us. I don't like to have to slap your hand, and I hate you when you make me do it. As you appear more and more helpless, and less and less responsible, my feelings toward you are driven around from respect to pity. If you become a burden on us, we will care for you, we will pity you, but we will no longer admire you except as the ghost of what you were.

And, the sad thing is that you have so much to be proud of. Unlike so many of my contemporaries, I wholly admire what my father has chosen to do for a living and the way he has done it. There is no guilt or embarrassment when I tell people my father is an English teacher; indeed, I have paid you the supreme compliment of following your footsteps. . . .

I hope my account has not seemed negative. As I have tried to say before, we are so concerned and so hurt because we love and admire you. It is hard to accept this new truth about you, but as I have suggested here your weakness is inextricably related to your great strengths, and you must draw on those strengths in the days to come. I would give anything to see you as you were at Cape Breton, healthy, relaxed, moving confidently, swimming well, smiling again. I would do anything, but it isn't up to me. The question is whether you will do anything, and I trust you will. If you can't bring yourself to do it for your own sake, and it is your own life and personality that you are slowly destroying, do it for mother's sake. She deserves better.

    Love,

    Thomas

❧

There are passages here that I cringe now to read, where I patronize Dad, where I hector him, sections that seem insulting and hurtful, even cruel. (Transcribing the original for publication was quite excruciating, and I confess that I usually skipped over it while reviewing and revising.) But I am also struck by the degree to which I take some responsibility for the distance between us.

In my experience, memoirs of fathers are typically motivated by a desire to repair a relationship with a parent who was absent in some significant way. That is certainly true of mine, but I acknowledge in this letter having absented myself from him. That removal, a form of passive aggression, must have been very painful for him. What might have comforted him is my admission that my withdrawal was a function of my sense of deep affinity with him—so deep it threatened my sense of individuality.

So while I can see how this letter may have seemed "devastating"—if I am remembering Mum's report correctly—I also hope that if he ever reread it—and why save it, if not to reread it?—he might have sensed the admiration, not just where it is explicitly articulated, but in the labor—psychic and emotional, more than verbal—that it took to produce such a letter. (A labor I have returned to in writing this memoir, this last letter to him.) I like to think that, as someone who I now know lived his early life in part through letters, he might appreciate my letter as an attempt to reach him through the fog of his depression. And if he heard echoes of his epistolary voice in mine—as I do—that too may have given him some bittersweet gratification.

Chapter Four

McLean Patient

1973

Dad's pattern of drinking was a severely pathological one. It did not rise out of, or have anything to do with, social drinking. Contrary to the actual effects of alcohol, which disturbs sleep, he may have begun to drink to induce sleep when anxious or depressed. As far as I knew, Dad never abused alcohol until he was in his sixties. I admit that I was slow to pick up on it then, but that's in part because of his habitual moderation; abuse of alcohol had never been an issue, so far as Jane and I knew. However his drinking began, whatever its roots, it had its own powerful dynamic; intoxication served some deep need—physiological, emotional, or both.

His drinking was solitary, furtive, and increasingly self-destructive. On those occasions when he could not quell the urge, he would acquire a fifth (or more) of gin and stash it in the closet next to his bed (the same one in which I found his archive after he died). After Mum fell asleep, he would retrieve the bottle and drink in bed—straight from the bottle. (Eventually, to protect his stomach lining, he resorted to mixing the gin with milk.)

Mum would awake to find him incapacitated—a truly rude awakening. When she could, she would wrest his bottle away and then help him sober up with a solid meal. Otherwise, he might stay drunk in bed for a couple of days. At first, his drinking was confined to weekends. This ruined weekends for Mum, of course, but it didn't interfere with his working. However, by early 1969, he was also drinking during the week. In this case, Mum would call in sick for him, go to work herself, and hope he'd be sober when she got home. The ploy of having Mum call the office soon became transparent, and his drinking must have been an open secret among his colleagues well before I and Jane were aware of it. When we found out, it was unsettling to think others knew more about our parents' lives than we did.

All of this took a heavy toll on Dad's body and mind. It certainly was hard on Mum. Her life had become a nightmare. She continued to work, less for the money than for gratification outside her home. Because of stigma and shame, this was a burden she was reluctant to share. As Dad's drinking became more difficult to conceal, she may have confided in a few close friends. I hope she was able to lighten her burden in that way, reasoning that it was better that they knew than that her children did. But she was far too loyal to—or ashamed of—him to tell others until his drinking had become obvious to others.

The more people knew, of course, the less Dad needed to restrain himself and the lower his self-esteem would sink. Shame and guilt deepened his depression, which led to more drinking—a truly vicious cycle.

When Dad drank, he drank to the point of oblivion. That was the whole point. His drinking was never about pleasure—if it had been, we could have indulged it. Rather, it was about killing pain, which must have been terrible to prompt behavior so inimical to the wellbeing of his family. He would not have done something so selfish—and so self-destructive—had it not afforded him otherwise unattainable relief from suffering.

~

One of the remarkable things about Dad, though, was his ability to rebound from a binge. With Mum's help, he could clean himself up and look presentable in a few hours—even to guests. Amazingly, Mum's diaries record days on which he was drunk on the morning of an evening social engagement. While she fretted, he rallied. At least for a while. By the early 1970s, he was no longer able to confine his drinking to our home. He began to overindulge at friends' and relatives' homes.

Despite his resilient constitution, this pattern became unsupportable—at least by Mum. Before Jane went to Viet Nam in the spring of 1971, the family—Jane, Mum, and I—staged an informal intervention; we gathered in the living room to confront him. Put on the defensive, he denied he was an alcoholic. I might have understood if he'd said, "I'm an alcoholic. I'm sorry, I can't stop drinking. But I'll try to do better." The admission would have meant much to me, even though I would not have put much faith in any promises. But, desperate to maintain some self-respect, he stubbornly denied his condition. I suppose he wanted to distinguish himself from stereotypical drunks reeling in alleys. (His being the son of a teetotaling Protestant Irishman must have deepened his shame.) At best, this was a refusal of a category that conflated him indiscriminately with others and denied his individuality and dignity. At bottom, though, his denial amounted to an existential lie—a falsehood about his behavior, if not his very identity. And it was counterproductive: denying he had a problem absolved him of the need to address it. I couldn't respect his denial then, and I still can't.

Frustrated, Mum took a medical approach. On the plausible theory that he was self-medicating for depression, she encouraged him to see a therapist. And he did: the estimable Dr. Robert Mezer, at his office in Boston's Back Bay. (Mezer had achieved a measure of fame when he testified for the defense in a sanity hearing in the 1967 trial of Albert de Salvo, who had confessed to being the Boston Strangler.) Thereafter, Mum's calendar records frequent visits to Dr. Mezer, as well as calls to and from him. Dad and Mum would sometimes visit the doctor together, and she would talk to Mezer privately as well. Ever hopeful, she made a note of each new drug prescribed to alleviate Dad's depression and/or moderate his drinking. And there were many. In addition to Antabuse, which causes unpleasant side effects when alcohol is consumed, over the course of his treatment Dad took all of the following tranquilizers, antidepressants, stimulants, and antipsychotics, alone or in combination—Elavil, Mellaril, Amytal, Dalmane, Parnate, Ritalin, and Thorazine.

But neither psychoactive drugs nor talk therapy did him much good. Dad could be very charming, and he apparently deceived his therapist into thinking he was feeling better—and drinking less—than he was. Once his enabler, Mum now had to function as his reality-check. At one point, she discovered that he had been lying to Dr. Mezer. She reported to me, incredulous and indignant, that Dad had told Mezer he was writing a book.

I wish he had been writing one: this one, the story of his life, which was far richer and more memoir-worthy than I suspected at the time, and which he could have recounted in more detail than I can, not to mention from a very different point of view. But of course, his very illness precluded his doing so. Being depressed—as distinct from having recovered from it—is not a position in which one is capable of memoir.

Antidepressants didn't seem to have any lasting effect. Worse, Dad sometimes took his drugs by the handful, which made him act very oddly. He would say things that made no sense, and we began to wonder about his sanity. His drinking became so constant, and attendance at school so spotty, that he could not continue as department head. In the winter of 1971, he and Mum decided that he would retire in June. He didn't make it even that far. That spring, Mum persuaded Dr. Mezer to authorize a medical leave for him, and he taught his last class in late April. In mid-June the school held a retirement party for him. There were over one hundred people present.

I was not among them. I'm not sure why; perhaps I had a conflicting obligation. I hope so. It must have been a bittersweet event for all—not the unalloyed celebration of a distinguished career that he deserved, and certainly not the inauguration of an eagerly anticipated new phase of life. Rather, it constituted a tacit admission of his inability to continue to function professionally in his prime. And, shockingly, he lived only four more years.

～

Retirement can be especially tough for men. But Dad didn't retire only to lapse into a depression because of a sudden loss of status. Rather, his depression necessitated his retirement, terminating his career prematurely, before he could retire properly, with dignity.

In the spring of 1971, he suffered two significant deprivations in quick succession: his daughter left the States for Viet Nam, and he lost his vocation. A double whammy, one would think. Oddly, though, both of these changes seem to have proved worse in the anticipation than in the reality. At least, judging from Mum's diaries, he remained pretty sober and functional for the remainder of 1971.

With the beginning of the new year, however, he began to drink again. And things worsened in the fall of 1972. With the end of the draft, I was able to go on to graduate school, after a three-year hiatus. Partly because of its proximity to home, I chose Brown University. For the first two years, I lived in Providence, Rhode Island, spending weekends in Cambridge, Massachusetts, with my fiancée. Being nearby, I visited or called home regularly.

For the most part, I did not witness Dad's drinking much until after Mum died; typically, she bore the brunt of it alone. But she summoned me to help her one night, and I witnessed him in the throes of delirium tremens. She had succeeded in getting his bottle away from him, but the sudden deprivation of alcohol precipitated withdrawal symptoms. I remember Dad lying on his back in bed, then convulsing so violently that he catapulted himself right out of it; miraculously, he landed on his feet, and his next convulsion vaulted him back into bed. I had never seen anything like it, and I hope I never will again. We decided that the best thing was for him to taper off, so we gave him some more gin. I could only sympathize with Mum, who must have suffered through such scenes over and over.

～

He and Mum were living two lives now. When he was sober—and, remarkably, he could be dry for weeks and even months on end—the two lived what appears, from her diaries, to be a rich, full life—as busy as when Jane and I were still living at home, but differently so. As always, they entertained guests and visited friends and relatives in New England and the mid-Atlantic states. They went to films, plays, lectures, museum exhibits.

But when he was drinking, he was a different person, and the two of them lived a very different life. When drunk, he was almost unrecognizable, and his behavior approached spousal abuse. Mum was reluctant to divulge the worst to me, but she hinted, saying that under the influence he would call her "terrible names." (Even now, I don't like to speculate what those were.) One calendar entry reports, shockingly, "Grif bit me"—probably as she tried to pry a bottle of gin from his hands. Alcohol seemed to utterly transform him. I began to think of him as a kind of Dr. Jekyll/Mr. Hyde. This was a way of reconciling myself to unpleasant new truths about him. This drunk was not my real father.

Mum was innately optimistic. This was a strong element of her appeal to Dad, with his susceptibility to depression. She was also very determined and independent. When he was on a bender, she would live as normally as she could. Only rarely did she stay home to tend to him. She would go shopping, even to movies or the beach, by herself. She would write to, call, or visit friends. Even if she did confide in friends and relatives, however, she must have felt isolated. And during his sober periods, she lived in a state of constant insecurity and dread of his next binge. She knew there'd be one; she just didn't know what would trigger it or when.

Understandably, his drinking angered her. It was ruining their life together, and it spoiled her anticipation of retirement. And it was always up to her to push him to seek treatment. This in itself made it less effective. When Dr. Mezer's therapy and drugs didn't seem to be working, Mum finally convinced Dad to enter McLean hospital for treatment in early 1973. What finally impelled him to enter McLean was her threat to leave him. His drinking was bound up with his depression, but the depression was the root problem, while the drinking was its most overt expression. This made therapeutic success difficult to measure: did a sober period constitute progress, if he remained depressed? If his mood improved, did that mean he'd never binge again? I think Mum would have settled for sobriety, which she saw as something he could achieve by willpower. But I think she desired a definitive resolution that was unlikely for either of these two conditions. Hence her desperate ultimatum.

Here is how Dr. Mezer presented Dad's case in a letter conferring him to the hospital's care:

> Mr. William [sic] Couser first consulted me on September 22, 1970 [my 24th birthday] for help with a depressive condition complicated by alcoholism. . . . Mr. Couser told me he had been depressed all of his life, but more severely so for the past two years. He had insomnia, loss of interest, some mild agitation, but no suicidal ideation. There were no delusions or hallucinations, and there was no thought disorder. *I could elicit no precipitants or crisis* [italics mine].
>
> I prescribed Elavil and saw him again on September 25th. There had been several calls from his wife because Mr. Couser had been drinking and had been unable to go to work. We discussed hospitalization as an alternative, but decided to continue with office care. He took a leave of absence from work, saw me regularly, and was able to return to work by the end of October.

However, the pressure of work was great, and it was a steady downhill course until the end of April, 1971 when he stopped working. This precipitated further depression and drinking, somewhat alleviated during those periods when his wife was on vacation and could be with him. Hospitalization was frequently discussed, but he would never agree to enter a hospital. Finally, in November of 1972, I arranged for his hospitalization at McLean, working this out with his wife, and he refused to go along with this recommendation. I pointed out that his failure to comply with my recommendation required me to refuse to continue with his case, and I told him he could see another psychiatrist; besides, he had been untruthful with me regarding his drinking, and I felt office management would no longer suffice. On January 12, 1973, I received a call from Mrs. Couser indicating that Mr. Couser was now ready to enter McLean. I assured her that this was the right thing to do and that this was an important forward step in his recovery, suggesting that electro-shock treatments would be carefully considered.

〰

I "sicced" the doctor's "William," because no one who knew Dad ever called him that. It may seem a small thing, but to me this misidentification suggests a fundamental lack of recognition and probably a significant lack of rapport. My other editorial act was to italicize the line, "I could elicit no precipitants or crisis." I don't fault Mezer for this. Dad had not been entirely forthcoming with him. Dad was protective of his privacy; the confessional mode was not comfortable for him. And no immediate precipitant for his condition was apparent to any of us. That made his collapse not only mystifying but frustrating; there would be considerable satisfaction in detecting a clear cause. Seeking one has been a prime motive of this memoir.

In listing Dad's meds, Dr. Mezer noted that Mum "has a distrust and dislike for all medications" and that Dad might have become dependent on Amytal, a barbiturate. Mum came by her distrust of medications honestly; it was rooted in Dad's history of abusing them. If a substance was mood-altering, Dad was likely to misuse it. The doctor added, "I'd see him at McLean whenever he thought it advisable," and concluded, presumably without intentional irony, "Good luck in treating Mr. Couser."

In the course of my research, I located Dr. Mezer in Florida, where he had retired. I wrote him to request any medical records he might have or any personal recollections of Dad. He responded that he retained no files; moreover, he did not remember Dad (letter of November 18, 2009). I confess I found the latter assertion troubling, given the length of time Dad had been his patient and the difficulty of his case. (Only later did it occur to me that I should have jogged the doctor's memory by sending him his letter of referral.) Perhaps Dad was not, to him, a very interesting patient. Or perhaps Dr. Mezer did not want to discuss the unsuccessful treatment of a recalcitrant patient.

One of Dad's physicians at McLean shared my dismay that Mezer had been "unable to come up w/ any material of psychodynamic usefulness relating to the patient!!" (Admission Note 1/16/73, emphasis original). Mezer's letter demonstrates that his depression was "treatment resistant" in more than one sense. First, it didn't respond to the drugs available at the time. More important, perhaps, Dad was hardly a compliant patient. When urged to consider hospitalization as a last resort, he obstinately resisted. Just as he denied he was an alcoholic, he resisted the implicit diagnosis of mental illness that inpatient status would convey.

His condition seemed to improve during Mum's vacations. He was lonely and at loose ends when not working, and doubly dependent on her for stimulation, company, direction, and support. He urged her to retire—an obvious solution to his depression, as he saw it. But she demurred: why should she give up a gratifying job to be at home with an alcoholic? And what if she decided to divorce him? She would need her income. She would retire only if he could pull himself together. Perhaps inadvertently, he had put the onus of his recovery on her. They were at an impasse.

Dad entered McLean's Appleton House (known then as the alcohol unit) in mid-January, 1973, and remained for more than three months. (In those days health insurance subsidized long hospital stays.) Located in Belmont, McLean was not far from our home; it was even closer to Arlington, where Mum taught, making after-work visits quite convenient. She visited many weekdays, making detours to Belmont part of her commute. It was also not far from Cambridge, where I was spending a good deal of time with my fiancée. So I was able to accompany Mum occasionally. And Dad was allowed to go home on weekends, when therapy was suspended. I could see him then, as well.

Widely regarded as one of nation's best mental hospitals, McLean has a lovely collegiate campus. It owes much of its fame to its long roster of celebrity patients, which includes Zelda Fitzgerald, Robert Lowell, Anne Sexton, Sylvia Plath, Ray Charles, James Taylor, Marianne Faithfull, John Nash, Lou Reed, Steven Tyler, and David Foster Wallace. It has been given compelling literary representation in Susanna Kaysen's memoir *Girl, Interrupted*, which tells the story of her eighteen months there in the late 1960s.

To write her memoir, Kaysen obtained her medical files and incorporated some documents into her narrative, along with her recollections and reflections. In researching Dad's life, I decided to take advantage of my right to his medical records. I hoped that seeing his case through the eyes of medical professionals might offer some insight into his psyche. At the same time, I was apprehensive about what I might discover—some truth darker than what I was already aware of? So I delayed until I reached this chapter in the narrative.

I summoned my courage and set the bureaucratic wheels in motion. After documenting his death and my status as his son and executor, and paying the requisite fee for photocopying and handling, I received a stack of records more than an inch high. Perhaps in this pile I would find the solution to the mystery of his deterioration.

For my sake, his sake, and the sake of the medical profession, I wish I could say that I did.

But one of the things that the medical files reveal is their own unreliability. This is not entirely their fault. Medical professionals are inclined to believe their patients' testimony in the absence of counterevidence, and patients—especially mental patients—are not always reliable. Perhaps alerted by Dr. Mezer, the staff at McLean did not take Dad at his word. I was startled to read this in his Admission Note: "Patient is 30% reliable." Thirty percent! How does one quantify such a thing? And what would lead to such a low estimate of Dad's credibility at the outset of his treatment?

As it turned out, however, Dad told some untruths in this new venue, as well. One seemingly gratuitous lie stands out: every account of his alcohol abuse in his medical file identifies his poison as bourbon—on the order of a pint or more per day (characterized as a "maintenance dose"). But while he may have served bourbon or rye to guests at home, I never knew him to drink it when bingeing. His poison—quite literally—was gin. (I hadn't just imagined I smelled it on his breath in the kitchen that day in the summer of 1969.) Why would he lie about this? After all, he admitted to heavy drinking. (Sort of: his actual pattern was not "maintenance" but intermittent bingeing, which was far more deleterious.) Why lie about what he drank? My guess is that bourbon seemed literary. He liked to romanticize his drinking, as though he was some sort of tortured genius, writing a book. Moreover, I suspect he enjoyed deceiving those with power and control over him; to do so was to get over, to assert and preserve some autonomy, some privacy. I cannot overlook these lies but I understand them as means of shoring up his ego, preserving some dignity in the institution.

I was right to dread and delay reading through his McLean files, which I have done at least three times; it is a dismal experience. These are the only documents in his archive—other than my letter to him—that I find truly painful to read. The other private documents were either written by or intended for him; though not meant for my eyes, they represent him favorably. Reading them, I don't feel like a voyeur; rather, I feel like a privileged auditor of precious private communication. Not so his medical dossier. It feels voyeuristic, even sadistic, to observe him under medical monitoring when he was so vulnerable, so fragile, so desperate. However, I cannot disregard documents that purport to offer authoritative medical testimony about him.

Physically, he was surprisingly hale at the time of his admission exam. In fact, the examining doctor described him as a "hearty male." Surprisingly—miraculously—his liver was barely palpable, and his blood work revealed normal liver function. He manifested "minimal organicity." This phrase that initially stumped me. I had no idea what it meant, but it didn't sound good. However, a psychiatrist friend—himself employed by McLean—informed me it meant Dad had "minimal brain damage." A good thing, then. And again, a testament to his extraordinary constitution.

While I was growing up, I perceived Dad as tall and quite strong, and he still looms large in my imagination, so it is shocking to be reminded that, at 5' 10" and 150 pounds, he was three inches shorter and thirty pounds lighter than I was at the same age.

Despite his relatively good physical condition, it is disturbing to read through the results of his physical, as every organ is subjected to medical assessment. What's far worse, however, is reading about his demeanor (downcast), his affect (depressed, flat), his conversation (monosyllabic), his attitude (resentful and resistant), and his behavior (agitated or withdrawn), his stance toward the other patients (fearful and isolated). Upon admission, and often thereafter, he would pace the halls like a caged . . . human being. Despite my sense, then and now, that he needed hospitalization, I suspect that some of this is a function of his environment—or at least his desire not to be in it. In any case, I find this report very affecting. My heart goes out to a frightened, troubled man.

The admission of a family member to a mental hospital is hardly an occasion for celebration, but Mum and I were greatly relieved to have Dad there. We hoped for the best for him. But, to be honest, we also took comfort in the fact that he was someone else's responsibility for a while. I'm afraid we gave that impression to the hospital and perhaps, more damaging, to Dad, who told the McLean staff that he felt the family had isolated him as a "sick old man."

I had my reasons for keeping my distance. Exactly a year earlier, during my first semester in graduate school, I had crashed emotionally. Over-whelmed with work and concerned about Dad, I seized up with anxiety and depression. I saw a therapist for the first time. Talking helped some, but the Valium prescribed hardly made a dent on my anxiety and had no effect at all on my depression. I learned what it felt like to be acutely depressed. I never considered suicide, but I came to understand the impulse to end one's suffer-ing by ending one's life. At the time I was reluctant to admit the extent of my distress to Dad and Mum, not wanting to add to their worry. I was especially reluctant to let Mum think (know) she had another depressive on her hands. By the time he entered McLean, I had rebounded somewhat, but my sense of affinity with his vulnerability made me keep my distance. Ultimately, of course, this was not good for either of us.

∼

Although Dad obviously needed psychiatric help, and I wish he had been a more compliant patient, I sympathize with his resistance to the hospital regimen. The whole set-up of such institutions seems inherently, and counterproductively, infantilizing: patients' days are regimented; therapeutic activities and appointments are scheduled; meds are doled out at prescribed intervals; meals are provided. At the same time, paradoxically, patients are urged to take responsibility for their recovery. The institution seems to send mixed messages, placing patients in a kind of double bind.

If Dad had any individual therapy, no records survived; at least, I received none. On a form optimistically titled "McLean Hospital Progress Notes," various medical personnel recorded his impressions of him. Their sense was that he wasn't doing very well. So, after a short unsuccessful trial with medication, he was given electro-convulsive therapy (ECT), popularly known as electroshock. For my generation, ECT was defined by *One Flew over the Cuckoo's Nest*, in which it is given forcibly to the protagonist Randle McMurphy (played by Jack Nicholson in the film version). So when it was proposed that ECT be tried on Dad, I was initially horrified. But nothing else seemed to have lasting effect. He acquiesced, signed the requisite waivers, and, over five weeks in February and early March, he underwent a dozen treatments. (A hefty chunk of the medical documentation I obtained consists of records of these treatments, graphing his EEG readouts—all of it inscrutable to me. In fact, I wonder how much it revealed to medical personnel, other than that the current remained within safe levels.)

After some encouraging initial improvement, the results were negligible: no lasting "lifting of mood."

∼

I remember visiting Dad during this period. It's very odd, visiting someone you love, especially a parent, in a mental hospital. Because of the stigma attached to mental illness, and especially to alcoholism, it felt intrusive to enter his unit, where other patients might fear being recognized or resent just being seen. Obviously, patients are there because they are deemed to be mentally ill, to some degree. And visitors are inevitably—and rightly—curious about how patients are doing. In the case of mood disorders, however, visitors can often read patients' state from their demeanor: they don't have to inquire. Indeed, asking may elicit an untruthful answer, and a patient's false claim of improvement may be counterproductive. On the other hand, a truthful answer may be unwelcome. So conversation trades in trivia; patients and visitors tiptoe around the pachyderm in the room.

I dreaded those visits, and I went along more to support Mum than to comfort Dad. Dad seemed rather vague to me—not quite all there. Not crazy, just not fully present—even more remote than his ordinarily distant self.

~

He was never a fully cooperative patient. In March, after ECT had failed to lift his depression, the staff (and Mum) pressed him to take "behavioral measures": to line up some volunteer work or paid tutoring, to attend AA, and so on. This seemed reasonable, but Dad equivocated, insisting that he would work these things out after his release. Finally, the staff confronted him. This was no more successful than our family intervention. Dad exploded and, as Mum wrote in her calendar, on March 30 he "walked out of McLean."

How did he get home, I wonder. Call a cab? Or ask Mum, who was furious, to come and pick him up?

Mum begged him to return and the hospital to accept him. The hospital said that if he agreed to return the following week, it would not discharge him "AMA" ("against medical advice"—a designation that protects the institution from liability). He didn't return immediately but was granted an extension. McLean agreed to readmit him to participate in the "transition program," but this seems a face-saving formality. He was readmitted on April 26 and discharged for good on May 1, 1973.

~

Here are some excerpts from his Discharged Outright Summary:

> A diagnosis of alcoholic addiction, chronic, was made. Simple drunkenness, neurotic depression, and a passive dependent personality.
>
> . . .
> Final Diagnoses:
> 1. Depressive reaction
> 2. Passive aggressive personality and alcohol addiction
> 3. Simple drunkenness. Improved.

Diagnosis of mental illness is an art, not a science. The many, ever-proliferating diagnoses in the *Diagnostic and Statistical Manual of Mental Disorders* do not refer to discrete conditions, nor are these conditions susceptible to definitive tests involving biomarkers. As Gary Greenberg has pointed out in *Manufacturing Depression* and *The Book of Woe*, only in psychiatry do symptoms in effect constitute diseases and vice versa (depression is at once a symptom and an underlying condition). So it does not surprise me to find varied diagnoses. Still, this summary seems a mixture of the obvious and the nonsensical. Dad was obviously—at this time in his life—pathologically dependent on Mum. But I suspect that the "passive aggressive" diagnosis has more to do with his resistance to treatment protocols than with any essential personality trait.

I confess that it amused me to come across the term "simple drunkenness" here. No one—but Dad—could deny that he was an alcoholic, and his denial of it was further evidence of it. But "drunkenness" is not a clinical term. "Alcohol addiction" sounds more medical. But I'm not sure even that is a valid diagnosis. If Dad was truly *addicted* to alcohol—rather than merely dependent on it in times of crisis—how could he live without it for weeks or months, or drink appropriately and moderately in social settings?

My skepticism of his diagnoses was heightened when I read the discharge summary written when he walked out a month earlier:

> 1. Alcoholism, alcoholism addiction medically improved.
> 2. Involutional depression, involutional melancholia—moderately improved.
> 3. Obsessive-compulsive personality—unchanged.

Granted, these two summaries carry the signatures of different physicians—Ralph S. Ryback (April) and David Browne (May)—but there is almost no overlap in the diagnostic terms offered. This seems like dartboard diagnosis, or as though the physicians are slapping diagnostic labels on Dad, like extra stamps on a package they want to be sure is not returned.

Obviously, he was depressed: chronically and at times acutely. But the diagnoses offered here are distinct. "Involutional depression" refers to depression related to, and presumably brought on by, the natural organic degradation of the body that occurs with ageing. But that's more of a description than an explanation: why is ageing accompanied by depression in some people but not in all? And, as his admission physical showed, aside from his depression and alcoholism—indeed, in spite of them—he was in remarkably good condition. (His siblings all lived well into their eighties or nineties, and likely he would have too, had he not been depressed.)

"Depressive reaction" refers to depression that occurs in response to some external event. But neither Dad, nor Dr. Mezer, nor McLean's best psychiatrists were able to identify developments in his recent life that might have precipitated his depression.

In medicine, the goal of diagnosis is to direct successful treatment, which did not happen in Dad's case. (His treatment ran the gamut without lasting benefit, so perhaps faulty diagnosis was not the only problem.) For me as a memoirist, the issue is that McLean personnel seem more concerned with classifying Dad than with understanding him. As a result, the medical file contains very little insight. What I seek is causation, explanation, and meaning, rather than accurate diagnosis. But I can't help thinking that had Dad and his carers been able to collaborate on a better narrative, that might have been more therapeutic than the pharmacopeia and electric current he was subjected to.

~

Also disturbing to me in Dad's medical records is the probing of family dynamics for clues. Some painful passages concern our relationship. Jane is nowhere mentioned; her response was that she felt hurt at having been left out. What about her being in danger in Viet Nam, for instance? I see her point. But her safety there was a matter for healthy, rational concern, which is not the issue here.

I'd rather have been left out than to discover the references to myself. This, for example, in a summary of a "Planning Conference" held soon after his admission: "He relates some of his symptoms of depression to his son's progress. The depression became increasingly severe five years ago when his son broke up with his girlfriend. Another of these exacerbations occurred at a time when his son was threatened with military induction."

I well remember that breakup, but what really shattered me was a friend's announcement, within months, that he and my former girlfriend were engaged to be married. (It's the only time I have ever fainted in response to bad news: when my friend informed me, I began to fall off my chair and barely saved myself from landing on the floor.) I was living at home at the time; my distress was obvious, and Dad and Mum inquired as to its cause. As I told them, I burst into tears. Mum, typically, said something meant to be comforting, about my girlfriend having been "caught on the rebound." (Mum may have been right; the relationship fizzled, and the couple did not marry, but I lost touch with a valued friend.) I don't remember Dad's response. Evidently, though, my fragility somehow infected him. Or so he claimed. Even if it wasn't true, it was unsettling to have him say that, as though he was my doppelganger, vulnerable to my changes of mood and outlook. Somehow he implicated me, my crises, in his slide into depression, as though he were living vicariously through me.

I was not surprised to hear his reference to the draft; I had long sensed that that had been a particularly difficult issue for him to negotiate, and reading my mother's datebooks posthumously confirmed that his drinking had accelerated then. The reference to my "progress" is picked up by suggestions elsewhere to the effect that he was threatened by my success and jealous of my mother's attention to me. This constructs the family dynamics as classically Oedipal.

Like any father and son, we were somewhat competitive. This manifested itself when we played tennis. We played only occasionally, usually when Mum suggested it, rather than as something one of us initiated. (I much preferred to play with friends, but Dad didn't have tennis-playing friends.) By the early seventies, I was fully grown, and the better player—bigger, stronger, fitter, and faster. I never knew how hard I should play, not wanting to beat him badly. One day—I can't remember why; in fact, I probably didn't know why at the time—I lost deliberately. I didn't make intentional errors; I just didn't exert myself, letting balls go that I could have reached. It was obvious to Dad that I was throwing the match, and he was justifiably disgusted. We drove home in silence, and when we pulled into the driveway, he turned to me and snarled, "Don't ever do that again."

What he referred to as my "progress" and success are my academic accomplishments. He and Mum had always had high expectations for my performance in school, and I had always assumed that he took unalloyed pride in it. I thought he'd been a good student himself, and I was just living up to his model, rather than surpassing it. Only after he died did I discover what a mediocre college student he'd been. He did a bit of graduate work at various universities before and after the War but never earned a graduate degree. By 1973, I was doing well in a doctoral program. Apparently, unbeknownst to me, my performance made him feel inadequate. And perhaps Mum looked to me to succeed in a way—and to a degree—that Dad had not, which may have exacerbated his sense of insecurity.

I remember only one overt incident in which I got any sense of this. We had all driven in to Boston to see the art film, *Elvira Madigan*, at the Exeter Street Theater. He and Mum were quite wowed by it. I made a disparaging remark about its having the visual quality of glossy magazine ads. He snapped, "Well, that's your conceit." And I think he meant that in two senses: it was my idea and a function of my intellectual arrogance.

For these reasons, I have long suffered from the suspicion that in some sense, like Oedipus, I unwittingly killed my father—more than once and in more than one way. I've already explained why I thought my letter might have been fatal. Pondering his psychiatric records makes me wonder if I had undermined him long before that. And I carry a degree of guilt—if not responsibility—for the circumstances of his actual death two years later.

～

So despite my hopes regarding his McLean dossier, I find nothing that explains the onset or root of his depression. Indeed, I find nothing more illuminating than my own amateur analysis in my letter of September 1969, which I am sure his doctors never saw—and probably never heard about, certainly not from Dad. Had he shared it with his therapist(s), though, it might have been very helpful.

His relationship with Mum also came under scrutiny, and various staff members found her wanting in empathy. There's some truth to that. The flipside of Mum's innate vitality was her limited patience with negativity. Her father had died at forty-two, when she was only thirteen, forcing her, the oldest of three children, to work as a live-in nanny while continuing to attend school. After completing high school early, at sixteen, she worked her way through the University of New Hampshire. She no doubt benefitted from her mother's model as a self-reliant and enterprising woman: trained as a nurse, her widowed mother dabbled in real estate, building and selling houses in her neighborhood.

For most of his marital life, Dad could rely on Mum's optimism and ebullience to carry him. For decades, that dynamic succeeded. But when his depression became serious and prolonged—and by 1973 he had been quite depressed on and off for about five years—Mum evidently lost patience and was relieved to turn him over to full-time medical care. As a result, she came across as somewhat insensitive to his needs. Various staffers (mostly women: registered nurses or social workers) reported that she spoke for, or spoke objectively about, him in his presence. They speculated that he harbored anger toward her that he could not express or even admit to them; rather, he would defend her: "She does it for my own good."

To be fair, she was trying to speak for a man who was slow to speak for himself—part of his understandable, but counterproductive, resistance to therapeutic regimens. Furthermore, she may have sought to say to hospital staff things she wanted him to hear but did not want to say to him directly. As far as I can tell, these dynamics were not typical of their earlier married years. (I suspect they were an effect, rather than a cause, of his depression and alcoholism.)

Ironically, however, by the end of his time at McLean, he and Mum were united in their bitterness at the institution for his lack of progress. This entirely unintended effect of his hospitalization may have been its only beneficial effect.

~

The second discharge summary carries no prognosis. Had it supplied one, it probably would have been the same as the first: "guarded." In fact, that might have seemed optimistic, and so it proved—in the long run.

But once again, Dad surprised everyone: he rallied a bit after his discharge. Over the next month, he abused his meds more than once, but otherwise remained sober, and he took up some of his spare time with new duties as a trustee of the Melrose Public Library. The really surprising coda to this chapter, however, is this: even as he was winding up his time at McLean, he and Mum were planning a trip to Spain, where they would meet Jane and David, who were returning from Viet Nam by way of Africa and Europe. The four of them spent ten days touring Spain and Portugal, and he and Mum returned refreshed at the end of June.

Jane had never been fully apprised of Dad's illness and had been completely unaware of his hospitalization, which was never mentioned during his travels—more family denial and repression. As unlikely as it sounds, she reports that she did not notice anything unusual or disturbing about his mood or behavior. He was able to consume alcohol—sangria and wine—without abusing it. He was, then, apparently functional and not obviously depressed. And the rest of the summer, according to my mother's journals, was blessedly uneventful.

How to explain this welcome turn of events? Had his hospital treatment had some delayed positive effect?

I doubt it. His "recovery" was probably another manifestation of the seasonality of his depression. When he had Mum's constant company—as during school vacations—he seems to have felt much better. When he felt better, he didn't drink. When he wasn't drinking, Mum could treat him like an equal partner. The dynamics of his relationship could return to a healthier pattern.

He probably suffered in part from what is now known as Seasonal Affective Disorder—depression caused by diminished exposure to sunlight in winter. But more than the additional sunlight of the longer days of spring and summer, it was probably the warmth of Mum's personality and companionship that revived him in the summer of 1973, when the two could spend more time together.

Chapter Five

Widower

1973–1975

The one negative note in Dad's summer reunion with his long-absent daughter was that Mum was experiencing abdominal discomfort. Given the stress she had been under, her doctor thought the problem might be psychosomatic, but the pain came on as her stress was abating. Typically, she soldiered on. After school started in the fall, her pain became insistent, and her calendar records exam after exam, test after inconclusive test. After various possibilities were ruled out, in mid-November she underwent "exploratory surgery." What a scary term. Always a last resort, such surgery rarely yields happy discoveries.

That evening, Dad phoned me with the results, his voice grave but controlled. He tried to put a positive spin on the outcome: the surgeon had discovered ovarian cancer but had "gotten most of it." I don't remember his naming a stage, but this was obviously a bad scenario.

∼

This was not Mum's first experience of cancer; she'd had breast cancer ten years earlier.

When I returned from summer school at Mt. Hermon Academy in August of 1963, my junior year in high school, I was greeted by an odd sight—my mother reclining on a chaise longue on the front lawn. Mum almost never reclined during the day—certainly not outside, in plain view of neighbors and passersby. Dad explained that she was convalescing from an operation . . . for breast cancer. That was the first I'd heard of it—having typically been protected from disturbing family news.

Mum had had a radical mastectomy, the removal of her entire breast along with muscle tissue and lymph nodes. At the time, reconstructive surgery was rare; for her, a foam prosthesis sufficed. The only evidence of her cancer I ever saw was this prosthesis dangling from the clothesline in the basement after a day at the beach.

Family and friends learned of this development from Dad's Christmas letter of 1963—the first—and the last—time any family member's health was ever mentioned in that medium: "The usual summer activities were somewhat curtailed. Late in the summer Ann had an operation from which she had a wonderful time convalescing. Jane stepped in and took over the various household and social duties." If readers blinked, they could miss this momentous news. This account is almost comical in its evasion, with its quick transition from Mum's operation to her convalescence and Jane's support. Its understatement of Mum's condition—not even named—is typical both of a period when cancer was highly stigmatized and of our family, which tended to suppress unpleasantness. At the same time, there's an element of truth here: if Mum was going to convalesce from a radical mastectomy, then she was going to enjoy the process, damn it! As much as she could, she relaxed into a passive role and basked in attention from her many visitors.

Her diary is somewhat more revealing, but not much. Without recording the discovery of a suspicious lump, in the middle of a busy summer of socializing and traveling she lists appointments with her GP and a local surgeon on Monday, July 29. The next day, she checked into the local hospital; the following day's entry reads simply, "Operation at 8:00. Turns out worse than expected." She had awakened from anaesthesia to find her breast gone.

A week later she went home; three days later I came home, and our family life resumed. Ten years later, she considered herself not just in remission, but cured.

❧

Sadly, but not surprisingly, Dad had begun to drink again after Mum returned to classes that fall. That was the last straw. In Mum's 1973 calendar, each day's horizontal slot is divided into three squares: Morning, Afternoon, and Evening. One of the most poignant entries comes on Sunday, October 28. Right over the date, near the left-hand margin, she inscribed a very large red "D" (for "Drunk"). To the right, under Morning, she wrote, "Grif drunk in bed until 3:00." Under Afternoon: "Told him this time I definitely want divorce!" Under Evening: "Wrote letters." Mum was not going to let the possible dissolution of her marriage prevent her from maintaining other relationships. On the contrary.

She had made the same threat a year earlier; that had finally impelled Dad into treatment at McLean. But that treatment had no lasting benefit, and this time she really intended to leave him.

Despite all I knew she had gone through, I simply could not envision this. It wasn't that I thought she wouldn't be justified in leaving him; I did. And it wasn't that I thought she wouldn't carry through on her threat; I knew she was serious: she didn't just record this in her diary, she told me at the time. She was determined not to live the rest of her life the way she had lived the last several years.

What I couldn't imagine, though, was her existence apart from Dad and outside of our nuclear family. I realize that this represents a failure of imagination on my part, rather than on hers. I had known her all my life only as my mother and Dad's wife. Also, I had a sense of his professional identity that I lacked of hers. I had known she was a teacher, but I had known Dad as *my* teacher: my sense of their separate lives and identities was quite unbalanced.

At any rate, I could not envision her life apart from his. Where would she live? Where would he? Where would my home be? (Although I hadn't lived in Melrose for years and was living with my fiancée at the time, I continued to think of the house in Melrose as home.)

I now recognize how unfair this was to her. She could have weathered a divorce far better than my father. Still working, she was financially secure. She had supportive friends. And she had intellectual and cultural interests to sustain her. He shared many of her interests, but, like many men of his class and generation, he lacked a network of friends. He had no social life outside of his marriage. More important, his depression and emotional dependence did not augur well for his prospects as a divorcé, whereas her independence would enable her to function, possibly even thrive, without the burden of his dysfunction. Her energy and positive outlook would ensure her wellbeing.

This diary entry of October 1973 is so poignant to me, though, not only because it signifies such desperation on her part but because I know what's coming: her illness would keep her from acting on this threat, and it would cut short her life. A year later she was dead.

～

Her illness took her life, but, ironically, it saved their marriage. Its intimations of her mortality had a complicated effect on Dad. For one thing, he appreciated that he and she would not have much more time together. His fear of losing her, and his guilt for having spoiled so much of her recent life, weighed heavily on him and rendered him all the more vulnerable to guilt-driven depression. But during Mum's final illness, he was sober for remarkably long periods of time. He made a valiant effort to support her. More than that, he tried to repair their marriage, which had been so damaged by his illness.

Mum's operation took place on November 12. For the next five weeks, her calendar is stunningly empty. A few of her earlier calendars have some inexplicable gaps—sometimes months long—but they are not ominous. In this case, it's clear that she had nothing to report, or no energy to report. She came home from the hospital two weeks after her operation, too weak to undergo chemo until the following week. That week her journal is also blank, except for this: "Nausea. Three days spent in bathroom." The following week's page has "treatment" in big letters, "naseau" in small letters. She was still and always an English teacher: the misspelling is an inadvertent expression of her distress. This must have been a miserable period for Dad as well; he had to witness her suffering without being able to ease it.

Mum had taken a medical leave in the fall, and she did not return to school after the holidays. Instead, Dad got his wish, sort of; they both finally, if briefly, lived the life of a retired couple: traveling to Boston to shop, to visit various doctors (for tests and evaluations) or the dentist (she was cavity-free on January 25). They saw friends. As news trickled out about the seriousness of her illness, her friends and relatives kept in closer touch, and I was moved to note how many visitors her calendar records. She continued to log phone calls, and I was pleased to see that I called frequently. In early February she reports "Valentines pouring in." On Valentine's Day, she reports "Christmas baking!"—her traditional Dutch holiday pastries, better late than never.

Knowing she would not live long, Dad and Mum indulged in a few luxuries—no point now in deferred gratification. Perhaps anticipating less theater- and movie-going, they bought a color TV at Christmas time. They bought her an avocado-colored Fiat. (Jane inherited this car; I always hated riding in it because it reminded me of chauffeuring Mum to various medical appointments in her final year.) And in 1974 they traveled abroad.

In March they traveled to Belgium and to Holland, her parents' homeland. This trip was marred, however, by Dad's drinking. On their return Mum reported to me angrily that one evening he left the hotel and did not return until morning, giving no explanation. I could hardly believe this, and to this day it makes me angry. Aside from that one lapse, though, he held himself together and the trip was gratifying overall.

In late April, Mum she flew to Copenhagen with two college friends, a trip that had different rewards.

On Mother's Day she reported, "Plenty of loot!" In June she accompanied Dad to his 47th Wesleyan reunion—as far as I know, the first he ever attended, and the last.

A recurrent motif in her diary is the phrase "blood tests." She would refer to these, jokingly, as her encounters with Dracula. The issue was not fear of needles but fear of bad test results. Behind her upbeat front lurked anxiety. Occasionally, she would record feeling ill—not her usual energetic self. This too must have seemed ominous, perhaps the beginning of the end. In the spring she experienced a build-up of fluid in her abdomen—so much that, if she hadn't been so old, she would have looked pregnant: I found her swollen belly very upsetting, as I'm sure Dad did. At one point she recorded disappointing news from one of her specialists: "No injection." Apparently, she'd had her hopes raised about some new treatment.

Then on June 10, she reports simply "The worst of news." The next day she had fluid removed from her abdomen ("10 lbs or 5 qts"). In mid-June she was treated with fluoromacil and methotrexate, drugs used against metastatic cancers. In mid-July, with radium. But these were last-ditch efforts, and one was experimental. Her doctors soon informed her that they could do nothing further for her.

❦

My fiancée and I had decided to marry in the summer of 1974. This involved reciprocal visits between my parents and hers, who lived in Manhattan, a home-and-home series I was a bit concerned about—needlessly, as it turned out. Dad was capable of drinking moderately in a social setting. And he could still be quite charming and vivacious. The prospective in-laws seemed to get along well. And the wedding plans took shape. We were to be married at the Crane Estate in Ipswich in mid-August.

So that summer I was deeply immersed in two conflicting narratives. I was preparing to start a new phase of my life as a part of a married couple; at the same time, I was watching my mother's precipitous decline toward death, which would end my parents' life as a couple. Though seemingly at odds, the narratives were linked: as my nuclear family disintegrated around me, I felt I needed to establish a home of my own—perhaps before I was really ready. In any case, these were not auspicious circumstances in which to embark on marriage. My life was overshadowed by Mum's cancer and Dad's depression; different as they were, both proved fatal. That was hard on both newlyweds, and my marriage lasted only five years.

That summer I was teaching at the Andover Summer School, not far from home, so I could visit frequently. Jane was living in San Francisco. As Mum's condition worsened and the wedding approached, Jane decided to come East earlier, and stay longer, than she had planned. It was a good thing, too, given what was soon obvious: that Mum's cancer was terminal.

In reconstructing this period, I scanned her calendar carefully for the date when she learned this. There seemed to be no explicit indication of it. On July 5, she was given her radium treatment, which knocked her out for a couple of days. Early the next week, she and Dad traveled to see friends and relatives in Maine. On Saturday, July 13, however, she wrote this:

!!

Tom for dinner; Peggy too. Grif a big help. Jane telephoned! She's coming home for maybe (?) a month. Tom now knows, too.

At first I thought that the exclamation points were the indication of her terminal prognosis. But it was unlikely that she would have got her prognosis on a Saturday. That, however, was the day Dad called me at Andover to deliver the news. What she had marked so prominently was not the date on which *she* learned she was going to die—which seems to have been June tenth ("The worst of news")—but the day on which *I* learned she was going to die.

As early as I could, I drove home. Mum greeted me at the door. We hugged—a rare gesture. I said, "I'm going to miss you," and she said simply, "I'm going to miss you, too."

My fiancée arrived, and we all sat down to a home-cooked dinner.

∽

Initially, Mum had wanted to protect me from this news. In fact, the only letter either Jane or I still have from her is the one in which she announced her prognosis to Jane but asked her to keep it from me:

July 3, 1974
Dear Jane
    This is going to be a difficult letter to write. Several years ago when I did not tell you the whole story of your father's condition, you were unhappy about the deception. So now I am telling you about a month ago the doctor told me I was not to recover. But the short time I have left shocked me. Of course, I didn't tell your father but yesterday the doctor told him. Neither one of us is going to tell Tom until after his wedding. Let him have his day! The doctor naturally doesn't know definitely how long—but he thinks it won't be more than September for me.
    Now, after all that—one other ray of hope. Today at noon I am going to the hospital for several days to have an isotope treatment. If that works, then the whole situation would be changed.
    And I'd love that!! So again we'll wait and see. After all, people are great believers in this radiation treatment so again I have great hopes.
    I look well, Jane, probably better than you do. Last weekend we went to Winnipesaukee to see the Russells [old Manchester friends, and my god-parents] where we had our usual good time. Sunday was a beautiful day. On the way home we stopped at Jean and John's [her brother and sister-in-law in Manchester] who always act so pleased to see us.
    Jane, as a daughter and a person, you have given me much pleasure.

So glad you're able to come for a week at the time of Tom's wedding. Did I tell you that I may even have the dinner before the wedding catered? I'll decide after this latest treatment.

Be of good cheer. My best to David.

All my love, Mother

How quickly she moves on from her prognosis to the experimental treatment and how cautiously she frames it: "People are great believers." She chooses to hope—but cannot not quite believe—that it will prolong her life. "And I'd love that"—more understatement. She then goes on to reassure Jane that she looks well. It was summer and she was tan, but she hardly looked healthy; she had lost a lot of weight, and aside from her swollen belly she looked gaunt. She then brings Jane up to date on her travels, thus embedding the news of her terrible diagnosis in a narrative of life as usual—but now with added poignancy.

～

I became aware of this letter only in the summer of 2011 when it surfaced by chance. Reading it, I sobbed so loudly it brought my wife running to my side. My outburst was triggered mainly by the mention of me: "Let Tom have his day."

Mum's decision to shield Dad and me from her prognosis is quite touching, but misguided—especially in view of what she admits to Jane about shielding her from the news of Dad's illness. Fortunately, she reconsidered, and I am grateful for that; I'd have been angry to have been kept in the dark about one more family secret.

Jane's reaction to this (to me devastating) letter was very different: she was hurt by such slight recognition in what was her last letter from Mum: "Jane, as a daughter and a person, you have given me much pleasure." As it happens, I never received an equivalent letter, but that is beside the point. I was around much of the time; I had much more of Mum's company and attention in her last years. I see Jane's point.

But this reflects the emotional style of our family—understated and tight-lipped, avoiding direct expression of any strong emotion, even love.

～

The weeks before and after my wedding are a bit of a blur. Dad and Mum made yet another trip to the coast of Maine, a favorite destination. On July 21, "Grif called Jane," presumably to tell her before she arrived that the radium treatment had failed. On Monday, July 22, Mum reports: "Wonderful mail [presumably "get well" cards]. Awful day. No marriage certificate nor birth!! Home all day. Notes."

The reference to vital documents has to do with her desire to arrange her affairs. Concerned—understandably but, as it turned out, unnecessarily—that Dad might remarry after her death, to the detriment of her children, she required him to give each of us $10,000—a substantial amount of money at the time.

Thus far, I've been relying on Mum's calendar to supplement my memory, but at this point, I can no longer do that: suddenly, shockingly, it goes completely blank. The next day's brief entry is the last of a twenty-year saga: "Everything for retirement set! Grif and I in town to [the dentist]. I rested. Then to movie *That's Entertainment*."

Well, that's Mum. Facing imminent death from metastatic ovarian cancer, she concluded her journal on an upbeat note. She had put her affairs in order. She'd had her teeth checked and cleaned. Her daughter was married, and her son was about to be. Her work as a parent was done. She could now die in peace. And for the moment she could enjoy MGM's compilation of scenes from old musicals, which must have been very nostalgic for Dad and her. It was just like her to end her diary with "That's entertainment."

~

She lived for nearly another three months, during which I was married and began a new academic year as a teaching assistant. She continued to get around. As long as she had the desire, we would take her to museums or theaters. In those days, before the AIDS epidemic, it was quite rare to see people in public who were obviously mortally ill. Her sunken cheeks and eyes, swollen belly, and wig—easily knocked askew—functioned as clear markers, and I resented the stares we drew in navigating her wheelchair around.

In the pictures of the wedding, neither of my parents looks well, but they did their best to carry on in a celebratory way, and it was a welcome opportunity for Mum to see many close friends and family at once, many of them for the last time. I didn't realize it then, but my wedding served as a kind of celebration of Mum's life before she died. In any case, it was a bittersweet affair.

~

Her ending her diary months before her death, when she was still quite active and physically able to write, meant two things. One was that she was finally, grudgingly, resigned to dying. The diary had become in part an illness narrative; at this point, the denouement was known. There was no further treatment to undergo and thus to report. She didn't need to write the ending; the challenge would be to live it. Once she knew there was no hope of survival, she resolved to make the best of her final days. So I read this premature ending not as a sign of defeat and hopelessness, but rather as one of acceptance of her fate. Her father had died at forty-two, her sister in her thirties; Mum appreciated that she'd lived far longer than either.

The journal's end also signals her willingness to surrender her perennial role in the family. For years—forever, in my experience—she'd been the care-giver, the organizer, the cook, the hostess—and, not incidentally, the family historian. At this point, she would let others do for her. She was certainly entitled, and I take comfort in knowing that she finally relinquished herself into our care.

Things eased a bit when Jane arrived, but even with her help we needed professional assistance. Dad was initially opposed to this, insisting—he, of all people—that we could cope by ourselves. But Mum was vehement: "Damn it, Grif. We can afford it, and you need the help." And that was that. Mum didn't require—and couldn't benefit from—much in the way of medical care. What we arranged was hospice care without the label. This freed us to be her family.

~

The wedding came and went. My wife and I honeymooned close to home—at inns in various picturesque towns in New Hampshire and Vermont. I called home every night, to be reassured by Dad that "Mother had a good day." In a sense, I think that was true.

Her final illness was, of course, especially hard on Dad, and occasionally he would drink or abuse medication. At one point late that summer, after Jane had come east, we discovered a pile of sticks, arranged like kindling, in the stairwell leading from the side yard down to the basement door. Jane and I were concerned—and overextended—so we conspired to commit him to McLean on the basis of this and other disturbing behavior. Jane persuaded a physician, whose daughter Dad had tutored, to come to the house and "examine" him; unbeknownst to Dad, the doctor signed a pink slip that empowered us to present him for involuntary commitment. I slept in the house that night, Jane at a neighbor's; the next morning Jane and I surprised him with the pink slip. Furious, he began to chug gin straight from the bottle before I could get it from him—another reminder of what Mum had had to deal with. I called the police to enforce the doctor's order. Dad countered by calling his lawyer, a genial former student and an acquaintance of Jane's.

After a brief discussion, the lawyer drove us over to Belmont in his late-model sedan—Dad in the passenger seat, Jane and I in the back. At the hospital, Jane and I claimed that Dad had become a danger to himself and/or others. In truth, we just wanted him out of the way and detoxified so we could attend to Mum's needs without interference. After interviewing him with his lawyer present, the staff physicians decided—no surprise, really—that he did not warrant commitment. (His history there was probably a factor.) So the lawyer drove us all back to Melrose, Jane and I staring out of our respective rear-seat windows.

Upon our arrival, we learned that the morning aide had not been able to rouse Mum. Without consulting us, she had called an ambulance, and Mum had been taken to the local hospital. There, she had been injected with steroids, which perked her right up. We were surprised, but pleased, to see her looking brighter and more alert. But as we entered her room, she flashed me an accusatory look. She wasn't pleased to have been brought back from the brink of death and to have to prepare to die all over again. I felt guilty for my complicity in her Lazarus-like resurrection.

But once again, events took a surprising turn. Aware that he had failed her, Dad sobered up and stayed sober for the few remaining months of her life. So her revival gave him a welcome do-over. He and she had a peaceful and harmonious final period. In her last months, she was not able to climb stairs, so she moved from the master bedroom into the first-floor guest-room. There he read poetry to her in what became her death-bed. Their relationship ended as it began, with two English teachers bonding over books.

In mid-October, 1974, about two months after my wedding, and a month after our birthdays—Mum's 65th and my 28th—Dad called me on a Sunday morning to say that Mum had died. I drove over to Melrose, where I had a few moments alone with her—or rather, with her body, my first corpse. Her skin was already waxy and cool to my touch. It was Mum, but not Mum. Her body was present, but *she* was gone. I leaned over, kissed her cheek, and said goodbye.

❧

When I look back over her last year, I take comfort in two things. First, judging from her diary, she did not suffer much physical pain, aside from what resulted from her medical treatment. That's a huge qualifier, of course. Recovery from this major abdominal surgery—now called "de-bulking"—is very painful. Chemotherapy is also extremely unpleasant; that was the only experience that effectively shut down her diary. And the whole sequence of events caused her a good deal of anguish. Reportedly, when asked by a hospital chaplain how she felt about her situation, she snapped, "How do you *think* I feel, you damned fool?" Although it was probably not the intent of the question to elicit such an angry response, that answer was probably cathartic for her, and thus beneficial.

But after treatment ceased, she was able to carry on many of her favorite activities until close to the end. She suffered much, but she was not in constant, or major, pain. And she had excellent, compassionate, professional care at home. In that sense, hers was a good death.

Second, and much more important, Dad and she were able to achieve a kind of rapprochement. Only her illness had prevented her from leaving him, and he knew it. He responded by behaving as the best partner he was capable of being. As is typical in such situations, she got lots of support; he got little. But he was finally able to offer her the unwavering support she deserved. And she appreciated it.

Over the longer span of their entire marriage, it seems that they had a very good partnership for many years. When she died, they had been married for more than thirty years; only in the last ten did she remark on his depression; only in the last five or so did it seriously disturb their lives. And even during those years, there were periods of peace and happiness. I think they had at least 25 really good years before dark undercurrents tore them apart. That was something to be grateful for, even proud of.

~

After a week of planning, the family gathered for a memorial service and then dispersed. And Dad faced life alone as a widower.

For obvious reasons, this was not easy for him. Without a network of friends, he was alone and often lonely, with little to do but lots of time on his hands. He went through bouts of manic activity, seeking out extension courses at Harvard and visiting museums. But he missed his dear companion. He managed the household reasonably well. But without Mum's touch, it deteriorated noticeably.

At one point, he turned to an old standby, swimming, at the local YMCA. He even won a ribbon or two in Master's races, which I admired. He could look the picture of health and fitness for weeks at a time. There were glimmers of hope that he might adapt to his new solitary life.

That Thanksgiving, the extended family gathered not in Melrose, where my parents had traditionally hosted the dinner, but in Concord, New Hampshire, at a cousin's home. It was painful for me to see relatives so soon after Mum's death, especially on a day that had usually featured her as hostess and chef. I didn't feel particularly thankful. It must have been even harder on Dad.

Christmas without Mum was even sadder.

Jane invited Dad, me, and my wife to join her and her husband in San Francisco, and we three flew west. To a New Englander's eye, San Francisco—with its foliage green in midwinter and without snow—sure didn't look like Christmas, so it would have been a strange holiday in any case. But without Mum it was particularly strained. I remember gray days and some desultory tourism.

Jane had neglected to buy a Christmas tree until the very last minute, and there were no decent ones left. She and David resourcefully scavenged two damaged trees and wired them together. Once decorated, it was a presentable simulacrum, but that tree sticks in my mind as a symbol of a holiday improvised by a grieving family, going through the motions. Mum's ghost loomed over us.

It must have been particularly hard for Dad: although I didn't know it at the time, during the War Mum had traveled across the continent to meet him in San Francisco before he shipped to Pearl Harbor. It must have been poignant for him, thirty years later, to remember the young couple in that iconic city of romance.

In any case, rather than bringing us together, our memories of Mum isolated us from each other. Worst of all, she was not there to cheer us up.

~

Back home, alone, Dad cycled between bingeing and sobriety. He seemed to rebound from each binge, but the drinking took a toll without Mum there to disrupt it or to help him recuperate. Moreover, he had to live with the guilt for having spoiled some of the last years of her life.

I kept in touch, calling regularly. My wife and I had him over for dinner occasionally. He interacted in his usual charming manner. So these occasions were pleasant, on the surface.

As a newlywed and grad student, I had concerns other than his welfare. I was preparing for my oral exams and thinking about a dissertation topic. I returned to therapy, where my concerns focused on Dad—not so much on our damaged relationship as on how I might respond to his desperate condition. I was asking questions then that I have continued to ask, ultimately in this memoir: how could such a fine man fall so completely apart in mid-life? How did alcoholism work? At one point I even asked my therapist to sign another pink slip, in the hope of committing Dad to McLean, but he rightly declined: he was my doctor, not Dad's.

As Mum had, I attended Al-Anon meetings, seeking support and advice about having an alcoholic in my family. There, I heard the AA party line: Dad's drinking was not in my control; there was nothing I could, or should, do. I needed to take care of myself. The best thing for the alcoholic is to let him "hit bottom." Only then might he recover.

This is all well and good, I thought. But what if "bottom" means dying, as I suspected, correctly, would be the case with Dad? I suppose the answer would be the same—do nothing—but I found it torturous to stand by as he deteriorated.

~

At this point, the narrative becomes especially difficult to write.

With Mum's death, it helped that I could foresee it and prepare for it, grieving in advance. Writing about it has brought it all back, but I derived some comfort from the way things turned out—her acquiescence and reconciliation with Dad. Dad's death was not a surprise, either, I suppose, but it couldn't be foreseen in the same way. More to the point, my sense of emotional kinship with him made it harder to protect myself. I found his depression contagious, and I was ashamed of his drinking. This made it harder to confide in my wife, my sister, and friends. I was a lonely witness to his slow, messy self-destruction then, and it is especially unpleasant now to reconstruct his last months. But it's a necessary part of this reconsideration of his life, and of mine.

I rarely remember dreams and almost never write them down. But not surprisingly, composing this memoir stirred my unconscious mind and manifested itself in dreams. I made note of two.

In the first, I am in the basement of the house in Melrose. There has been some sort of flood, and things in the basement are soiled with silt. I attempt to clean them, but the washing machine doesn't work. I take it apart in an attempt to fix it, to no avail.

As it happened, soon after we moved to Melrose in the summer of 1954, a hurricane did flood our basement. In Manchester, we'd never had a flooded basement, and this occurrence may have been particularly unsettling to me in my new home. In context, however, the dream seems to reflect my sense as a memoirist that, in endeavoring to purge the house of unpleasant memories, I am laundering "dirty linen" in public.

In the other, I am struggling to write a letter to my father. I am using an odd hybrid machine: it's small, like a laptop computer, yet it has paper running through it like a typewriter—irregular and unsubstantial. The letter keys are in the right places, but the function keys are erratic; formatting is problematic.

On one level, this dream may reflect the memoir's reliance on both old-fashioned correspondence (some handwritten, some typewritten) and new-fangled digital technology. On a deeper level, of course, it has to do with my memoir as a fallible medium of communication with a father I had injured with an earlier letter.

~

Like Mum, I could not prevent Dad from getting alcohol and consuming it. As I never knew when he would binge, I lived in constant fear and uncertainty. When he was bingeing, he would not answer the phone. That's how I knew. After a day or two, I would drive to Melrose to check on him. One such time, he didn't respond to the doorbell. Finding the door unlocked, I walked in. I found a lot of cash spread out on the living room couch near the front door. I'd never seen that before. This puzzled me at first, but then I tumbled: this was to pay for a liquor delivery. I wondered whether the delivery came in an unmarked car or whether a company van announced Dad's habit to the neighborhood. Either way, I knew that if he could have liquor delivered on demand, there really was no stopping him. He could continue to drink well after he reached the point at which he was unable to drive to the nearest package store. (Ironically, Melrose was a dry town.)

Another time, I found him looking as though he had been beaten; he had a black eye, swollen lips, and a grotesquely swollen nose. But he had not been the victim of an intruder; he had fallen flat on his face, too drunk for his reflexes to protect him.

There came a Friday in mid-June in 1975 on which, once again, I was not able to raise him by phone. That afternoon, I drove to the house to find him in bed in the guestroom. When bingeing, he slept there on the ground floor, rather than in the master bedroom upstairs. This meant that he was sleeping in Mum's deathbed. He may have found some comfort in that; they had not slept in the same bed when she was alive. I found him grizzled, haggard, disheveled—barely recognizable. His situation seemed desperate.

With no one to stop him from drinking or to help him recover from his binges, it seemed obvious to me that he was a danger to himself. But my experience with McLean the previous summer had convinced me that the only way to get him into detox was by his own volition. I begged him to let me take him to the Danvers State Hospital, not far away. Predictably, he balked. Of course, he was hardly in his right mind. But I felt powerless to force him.

I drove to the police station, thinking that I could persuade someone there to call an ambulance to take him to Danvers. The cop at the front desk was polite but reminded me of the law: Dad could not be taken against his will. I told him Dad might well die without detox. The cop did not budge. The law is the law.

So I did the only thing I could think of: I called the visiting nurse association and arranged for home care. I can't remember how I finessed that; I certainly did not tell the truth about his condition. To my relief, they agreed, but they could not start until the following Monday morning.

I spent the weekend trying to distract myself. As far as I could tell, Dad had exhausted his supply of liquor but did not seem in any shape to care for himself—perhaps not even to rise out of bed.

I hated to think of his condition. I could think of little else. But I did not intervene.

Monday morning came at last, and I drove over to Melrose. I found an unfamiliar car in the driveway and the front door open. I was relieved to have arrived after medical help. Inside, I found two nurses cleaning Dad up. He had apparently spent the entire weekend in bed, too weak to get up. As a result, he was wallowing in his own feces and urine. He'd vomited, too, and his grizzled chin was streaked with it. It was a horrific scene. But the two women—bless them—carried on without comment. They didn't point out that I had misrepresented his condition. Nor did they seem upset about it.

They were purely professional. Never have I been so grateful for nonjudgmental medical help.

They called an ambulance, which took him to the Melrose-Wakefield Hospital, the site of Mum's initial treatment for both her cancers. I followed in my car. When I identified myself in the emergency room, a doctor asked if I wanted him to treat Dad. I said "Yes, of course." At the time, I thought he was asking if I wanted *him*—rather than, say, our family physician—to treat Dad. Only much later did it occur to me that he had been asking whether I wanted Dad treated *at all*—whether I thought it worthwhile to try to revive him. As the closest relative of an incompetent man, I had made an end-of-life decision without even knowing it, much less thinking about its implications.

For the next week or so, I visited him daily at the hospital. After I told Jane how serious his condition was, she flew east immediately. She had recently learned that she was pregnant with her first child, which would have been Dad's first grandchild. But because it was early in the pregnancy, and because she expected Dad to survive, she didn't share that delightful news with him. We both wondered later whether it would have made a difference.

In the hospital he looked a good deal better. He'd been cleaned up, fed, and rehydrated. But he was on an IV and oxygen—he who had won a ribbon as a master's swimmer only months earlier. To remind him of that achievement, I brought him the ribbon from home. He looked at it vacantly.

In fact, I am not sure that he spoke at all during those days. He looked better than he was. His drinking had damaged vital organs; the doctors did not expect him to recover fully. This stunned me. He had rebounded so many times before that I expected he'd recover once again—perhaps better than before, because this time he had medical support. Maybe this near-death crisis would constitute his "bottom," and he would finally stop drinking.

Instead, I was told that, at sixty-nine, he needed to be put in a nursing home—like his mother, who had had Parkinson's. This time, there was apparently significant "organicity"—brain damage. Hence his uncommunicativeness. He didn't seem fully present. He didn't brighten when we visited. He didn't interact with Jane and me. We talked at him, not with him. He seemed to listen but never responded. Worse than being incommunicado, he looked indifferent, as though he didn't really know or care who we were. It was deeply unsettling. I thought visiting him at McLean had been difficult. This was far worse. And unlike Mum, who once recorded having had a dozen visitors in a day, he had only me and Jane.

Jane and I inspected some local nursing homes, then she flew home.

A few days later, on June 25, 1975, I got a phone call just as I was waking up. It was Dad's doctor, informing me that he had died during the night. I clearly remember what I said in response: "Okay."

Of course, it wasn't okay. I had not really accepted that he could never return home. I certainly had not expected him to die. I do remember that during one visit, I pleaded with him to "come back to life," in just those words. By that I meant not only, "Please recover from this near-death condition" but also "please rejoin those who relish life." His status was like an extreme somatic manifestation of his chronic depression. He left his life before he actually died. Perhaps, aware of his children's plan to institutionalize him, he'd lost his will to live and let go.

In any case, I felt keenly that I should have called an ambulance that Friday afternoon. I could have feigned ignorance as to his condition, or lied about it, to get an ambulance to the house; once there, they'd take him to a medical facility, wouldn't they? Instead, he'd been left without food or water all weekend, to choke on his own vomit. The interval had probably pushed him past his physical limit. Once again, I felt I had killed my father—this time quite literally, by neglecting to save him.

I drove to the hospital to collect his belongings. I went straight to his room, only to find his bed empty. Of course. They don't leave dead patients in their beds until the nearest relative arrives. They hustle their bodies off to the morgue. I authorized an autopsy, took his things, and returned home to Concord.

Like Mum, Dad wanted to be cremated. But not having had a chance to say goodbye to his body, I requested a viewing at the funeral parlor. It was an eerie experience, very different from seeing Mum at home. That had been unsettling, in its way; she'd been my first dead body. But that encounter allowed me to register her death, her utter absence, in a direct way in an intimate and familiar setting.

Seeing Dad composed in a coffin, in dress clothes, was an entirely different matter. I suppose I provided his clothes, but I don't remember which— whether, for instance, he was wearing his signature bow tie. What I do remember was that he had a mustache. In the hospital, when he'd been cleaned up and shaved, he'd been left with a mustache and, not speaking, he hadn't objected to it; I went along with this, having other concerns. But had I not given the funeral parlor a picture of him in better times for them to simulate with their dark arts? In any case, the strange facial hair was very disturbing. It was as though he'd been disguised, as well as embalmed. Even dead—especially dead—he needed to look like my father. I demanded that the mustache be shaved before he was cremated. But I didn't return to check and never saw him again. The whole experience reinforced my sense that the man in the coffin, the man who had drunk himself to death in his sixties, was not the man I'd known, and loved, as my father.

It devolved upon me then to call his siblings and close friends to give them the sad and, to most, surprising news. Ashamed of the circumstances of his death, I didn't know how much people already knew and thus how much to tell them. To the extent that I accounted for his premature death, I said merely that he hadn't taken good care of himself since Mum died. That was certainly true, but far from the whole truth; like father, like son—more Couser understatement and evasion. In retrospect, I realize that many people must have known of his drinking. Fewer would have known of his stay at McLean and the seriousness of his depression. But his death may not have been as unexpected I thought. Ironically, it may have surprised me more than it did them, for I had witnessed, and continued to believe in, his amazing resilience.

I did find myself thinking, though, where were his siblings during this downward spiral? Did any of them keep in touch and offer support? For a time, in addition to my own guilt, I was quite angry at them. But I had never asked them to intervene; to do so would have meant violating his privacy and our wholesome family image. And, ultimately, I realized that no one could have saved him without his wanting to be saved and willing his own recovery.

Officially, his death was caused by "bronchopneumonia, E.coli, pyelonephritis, chronic and acute." So, surprisingly, the cause of death was not cirrhosis but pneumonia and kidney disease (a different form of which had killed his father). But clearly it was the drinking that did him in, and that was at least in part a response to his depression, which is what I take to be the ultimate cause of his early demise. Today, when I refer to the circumstances of his death, I am inclined simply to say that he "died of depression." It's not the whole story, but it's undeniably true. And it needs to be said.

In the end, I tell myself, his death was probably as inevitable as Mum's. It was a question of when, not whether, it would occur. And without Mum there to rescue him, and with the added burden of guilt for spoiling much of what proved their last years, it happened sooner. Nothing anyone could have done would have saved him, if he couldn't, wouldn't, save himself.

I thus absolve myself.

~

Given the circumstances of his death, it was hard to make his memorial service the celebration of a life that Mum's was. But in the days after his death I discovered in his closet, and quickly surveyed, the archive on which this memoir is based. Jane and I drew upon some evocative and poignant documents for texts to be read at the funeral. In that service lay the seeds of this memoir, which I hope may serve as a better memorial, some thirty years later, than the event that first marked his death.

Chapter Six

Endnotes

A Life in Scraps, 1974–1975

He had always wanted to go back to the Pacific, where the only daring part of his life lay, and travel across it, its vastness, passing the great forgotten names, Ulithi, Majuro, Palau, perhaps visiting a few graves, Robert Louis Stevenson's or Gauguin's, ten days by boat from Tahiti. Sail as far as Japan. They would plan trips together and stay in small hotels.
—James Salter, *All That Is*

In the immediate aftermath of Dad's death, in addition to the archive in his closet, which documented his premarital life, I discovered written traces of his final months scattered around the house. Unlike his letters, they are fragmentary and not always coherent. I puzzled over them briefly, before consigning them to the box that I stored in my attic where they languished for decades.

When I finally took the time to review and assess them, however, they offered tantalizing glimpses of Dad's state of mind in his last days—the eight months between Mum's death in October of 1974 and his own the following June.

∾

Most were written in ink on quarter sheets of unlined 8 x 12 paper—home-made note paper. They seem to have been written spontaneously, at odd times, whenever a thought occurred to Dad. Undated, they can't be sequenced. Nevertheless, I regard them as a kind of unbound diary or journal in which he reviewed his life as he prepared to die. They do not comprise a suicide note, exactly, but I have come to think of them as notes *toward* a suicide because in them Dad seems to anticipate his death—aware, on some

73

level, that he was bringing it on himself. In any case, these notes gave me intimate access—sometimes disturbing, sometimes reassuring—to my father's final frame of mind.

I found most of them adjacent to what became his favorite chair in the living room. In the final phase of his life, he spent much of his waking time in that green velvet club chair diagonally across the room from the TV, which was on much of the time, even during the day. This arrangement was a departure from the past and a sign of his distress. When we first got a TV, it was placed in the basement, and it remained there until Mum got too weak to climb stairs. When she moved down from the master bedroom to the first-floor guest room, the TV was brought to the first floor.

After she died, I thought Dad might move it back to the basement. That he didn't was a sign of his loneliness and dependence on it for distraction and company. I doubt that it gave him much gratification; there wasn't much he actually enjoyed watching. He'd never been a sports fan or news junkie. His taste was too refined for most TV of the time. But after Mum died, the box continued to perch awkwardly in the living room, dominating even when it wasn't on, or was on but muted. It pained me to know that he spent so much time with a medium he scorned. If it served him as an opiate, it was a poor one.

Dad's first months as a widower were obviously difficult. After the initial wave of support ebbed, he was very isolated. Mum's death deprived him not only of her company but of other social contact as well. Like most married couples, they socialized mostly as such. While Mum had several female friends, Dad had no male friends that I am aware of—no pals. Thus, in contrast to the rich social life of his bachelor years, when he had close friends of both sexes, he was quite bereft after losing his wife.

In every way, his last months lacked the dignity of Mum's. His illness—depression manifested in, and complicated by, binge drinking—was messy and somewhat shameful. Friends—and even relatives—do not seek the company of someone depressed to the point of dysfunction, much less someone drinking himself slowly to death. No one wants to witness that sad spectacle. I certainly didn't want to, but I had no choice. Indeed, no one wants to acknowledge what's going on: the terminality of his condition could be acknowledged only in retrospect. The unfair effect of this was to deprive him of the comfort usually offered to the terminally ill. No one came from afar to say goodbye, not even his siblings.

After her return from Viet Nam in the summer of 1973, Jane lived thousands of miles away in San Francisco, so she was not in a position to offer company, except by telephone. I and my new wife lived only about fifteen miles away, in Concord. I did call Dad regularly and saw him at least every couple of weeks. But, prone to depression myself, I feared being dragged into his emotional morass if I didn't keep some distance. I provided some company and distraction, but I didn't afford him much real comfort. I was grieving, too, and mourners can be self-absorbed. Perhaps his early death, a mere eight months after Mum's, was not surprising, although it shocked me when it finally occurred.

～

At some point, drinking, which we had regarded as his problem, became for him a solution—indeed, his final solution. It was also a way of terminating his life without acknowledging it. Rather than committing suicide in a forthright and unambiguous way, he engaged in a slow-motion suicide, a suicide with plausible deniability. That is, his drinking became a suicide that he—and we, his survivors—could deny he had committed. And so we did, Jane and I, for many years—to our detriment. We would have been better off admitting it right away.

Of course, one can never be *sure* such a death is a suicide. At the time, I let people draw their own conclusions. In fact, I was deeply ashamed of the circumstances and the cause of his death. Encountering high school classmates, many of whom were his students, at reunions, I find myself not wanting to say more than that Dad died in the mid-1970s not long after Mum.

～

It is significant that no letters survive from this period of his life. All I have as documentary evidence of this phase, then, are these notes, literally scraps of paper. Though brief, scattered, and enigmatic, they are poignant vestiges of this period. Their impulsivity and fragmentariness are themselves revealing of his state of mind. And in the absence of more extensive documents, they are precious to me—discrete, isolated relics of the last stage of his life, during which he grieved, reviewed his life, and prepared, more or less consciously, for his death. As his son the English professor, I come honestly by the urge—or compulsion—to read texts closely. In reading them, deciphering his dying, I am his student as well as his son, learning my final lesson, realizing my legacy.

～

Of all the notes, this one probably best encapsulates his condition after Mum's death—bereft, "retired," with much too much time to fill with idle pursuits, and relying on alcohol to fill the void and kill his pain.

> Knocking around at loose ends. Mowing the lawn, raking up, reading some poetry in French, getting mad about that bastard Nixon and all the time being a little lonesome. Can't you cure that. Have to make myself a little drink.

The reference to yard work suggests that this note was written in the spring, perhaps in April, Eliot's cruelest month. Dad always took meticulous care of our yard. In one of my lasting mental images, house-proud Dad patrols the yard, picking up branches fallen from one tree or another. Watching him from my bedroom, I would think, "Get a life, old man." Of course, now I do the same thing. I don't have a son to watch me with a critical eye, but I provide my own self-mocking commentary. It's only fair. I am his son in more ways than I like to admit.

Landscaping and gardening could not have consumed much of his abundant free time, however, and none at all for the months immediately after Mum's death in October. The confinement of that first winter must have been especially hard. So it's no surprise to hear him refer to yard work as a source of solace and distraction.

As for his hatred of Nixon, that comes as a bit of a surprise. Nixon had resigned in disgrace in August of 1974, only a few days before my wedding, and Ford had pardoned him a month before Mum died. Why get worked up about Nixon? He seems an odd villain for Dad to obsess about, given his own plight. (I can't remember how much was known at the time about Nixon's pathological drinking; there may be an element of projection in this reference to a disgraced public figure.) In any case, I take some satisfaction in the evidence that he had not stopped following the news, and he was not so self-absorbed as to be indifferent to public events.

Obviously, though, his main concern, which underlies all the others, is his "lonesomeness." He must have been devastatingly lonely. He and Mum had been married for nearly half their lives. In recent years, of course, the marriage had been strained to the breaking point; the relationship had been tested and almost shattered by his depression and drinking. Still, her death deprived him of a partner he had relied on for decades for conversation, intimacy, company, and all the rest of the obligations and pleasures of married life. So her loss was his main, even obsessive, concern.

I initially read the last line, "Can't you cure that. Have to make myself a little drink" as ending "have to make myself a little *drunk*." But the effect is the same: the point of a drink was to make him drunk (and not just a little). But of course, drinking, which he liked to imagine as a "cure," was at the same time his disease. And like Mum's cancer, it proved terminal.

❧

Despite his very heavy drinking, he remained a handsome man. Although his hairline had long since receded, his remaining dark brown hair had only begun to be flecked with gray when he died. He had a slender frame and maintained it; when sober, he could still cut quite a debonair figure. Though no dandy, he was a dapper dresser. Partly out of a sense of fashion, partly to conceal his baldness, he wore a fedora as part of his dress outfit—i.e., to work, to church, to the theatre, and so on. He also wore garters to keep his stockings up: no exposed shins for him. He typically sported a bow tie. I've almost never worn one, but thanks to him, I can tie one. He had very nice sport coats, some of which were custom-made by his clothier friend and former Aleppo student Richard Parseghian. On a modest budget, he managed to dress very well.

In any case, when fit and feeling good about himself, he began to think about the opposite sex, relatively soon after his bereavement. At least that's the implication of the brief text on the back of note #1, which suggests he had at least fantasized about an alternative to "knocking around at loose ends":

> Old warrior like myself to be despondent is one thing.
> But you think I'm a really cock-eyed weirdo & wish I would go away.
> A girl who is more interested in lusty young men.
> Get hornier & hornier and my performance improves.

I have no idea whether this refers to an actual young woman he might have known and lusted after, or to some imagined partner. If the former, it was no one I was aware of. Perhaps he came into contact with an attractive younger woman in one of his continuing education classes and tried to strike up a conversation, even a relationship. This would not strike me as being inappropriate in the wake of his long-time partner's death. Rather, it would suggest an affirmation of interest in the future and a reassuring sense of his attractiveness and worth. He could be charming, especially with the opposite sex. Whenever he wrote this note, however, it was probably too soon for the "old warrior" to engage in romance and sex again, and this person was apparently not very receptive. Realistically, too, his pathology would eventually have been evident to anyone who got to know him. Still, it's gratifying to think that he could still (or again) see himself as a romantic partner. That would be a major step after such a blow as his partner's lingering death.

As to his performance, he must have been referring to masturbation, not an unlikely or unwholesome preoccupation for a lonely, aging male. (I found a stack of *Playboys* in his closet after he died.) He must have found it encouraging that, despite his heavy drinking, he could still perform, at least in that way, when there was little at stake.

~

If at times he fantasized, at others he philosophized:

> Wm Sloane Coffin: If you're religious you have a kind of thumb-nosing freedom towards contemporary values. As Luther said, "A mighty fortress (& rest of that hymn)."
> Unmerited evil is the toughest question to answer. Why must the first quality go & the 2nd, 3rd, 4th raters stay.

[verso]

There are those who will fall on a grenade because there is no time to throw it back.

Whose world is it?

It's your world, Couser

We're always looking for answers to our intelligently selfish questions.

Do we stand by God in his suffering on the cross?

The quotation from Sloane Coffin, the progressive pastor of the Riverside Church in Manhattan, expresses Dad's sense of religion as a system of ideas rather than of faith. And at this point in his evolving political development, he was attracted to the Christian left's critique of contemporary American values, as manifested in imperialist ventures like the Viet Nam War and pervasive materialism. Being able to thumb his nose at the "world" of conventional morality would have been of little solace, however, in his current predicament, which was wholly defined by the loss of Mum, the center of his world.

So he addressed the problem of evil as he felt it: how could God allow a woman like Mum to suffer and die when so many mediocre people endured? I share his sense of the injustice of Mum's death at such an early age, when she was still so vital and engaged with the world. But I don't struggle with it as a theological problem. I don't think that it follows from Mum's suffering that there is no God. Dad was religious enough to feel this as a theological matter. For me, theology, or perhaps theism, is the problem.

But apparently Mum's death turned Dad's thoughts to suicide. How could he survive without her? And indeed, why should survive her? Did he deserve to? The metaphor of falling on a grenade comes out of nowhere and seems incongruent, if not incoherent, here. In a military context, it's a classic image of altruistic heroism, giving one's life for others. But who is throwing the grenade here, God? Who falls on it—Mum, in dying first? Who is saved then? Certainly not Dad.

I think the answer may lie in what follows: "We're always looking for answers to our intelligently selfish questions." He may have recognized that his concern here was quite selfish. He wasn't deeply concerned with The Problem of Evil. He just missed Mum, didn't think it fair that she had died; he needed her and wanted her back. If she was not to be restored to him, he might as well kill himself. Falling on a grenade would not save anyone else, but it would end his own suffering, and perhaps assuage his guilt.

~

Another note reinforces my sense that he felt utterly isolated:

Someone, perhaps a cynic [actually, the Concord Transcendentalist, Thoreau—an odd lapse for an English teacher], has said we live lives of quiet desperation. After an event such as this, life seems even more desperate & it is certainly much more quiet.

I don't think I often thot that way when Ann was alive.

Quietude is one thing. Desperation is another. Dad's life was not desperate when Mum was alive; she was a powerful life force, devoted to living energetically and fully. But Dad's depression rendered him gloomy, uncooperative, uncommunicative, self-absorbed, and passive. Perhaps that kind of suffering is different from what "desperation" connotes here. It certainly was less amenable to remediation of any sort. That is, his "desperation" might have been relieved by Mum's resurrection, but he still would have been prone to depression. And that depression, exacerbated by the desperateness of his new physical and emotional solitude, was slowly killing him. So he would have found new resonance in this familiar passage from Thoreau.

~

The connection among these seemingly miscellaneous notes is retrospection in the face of Mum's recent death and his anticipated one. He mixes reflection on death with a review of his life in terms of those who influenced him.

Coffin wants to write a course on death. Ann wrote a course in death for me. You have to die, to live. She met death magnificently. Who were the greatest influences on your life?

Rabbi Herschell [possibly Herschel Schacter, the first Army chaplain to enter Buchenwald].

My students, my children, my wife, my father & mother, some teachers, [William] Sloane Coffin. Some colleagues, Judge Branch, Dr. Merrill, Fouad Aintabi, R. Parseghian, Dan Moriarty, Sam Tatelman, George Saylor, Mary Ford [his student and a fine tennis player who became a nun], Lou Thomas [his close friend from Manchester, later an executive with RCA, who died in early middle age], Adm. Keliher, Capt Gainard, other Navy colleagues - John Davis.

There was more in this vein, as he combed through his past in search of significant others, role models and heroes:

People who have influenced my life

Rev. Lorimer, Wally Anderson [minister at his Manchester church when he was in Aleppo], even Mr. Dillon, Hana Scheer, Jim Mahoney, Joe Mac-Dowell, C. Revson [his high school classmate and founder of Revlon], Jim Milner, Eric Lifoergren, Jim Doyle, Dan Wilkins & sister

Women: my mother, cousin Gertrude Steen, cousin Madgalene, Helen Knox, Mary Clarke, (first always—my wife) Marion Emerson, Rhody Parker [a high school classmate and girlfriend in his twenties], several young women teachers _____ Day, Laura Rosberg, Ruth Foster, Jane Fonda, Ann Radice [a college friend of Jane's whom she'd mentored], Mary Russell [my godmother], Mary Jane Leonard, Vera Mahoney [his banker]

Navy colleagues: Charlie Meany [or Murry], Dave _____, Geo. Nichols, several chiefs and sailors, Mitch Rosser.

Then this, on the back side:

> It is difficult sometimes to distinguish between the people who have had strong influence & those you admire (there's always an influence from those you admire & respect)

These lists of influential people in life impress on me how little of his life I shared temporally and thus how little, in a way, I knew him: I can identify very few of these individuals—even with today's electronic resources. I have annotated most of the names I recognize. The vast majority I don't remember ever hearing. Some figures, like Admiral Keliher and Captain Gainard, can be identified because they left historical traces, and their inclusion here helps to document his naval career. Dad did sustain a few relationships with Navy pals after the War, until early in our Melrose years; we may have had one or two to the house at one time or another. But those relationships soon faded. And the overall impression here is of scraping away at his life's palimpsest to reveal buried images, of wondering about others' lives as his own dwindled to its end. (In my sixties, but not anticipating my own death, I too find myself wondering how long-lost friends have fared.)

His otherwise surprising mention of Jane Fonda is owing to my sister's acquaintance with her. Both were outspoken critics of the war, and the two Janes were in contact in the early 1970s—after Fonda's infamous visit to North Viet Nam. Dad obviously came a long way from the veteran who resented our marching in anti-war protests to one who could admire "Hanoi Jane."

Other names are those of colleagues, all female. As chair of the English department, he hired and supervised mostly women—a function of the gendering of the subject. The fact that I recognize few of their names again reinforces how much of his life was unknown to me. But I credit him for acknowledging their influence on him. It speaks well of him as a male administrator in a time of considerable sexism—the era of *Mad Men*.

The inclusion of Irish cousins (Gertrude and Magdalene) is a bit surprising since he had not seen or corresponded with any of them, as far as I know, since his visit to Ireland in 1930 en route to Aleppo. His reaching so far in time and space for influential figures suggests how comprehensive this review of his life was, how diverse the contexts of his significant relationships over the course of that life.

I wish I could annotate the list fully. More than just wishing to know who these individuals were and why they mattered to him, though, I wish I could have actually known them individually, informed them of his death, invited those who were still living to reminisce about, or otherwise memorialize, him. Many were friends he had already lost touch with before I was born. But some were people who were important to him after I was out of high school. What I find most impressive about this list is that he could think so admiringly and respectfully of so many people from so many different walks of life and from such distinct periods of his life, as his world contracted. I would be hard pressed to compose such a long list myself.

The other, more powerful, impression that this census makes on me is its sense of finality; I can understand it only as a ultimate reckoning and a valedictory gesture.

∼

The recurrent prompt is always Mum's death:

> I've learned more about hell in the last six months than I ever knew before. I thot I'd seen my share during the war, lots of horrid death, friends ship mates blown to pieces. Even after the war came the typhoons—men & ships just disappeared (the story of Billy McKay[?])—Enough to endure, to make me indestructible. Tried to bring my kids up to believe that. The most flattering thing I thot then that my children ever said was when Jane once said, Dad, You're indestructible. And I thot I was. How fallible I have found myself: how destructible. I live on the edge of tears. This is the toughest campaign I've ever been through.

The scattered references to his time in the Pacific suggest how important that period was for Dad's sense of himself. That phase serves as a basis of comparison to his latest challenge (the death of his wife), but it also evokes nostalgia for a struggle that was both morally unambiguous (as he saw it) and ultimately victorious, something he could look back on with pride. My sense that he viewed his wartime years this way accounts for my epigraph from James Salter. I suspect that Dad would have reveled in the opportunity to revisit the South Pacific, to travel across "its vastness, passing the great forgotten names, Ulithi, Majuro, Palau" (he would not have forgotten them),with my mother at his side, as many WWII veterans have done.

∼

I'm not surprised to see him associate his service in the Pacific Theater with this most recent "campaign." His service in the World War Two was a formative experience, even if it came rather late to fit neatly into that category. I don't think he actually witnessed bodies, let alone buddies, being blown to bits. But he certainly lost acquaintances and friends. At most he was at one remove from disaster. So I take these references to the war seriously.

However, it was unrealistic to expect that experience to inure him to what he underwent with Mum's terminal illness. One shouldn't expect much carryover from the knowledge of one's comrades' deaths in war to witnessing, up close, the decline and lingering death of the person one loves most in the world, and whom one has known and depended on for so long. So if he was surprised at his vulnerability, he shouldn't have been; there was certainly no call for shame, either. The irony of Jane's calling him indestructible, and his seeming to believe it, is just too sad. He had never been indestructible. Evidently, there was some fissure just below the surface of his usually composed façade. And at some point, inner stresses cracked that fissure open.

Perhaps the saddest thing about his repeated references to Mom lies in his assertion that by facing her death magnificently (which she did) she had taught him a course in death. On the contrary, these very notes from his last months suggest that he could not apply the lessons of her death to his own.

There's no shame in that. Mum resisted her death as long as she could, then grudgingly accepted it, made peace with Dad and died gracefully; not everyone is capable of such equanimity and, to be fair, Dad helped to make her composure possible, in the end.

But his dying was of a different order, a different genus; he courted death in a way that was an extension and exacerbation of a long-standing pathology; it was emotionally draining on those who loved him. And while suicide by the bottle is not as messy as suicide by, say, gunshot, it was terrible to witness firsthand, as I did.

I suppose Dad's life was his to waste or terminate, and it is not for me to blame him—or forgive him—for ending it. It may not even be for me to forgive him for doing it in front of me, or at least in proximity to me; I don't think he made a conscious choice to do it that way, or to make me suffer through it. Even if I were to forgive him, however, I would never—will never—get over it. I have come to think of the deaths of my parents in quick succession as the trauma that has haunted my adult life.

But I take considerable solace now—and I am surprised that I didn't take more when I first read these notes after Dad died—in the lines that reveal that Dad did think of himself as in the process of committing suicide. I can now begin to appreciate the invaluable subtext of the suicide note as a genre: "This *is* a suicide" (i.e., I intend to end my life). The reference to falling on the grenade strikes a false note. It purports to make the act seem heroic and selfless, a sacrifice of something valuable or for a greater good, whereas I think his death was instead the termination of an existence he came to find insupportable. Looked at hard, these are rationalizations rather than rationales. But I take comfort in the knowledge that he knew what he was doing, even if he didn't quite admit it, even to himself.

Moreover, if he was not merely falling off the wagon occasionally but bent on killing himself, then I am not to blame for not saving him. Nor is anyone else. If he had to kill himself (as it seems he had to), then I am grateful for these scraps of evidence that the act was, if not premeditated, at least to some extent and in some way, chosen—not a bluff, the clichéd "call for help," and not an accident.

The good news is that his suicide was not about us, his children; we did not drive him to it or fail to prevent it.

The bad news is also that it wasn't about us: abandoning us was a price he was willing to pay to end his pain.

That hurts. And it will always hurt.

II

The Father I Never Knew
(But Now Know)

Chapter Seven

Mill Town Lad

1906–1930

A classics major in college, my father would have known that the three Greek fates were personified as weaving, measuring, and shearing cloth. So he may have appreciated the fact that the first two decades of his life were spent in textile mill towns. He was born in an Irish mill town, Bessbrook, near Belfast, in 1906, and after his parents immigrated to the United States in 1910, he lived in mill towns in Wisconsin, Massachusetts, and finally New Hampshire until he went to college. Only belatedly, however, by reconstructing this period of his life, did I come to appreciate that aspect of his life—so different from my own suburban youth.

~

In contrast to the great Irish migration of the previous century, Dad's family's relocation had nothing to do with poverty or hunger: his people were textile workers and small business owners—middle-class (and Protestant). Nor did it have anything to do with Irish political turmoil: the Easter Uprising and the Irish War of Independence came later. Indeed, Bessbrook was blessedly free of the animosities endemic to Ireland. Founded as a model mill village in the mid-1800s, Bessbrook prided itself on its lack of pubs and pawn shops—and hence of police. Moreover, it was characterized by remarkable harmony between Catholics and Protestants—the legacy of the Quaker mill owners, the Richardson family. (Ironically, during the Troubles, the disused Quaker-owned mill was fortified and used as a garrison by British troops, and the grounds housed Europe's busiest heliport.)

Isaac was the eighth of ten children, Maria the fourth of eleven. (As if running out of inspiration, her parents had named their seventh child Septimia.) So their expatriation entailed abandoning many relatives. All of their siblings remained in Ireland, where they lived quite comfortable lives. For a young couple to leave so many siblings—not to mention parents, uncles, and aunts—is hard for me to imagine. As young child, Dad would have had weaker emotional ties to his Irish grandparents, aunts, uncles, and cousins, but even for him, immigration must have had an emotional cost.

The evident motivator was Isaac's status as a master card-cutter—an expert in Jacquard weaving. This expertise was Isaac's ticket to America—as attested to by a letter of reference from Bessbrook Spinning Company of October 8, 1910: he "has been in our employment as Foreman Cardcutter for the period of twelve years, during which time he has proved himself to be a most reliable and steady workman and one who understands his business thoroughly." (In a letter of introduction to churches in America, his Presbyterian pastor vouched for his membership in the local branch of the "Men's Protestant Total Abstinence Union"—another valuable credential for an Irishman approaching prospective employers in America.)

From the beginning of the textile industry in England in the 1700s, British expertise and technology had been in demand in the United States, and Isaac saw an opportunity to capitalize on his skill. Or thought he did. Unfortunately, at the time of his immigration, linen was being surpassed in popularity by cotton, which was cheaper to grow and easier to process. Unbeknownst to him, the linen industry had peaked and was in decline.

This may explain why Dad's family moved so often over the next decade, from mill town to mill town—Beloit, Wisconsin; North Brookfield, Massachusetts; Franklin, Massachusetts; and Manchester, New Hampshire, before finally settling in Dover, New Hampshire, in 1922. During this time, Maria bore three more children (Irene, Jim, and Ken); you can trace the family's itinerary by connecting their several birthplaces. I wonder whether this peripatetic life among strangers was really preferable to the settled life the family might have lived amid their extensive families in Bessbrook—especially for Maria, who was uprooted every few years and had to bear and care for children in new and unfamiliar surroundings. It must have been lonely for both parents, and I wonder whether they ever questioned, or regretted, their decision.

As a provider, Isaac seems to have been resourceful. As his skill with Jacquard weaving became less marketable, he shifted into cotton weaving, serving as a foreman and overseer—even patenting an improvement to one of the looms he supervised. And of course my father's generation had opportunities they would not have had in Ireland. Expatriation paid off for them and in that way for their parents as well. Even so, it is hard to believe that this rupture came without significant emotional pain, the inevitable aftereffect of exile. Despite their relatively fortunate circumstances, Isaac and Maria must have experienced a strong sense of loss.

The only personal letter in my father's archive that originated in Ireland offers a poignant testament to the cost of this episode in the family history. Scrawled in spidery script, it conveys Isaac's mother's heartache to him years after his departure.

August 15
my Dear Son,
I wright you a fue lines to let you know I ame breathe[ing]
I wish I could see yo
I would tell you more than I could wright
I ame all alone to day only Misses Brown is with me
I fiel it very mutch to be alone but it will come to an end some day
They are all good enuff to me
You said when you went away you would come to see me in to years
Manny a time I wonder will I ever live to see you agane
Remember me to wife and children
May god bless you all
I field tired an can right no more
You can harly be able to read this
So good by from your loving mother to death
Jane Couser
God bless you all. [emphasis mine]

In her memoir, *The Family Silver,* Sharon O'Brien says, "we inherit our ancestors' emotional histories, particularly their unexpressed stories of suffering, exile, and yearning. . . . From what we know of trauma now, it's clear that both those who stayed in Ireland and those who left, never to return . . . , were marked emotionally and psychologically, and that inheritance has to have marked their children and grandchildren."[1] My great-grandmother Jane's letter, written one hundred years ago, attests to the emotional toll of immigration on both sides of the Atlantic and hints at the guilt emigrants might feel. I suspect this affected Dad, the only child in a position to remember the transatlantic move.

∽

Given Isaac's point of origin, it was altogether appropriate that the Cousers found their way eventually to Manchester, New Hampshire: like Bessbrook, Manchester was a model company town—only on a much grander scale. The "Queen City" took its name from its English counterpart, the world's first industrialized city. The New World Manchester was meant to outshine its namesake, avoiding the squalor and poverty that had caused Blake to condemn the "dark, satanic mills" of England's Industrial Revolution.

For a while, it did. Developed in the early nineteenth century, it presented a benign image that survives today: the mile-long mills that anchor the city plan are arranged in a gentle curve along the Merrimack River. The long, handsome facades are punctuated by large windows, bell towers and ornate archways. Tree-lined canals diverted water from the river above a fifty-foot waterfall and returned it through turbines that drove the looms by an extensive system of belts and pulleys.

Rising up the hillside from the mills were streets flanked by brick housing—boardinghouses for workers, townhouses for managers—in the same style as the mills. Extending across the hilltop was a tidy urban grid. Workers like my grandfather could quickly walk to work in one direction; their families could easily walk to stores, schools, parks, and churches in the other. At Manchester's peak in the early twentieth century, the thirty Amoskeag Mills, as they were collectively known (after the river's Indian name), constituted the largest textile plant in the world.

Toward the end of my father's life, I took a graduate course in American Studies that focused on Manchester's Massachusetts equivalent, Lowell, located thirty miles downriver. Only then did I learn that my grandfather had been employed at the Amoskeag Mills and that my father had lived, as a youth, in mill housing. I hadn't imagined that as part of Dad's past. But he didn't seem interested in revisiting that part of his life in detail—or perhaps I didn't show sufficient interest—and our discussion went no further. (This was all too typical of our relationship; we missed connections again and again.) Mill town life remained for me an academic matter.

Writing this memoir changed all that. I returned to Manchester to do research in the public library (from which I had borrowed books as a child), the Manchester Historic Association, and the Manchester Millyard Museum (housed in a former mill building). Visiting the latter, one gets a visceral sense of the size of the complex and the scale of the power involved: mill walls are punctured by pipe openings ten feet in diameter through which the river water churned.

On his arrival in Manchester, Isaac was hired as an overseer in a cotton mill and the family lived in a townhouse on Stark Street. During the first quarter of the 20th century, however, with alternatives to hydropower and cheap labor available in the South, textile manufacturing abandoned New England. In 1922, attempts to organize unions in Manchester, a paternalistic company town, led to a nine-month mill closure. Many workers lost their jobs. Isaac was not laid off. But, as I learned from a city directory—which lists occupations alongside addresses—he was demoted from overseer to laborer; as a result, he had to move his family of seven to a boardinghouse. This abrupt downward mobility shocked me, and gave me a sense of the vulnerability of his family. The decline of the textile industry was nearly devastating for them. I wonder how it affected Isaac; did he think himself a failure, the whole American venture a mistake? And Maria? Was this the payoff for leaving her homeland and large family, then relocating every couple of years from one mill town to another through the Midwest and New England? Surely they had moments of doubt, if not outright regret.

Once more, however, Isaac moved his family, this time to nearby Dover, where he found a managerial position at the Pacific mill. This proved fortunate: the entire Amoskeag complex shut down for good in the 1930s, and Manchester went into steep decline. Somehow, Isaac managed to stay employed—though not at the same mill—throughout the Depression. And the family never had to move again.

Dad's younger siblings grew up in the house at 274 Washington Street in Dover; the endpoint of their wanderings, it became home to them. Isaac and Maria lived there until Isaac died in 1951; after that, Maria stayed on alone as long as her Parkinson's disease permitted. Throughout my childhood, I knew it as the family homestead.

But when the family moved to Dover in 1922, my father stayed in Manchester to complete high school. This intrigues me: did he insist on finishing school with his classmates, even if it meant living apart from his parents and four siblings? And where, and with whom, did he live for that final year? With another family? At the YMCA? Wherever he lived, he must have had to work to pay his room and board. This seems an early demonstration of his independence and determination, his deviation from the path of least resistance. In any case, Manchester had become home for him, and he lived there—with significant, but short, absences—for the next thirty years.

After graduating from Central High School in 1923, he went on the University of New Hampshire, the first of his family to attend college. After his freshman year, however, he transferred to Wesleyan College in Middletown, Connecticut. This too stimulates my interest, as it seems so unlikely: his parents could hardly have afforded to send their oldest child to a private liberal arts college. He must have received a generous scholarship. But whose idea was this transfer in the first place? Was he encouraged by someone who sensed his potential—one of his teachers at Central, perhaps? This might help to explain his pleasure at returning to teach there himself and his own generosity to students who showed promise beyond their expectations.

~

At Wesleyan, he found himself amid a different class of students, in socioeconomic terms; indeed, the term "classmates" may have seemed ironic. Many came from affluent backgrounds and prepped at boarding schools. Although certainly bright enough, Dad was a mediocre student for his first three years at Wesleyan. Could he not keep up? Or did he just lack confidence? More likely, he was just disengaged—or otherwise engaged: his fraternity, Delta Kappa Epsilon, ranked last in the fraternity scholarship competition. He seems to have taken advantage of being away from home to cut loose a bit, majoring in Greek figuratively as well as literally. He was evidently not a teetotaler like his father, and I wonder what role drinking played in his college career. Did he develop a habit, a thirst, a dependency then, that came back to haunt him in later life?

In any case, his transcript reveals a spotty record—mostly C's and D's until his final semester, when he redeemed himself, earning A's and winning two prizes in his major. I was not merely surprised, but downright angry to discover that he had held me to a standard he had not met as a student. Now, however, I can see that this double standard may have been less a matter of hypocrisy than of his wanting me to get the full benefit of my opportunities. He may have wanted me to surpass him, even if that threatened his ego.

After graduation, he returned to Manchester, where he roomed with a friend, Bob Riedel. The next year he worked as the membership secretary of the YMCA, an institution that played a large role in his life. New facilities featured the state's first indoor pool, a gym, and an indoor track. For a teenaged boy in a mill town, the Y was a home away from home, a place to make and meet friends as well as to burn off energy. It's there, I think, that he first befriended Bob, who had attended a different high school. It may be there, too, that he had his first exposure to gay subculture, another aspect of his life that was hidden from me while he was alive.

To research this part of his life, Jane and I returned to Manchester to locate and photograph his various residence there—mill housing, several rooming houses where he lived as a bachelor, the first house he and Mum occupied, and the house we lived in immediately after the war. We were struck by how close together these various sites were, how small a world he occupied, in a way. But we were particularly impressed with how close to his first home the Y was—so close that the mill housing in which his family had lived was eventually demolished to make room for an addition. How appropriate that the Y eventually swallowed up his boyhood home.

After a year in Manchester, Dad moved to nearby Concord to begin his career as a high school English teacher. After a stint teaching in Aleppo, from 1930 to 1933, he returned to his home town to teach at his alma mater. It was there that he met, courted, and married Mum, after she joined the English Department at Central High School. (She had grown up in Manchester, but across the river on the west side, attending a different high school.)

Thus, my father's life to that point could be traced from one mill town across an ocean to another, with stops at several in between. He was, then, in a sense, a mill town lad, the product of a very distinctive environment and culture. But his route was far from circular. Manchester was nothing like Bessbrook: it was much larger and more diverse, with significant numbers of French Canadians, Greeks, and Eastern Europeans; Protestants, Roman Catholics, Orthodox Catholics, and Jews. In any case, unlike many mill town lads, he did not grow up to work in a mill himself; his parents made sure of that.

They valued education, and so did he. Indeed, he made it his vocation, his life work.

Despite his uneven record at Wesleyan, going there may have made all the difference. Its emphasis on the liberal arts suited him, and the experience seems to have extended his horizons. It may have been there that he somehow set his sights far beyond his immediate environs, Manchester and New England, on Aleppo.

His decision to go to Aleppo is the next conundrum to me. There's no obvious preparation for this in the life of a mill town lad, even a college graduate. But while his archive yields no definitive explanation, it does shed a good deal of light on why he went there, what he found there, and how that experience shaped him, far more than his father's experience with the textile industry. Again, his letters help me understand an important part of his life that ended long before I entered it.

Chapter Eight

"In Aleppo Once"

Syria 1930–1933

Growing up in the 1950s, I knew that not long after Dad graduated from Wesleyan College, in 1927, he went to Syria to teach at an institution called Aleppo College. I grew up literally surrounded by evidence of his sojourn; souvenirs of his time there decorated our modest house in Melrose: tear bottles, scarabs, coins and buttons, Oriental rugs and fabrics. (If anything, the souvenirs were *too* familiar; rather than being curious about them, my sister Jane and I took them for granted.) We also had human reminders of his stint in Syria: as a family, we socialized with some of his former students who had immigrated to the Boston area. But they were ethnically Armenian: why were they not Syrian?

So that period of Dad's life was mostly a mystery. Where exactly was Aleppo? What was "Aleppo College"? What exactly did he do there? And what drew him there? That episode of his life was remote in time as well as space. It was hard for me, growing up in a white-bread Boston suburb, to have any sense of what it must have been like for him to venture so far at so young an age. And he didn't volunteer much about it. What I knew I picked up by overhearing conversations with former students or College staff who visited us in the 1950s and 1960s.

Among the documents in Dad's archive, however, many were related to Aleppo. It was only in perusing them that I have come to appreciate what an extraordinary thing Dad did in his early twenties, leaving behind family and friends to teach in the Middle East. Like his parents, who emigrated from Northern Ireland in 1910, he broke away from the known and familiar—but he did it entirely on his own. I certainly did nothing so adventurous at that age.

That sojourn was critical in making him the person I knew, and it sheds retrospective light on him as a young man, so long before my birth. With the help of documents in his archive, I've come to a better appreciation of this period in his life. That understanding was deepened by a pilgrimage to Aleppo in the spring of 2010.

One surprising discovery was that Dad had been a missionary, at least in name: from 1930 to 1933 he was employed by the American Board of Commissioners for Foreign Missions (ABCFM), a body founded in 1810 by New England Congregational and Presbyterian churches. The first American foreign missionary organization, it sent emissaries far afield—to Japan, China, Africa, and Southeast Asia—as well as, during the nineteenth century, to Indian tribes in the American West. Ironically, I first heard of it when I was a graduate student in American Studies; at the time, the ABCFM seemed something out of the remote past—and its agenda seemed somewhat suspect, tainted with colonialism. I had no sense of the organization's work in the twentieth century, much less of Dad's involvement in it. I am struck by how his life history has complemented my book learning, and vice versa. Indeed, my appraisal of the ABCFM has changed as a result: its mission in Syria seems to have been remarkably progressive—even, or especially, today.

When I first read through Dad's papers in 1975, though, I had trouble reconciling my sense of him with my image of a missionary. Although he was a life-long church-goer, he did not seem particularly religious, much less driven by evangelical fervor. Becoming a missionary in his mid-twenties seemed an uncharacteristic choice for the man I knew. And my research suggests that his venturing to Aleppo was a more a matter of pedagogical than of religious fervor, mixed with inchoate romantic impulses.

I certainly found no evidence of nascent interest in religion in Dad's college records. As its name suggests, Wesleyan was founded by Methodists, and it has a history of producing missionaries, but Dad was not among them. His college yearbook revealed that he had not been a member of the Christian Association; his transcript, that he did not take a single course in religion. I have no idea where, when, or how he was recruited. But his letters suggest that he had met the director of Aleppo College, the Reverend John E. Merrill, before he went to Syria perhaps at Dad's church in Manchester. However they met, Merrill made a powerful impact on him, but it seems to have been more vocational than spiritual.

In Aleppo Dad's primary responsibility was to teach English. His extra-curricular responsibilities dealt with bodies, not souls. He coached soccer (in which he lettered at Wesleyan), tennis, and track; organized a basketball league; and even—implausibly in Aleppo—taught students to swim, using local farmers' irrigation pools, which were filled, as he wrote home, "from adjacent wells by chain-bucket wheels turned by blindfolded donkeys or camels." He was proud of that adaptation of traditional technology, and I admire its ingenuity.

In any case, his mission in Aleppo was not to preach Christianity to Muslims (which wouldn't have been allowed) but to teach English to Christian Armenian refugees from the genocide at the hands of the Ottoman Turks. His fundamental concern seems to have been to give them the educational wherewithal to improve their individual lives—and thus their collective prospects. In a letter sent to his parents his first fall in Aleppo, he wrote,

> One has a feeling of contributing much more than is possible in an American school. For most of these boys who come from very poor homes, the school is absolutely their only chance of providing themselves with the means of advancing. They are the raw material out of which their civic leaders will come. Much will depend on the leaders because as a new people here they are faced with hundreds of problems in adjustment. (October 19, 1930)

His Armenian students were recovering from a historic trauma. That fact—still denied, outrageously, by the Turkish government (and not yet fully acknowledged by ours)—endowed his work with particular urgency.

From my research, I now know the back story of the institution he served. One of several ABCFM educational institutions founded in the Muslim world—including Robert College in Istanbul and the American University of Beirut (originally the Syrian Protestant College)—Aleppo College was the successor to Central Turkey College, which had been established in 1874 in Aintab. The first nation to adopt Christianity as a state religion, in the 4th century CE, Armenia became part of the Muslim Ottoman Empire in the 16th century CE. The mission of Central Turkey College was to educate Armenian "evangelical" Christians—i.e., Protestants, rather than members of the Armenian Apostolic (Oriental Orthodox) or Armenian Catholic Church. These Protestants were a minority within the Christian minority in a Muslim empire. During the genocide (1915 to 1923), however, the College was forced to close, and many Armenians sought refuge in Aleppo.

After the First World War and the dissolution of the Ottoman Empire, the League of Nations established a French mandate in Syria in 1922. From our current perspective, it is clear that this post-war division of territory by European powers involved the suppression of minorities. Recent developments like the "Arab Spring" can be traced in part to long smoldering conflicts among different sects of Islam and other religious and ethnic groups. At the time, however, the fact that Aleppo was part of French-controlled Syria, rather than Turkey, was reassuring to Christian minorities; the Armenian community took root there, and the ABCFM founded primary and secondary schools for girls and boys. Two higher grades comprising Aleppo College were added to the boys' preparatory school in 1927, and in the year of Dad's arrival, 1930, Aleppo College was formally accredited as the successor to Central Turkey College.

Several distinctive aspects of the school were attractive to Dad, himself a first-generation college student. It was geared to students of limited financial means; tuition was low, financial aid was available, and work-study was common. Moreover, its educational philosophy was remarkably progressive. The official institutional ideal was a "constant, continuous, co-operative, democratic, friendly, and human relationship between teacher and student"; the ethos, then, was anti-hierarchical and anti-authoritarian—protestantism with a small p. Finally, the school was remarkably ecumenical. In the early twentieth century, the ABCFM became non-sectarian, an aspect that helped it penetrate regions, like the Middle East, where evangelism was unwelcome. Although its student body in the early thirties was largely Armenian Christians, the school was open to students from any religious background. And a brochure from this period boasts that the small staff included people of six nationalities and six "religious communities." Remarkably, the compulsory religion course covered not only Hebrew and Christian scripture but an introduction to the Qu'ran. This, despite the fact that its first students were Christians whose families had been brutalized by Turkish Muslims. Or perhaps this ecumenicism was a conscious response to sectarian aggression. In any case, the school's philosophy seems remarkably enlightened.

Later, during Alford Carleton's presidency (1937-53), the student population evolved to the point at which a third of students were Armenian, a third Christian Arabs, and a third Muslim. Clearly, then, the aim of the College and its related schools was not to make Christians out of infidels but to encourage mutual understanding among members of separate "nations." In the light of recent history this approach seems all the more compelling.

~

Dad's long absence from home meant that he could communicate with family and friends only via correspondence. Fortunately for me, his family retained his letters. Ironically, then, his distance from them brings him close to me, giving me precious access to his frame of mind. The most direct expression of gratification in his work comes in a letter to his parents as he contemplated his return to the States.

> I am indeed very busy here, but it is a kind of duty that does not present itself as work. I become completely absorbed in this or that phase of it but am not conscious of any effort required to do this. . . . One is called upon in so many ways to produce, that when I think of teaching again in America, it seems like taking on only half a job, like using only half of myself. (May 1933)

Figure 8.1. Aleppo Boys High School, Class of 1932.

Whatever sense of mission he felt about his work seems to have followed from, rather than led to, his initial decision. Later, back in the US, particularly in Melrose, where his students were quite privileged, he may have suffered from the sense of being underemployed that he anticipates here.

As I delve into his past, though, an obvious question is what motivated him initially to venture so far from home. Of course, there was the Depression, when unemployment blocked many in his generation from getting footholds in the economy. But by 1929 Dad had a seemingly secure job in a "safe" profession, teaching English at Concord High School; there would always be students to teach in the States. I believe his decision to spend his middle twenties in a remote and alien environment was impelled mostly by wanderlust, curiosity, and sheer adventurousness. Literally of provincial origins, he had grown up and been educated mostly in New England. His years in college, especially Wesleyan, presumably broadened his awareness of the outside world. His major, classics, would have educated him about ancient civilizations in the Middle East. And his graduation coincided with the publication of *Revolt in the Desert,* T. E. Lawrence's account of his exploits there during World War I, first as an archeologist, later as a military leader.

Lawrence came alive to me as a teenager through a very different medium, David Lean's film *Lawrence of Arabia* (1962), which we made a
family excursion to see at a Boston movie palace—where a red velvet curtain
rose slowly before the show and the film was long enough to warrant an
intermission, like a theatrical performance. I subsequently wrote a research
paper on Lawrence, whom I found very appealing—smart, brave, dashing,
and devoted to Arab independence. Dad was an informed reader of my paper,
but I don't remember his volunteering that he had traveled in Lawrence's
sandy footsteps. At that moment, as at so many others, I would have welcomed the benefit of his rich life experience. Intriguingly, in my research for
this memoir, I learned that one of the people Dad knew in Aleppo, Dr. Ernest
Altounyan, was a close friend of Lawrence; they met when Lawrence was
doing archeological work at Carchemish before World War I. Dad must have
been thrilled to meet a man personally acquainted with the legendary Lawrence. But, oddly, he never shared that with me.

Even if travel was not his stated motive for going to Aleppo, he took
advantage of being there to explore. To begin with, he took a leisurely route
to his destination; he detoured to Northern Ireland to meet relatives. The first
family member to return to his homeland, he must have seemed a prodigal
son. In Ireland, he established intercontinental connections that have continued to my generation and beyond.

From there, he traveled through Europe with his best friend, Bob Riedel,
stopping in Vienna and Budapest en route to Istanbul. On a modest budget,
they managed to travel in style: his archive contained pictures of the two
"hiking" in the Alps in three-piece suits and, in Dad's case, plus fours. Bob
seems to have accompanied him all the way to Istanbul, where Dad took the
train to Aleppo by himself.

∿

An ancient city inhabited mostly by Arab Muslims, Aleppo was some
5,000 miles away—and about as different as it could be—from Dad's home
town. No matter how much he might have read about the area and no matter
how slow his approach, he must have experienced some culture shock on
arriving at the city where he was to spend the next several years. There he
was, a New Hampshire Yankee in the storied Levant. But he gives no evidence of discomfort in his correspondence, only delight in its exotic character. Was he putting on a brave face for those at home, or was he really so
open to new cultural experiences? It's hard sometimes to sense his true
feelings in his circumscribed and formal letters home. But my sense is that
this sojourn fulfilled some deeply felt need to escape the prosaic mill town he
grew up in.

Here is how he described his new home to his congregation at home:

From the first Aleppo struck me as the real thing, a "real" Eastern city, fascinating beyond words. Though the day when I thrilled to find it so is long past, I venture even now to say that it is comparable only to what one may imagine. Not what I dared imagine Aleppo would be, but like the rare and romantic places one's imagination has a special suggestion for.

Densely built, the city spreads widely over the bottom of a great basin the lip of which is a circle of low, bare hills. Conspicuous on a mound in the center is the citadel, aptly described by Lawrence of Arabia as like a cup bottom-up in its saucer. About it spreads the mysteriously intricate pattern of flat grey roofs giving a common color effect that accounts for the name "Aleppo the grey."

After passing through the city one sees that a line may be drawn between what is genuinely and what less genuinely Oriental. Native Eastern costume of all cuts and colors is met throughout the city, even in the Franco-Syrian quarter where the newer shops and the tram-line are. Eastern dress prevails in the oldest and largest section, the Moslem or Arab quarter. The Great Bazaar is in the Moslem Quarter, in the heart of the old city, and there one's senses are simply filled with the East. I shall not attempt any more of this; really the bazaars beggar one's descriptive powers.

Dad was plunged into an environment that must have seemed alien in every respect: topographical, climatic, linguistic, cultural, architectural, ethnic, and religious. The formal, detached tone of his epistolary account gives a sense of the outward impression the city made, but not whether or how it may have unsettled him or made him homesick.

To avoid Aleppo's scorching heat, he spent summers in Europe. On a limited budget, he took deck passage, self-catering and sleeping in a custom hammock on deck. (In the 1950s one such hammock hung between two fruit trees in our Manchester backyard.) His itinerary took him along the northern Mediterranean coast, stopping in Turkey, Cyprus, Rhodes, and Athens. The first summer, he disembarked in Brindisi, on the heel of Italy's boot, traveled up the peninsula to Geneva, where he dropped in on the opening session of the League of Nations Assembly, which much impressed him. He considered studying French there, but found Switzerland prohibitively expensive and traveled to Grenoble instead. At summer's end, he returned to Italy and embarked from Genoa.

He took advantage of shorter school vacations to travel on an Indian motorcycle to various sites in Syria, including Palmyra, Hama, and the famous crusader castle Crac des Chevaliers, a site studied by Lawrence. (He kept the motorcycle a secret from his parents.) He traveled to Baghdad by train. During the Easter vacation of 1932, he and a Swiss colleague, Ernest Bille, took a trip by train to Beirut. From there they motored with two female teachers to Jerusalem, driving literally on the beach from Acre to Haifa.

After a brief tour of Biblical sites, they took a train through the Sinai desert to the Suez Canal, ferried across it, and continued by train to Cairo, to see the pyramids at Giza. They trained on to Luxor and Karnak to view temples and ruins. There's a wonderful photo of Dad in khaki shorts and pith helmet at Luxor; the shadow of the photographer, presumably Ernest, is visible in the foreground—a tantalizing trace of a person who remains mysterious, despite the fact that he was an important figure in Dad's life at the time. (In a letter, Ernest refers to him as his "best, his only, friend.")

Even when he wasn't traveling, he was living in Aleppo, and that in itself was delightfully different from the world he had known growing up in New England. Aleppo bears traces of Roman, Hellenistic, Muslim, Byzantine, Ottoman, and of course French, culture. The city is divided into various "quarters"—for Muslims, Jews, Christians, and foreigners. It is clear in letters from Ernest, who was very nostalgic for Aleppo after his return to Switzerland, that both greatly enjoyed the souks and the local food.

I doubt that this travel was an afterthought or an unanticipated perk of his position; rather, I suspect the missionary stint was a way of subsidizing such exploration. His decision to teach in Aleppo arose out of the same motives, and brought the same rewards, that characterize service in the Peace Corps—the opportunity to see the world in a non-military capacity and the opportunity while doing so, to do some good. As it happened, once he married, settled down, and had children in the 1940s, his opportunities for travel were greatly reduced. Aside from escorting a wealthy young man to Europe and Russia in the summer of 1934 and a tour of duty as a Navy officer in the South Pacific during World War II, he did not leave the United States again until our family tour of Europe in the summer of 1961. But in his twenties he ventured far to explore sites with ancient pedigrees, sites few of his contemporaries visited.

In his first surviving letter home, written in early October, he refers to having received a series of letters from his family, beginning in August. In his first letter home, I sense an undercurrent of homesickness when he refers nostalgically to late summer activities like apple-picking: "I suppose that by the time this letter reaches you the leaves will have begun to turn. I shall not see much of that this year but shall experience the autumn of another land. Already I know it as a land of many colors although there are fewer trees than I have been used to. One depends on other natural causes for the color and they supply it." (5 October 1930)

Having been to Aleppo, I know "fewer trees" to be a gross understatement. In sharp contrast to New England, in Aleppo most of the trees are located inside people's homes—within high-walled courtyards. Only a few major streets are tree-lined, and parks are few (and usually of European origin). Dad's letters to his parents may have minimized how alien his new home felt to him. Typically, his tone is quite formal: "I shall not see" and "one depends." It must have seemed so even, or especially, to his parents, who lacked his higher education. But he knew his letters might be circulated; some were read in church. He was conscious of his audience, managing their view of Aleppo. He wanted to convey its exoticism without reinforcing stereotypes.

He was been remarkably non-judgmental about the local population. The only evidence of stereotyping Muslims comes in a letter to his brother Tom. Interestingly, it has to do not with religion or "culture" but with sport; he invidiously compares their athleticism to that of his Armenian students:

> The Armenians take to games as if it were instinctive with them; they seem actually born to sport. This is quite in contrast with the attitude of the Mohammedans who, though quite interested in sport, are interested in it as a spectacle; that is, from the spectator point of view. The idea of participating seems to suggest to them losing their dignity, soiling their hands, in other words being plebeian.

If he had not really registered the French hegemony in Syria before he went there, he was reminded in a dramatic way his first fall:

> Dr. Merrill was officially invited to attend the review of troops before the French general. Being unable to go, he sent me as his representative. You may be sure that I relished the idea very much. Wanting to do the thing properly and with fair style I got me a carriage and drove to the field, arriving there amidst the other dignitaries. And it surely was a spread-eagle affair. The grandstand contained a bewildering variety of official costume and dress. . . .
>
> There were infantry and artillery battalions of Syrians, Madagascarites (Negroes), and Algerians. But the Moroccan horsemen, called "Spahis" and the Arab cavalry were the most impressive, both men and horses. The Spahis wear white cloaks with red or blue lining, and turbans. . . . On the gallop they are a thrilling sight with their head cloths streaming behind.
>
> After the Spahis and Arabs had passed in review, they formed a great long line on the hill, and did the finale of the afternoon by making a flying charge down the hill directly towards the grandstand. The few moments this took had all the sensations one gets imaginatively from reading two or three fighting romances of the "Beau Geste" variety. I got an immense kick out of it. (November 1930)

Prepared by reading T. E. Lawrence, he clearly relished this display of native pageantry and horsemanship—literally something to write home about. His travels gave him a taste of exotic, swashbuckling spectacle that was fun to retail to folks in New England.

Far from home, he was privileged to become part of a small social circle revolving around the Altounyan family. In a letter home of early November

1930, he reported with pride that he was a charter member of "the Etcetera Club," which was organized by the Altounyans and held a different sort of gathering each week. The patriarch of this family, Aram Assadour Altounyan (1854-1950), was born in Anatolia, the original Armenian homeland. After graduating from Central Turkey College in Aintab in the 1870s, he went to medical school in England, practiced medicine in New York, and returned to Anatolia, where he married Harriet Riddell, a nurse from Dad's birthplace, Northern Ireland. (The Irish connection must have pleased Dad.) Aram then established a medical practice in Aleppo (then within the Ottoman Empire), eventually building his own hospital. Having treated Ottoman rulers before World War I, he was shielded from persecution during the genocide; indeed, he managed to extend protection to other Armenians. His wife is credited with founding the Protestant church in Aleppo, which served the Armenian Protestants.

In 2010, Jane and I traveled to Syria to see Aleppo for ourselves. Although it had grown tremendously in the eighty years since Dad's sojourn there, its historic core was much the same. The Syrian Catholic and Armenian Orthodox churches are located in the Christian quarter of the old walled city. Built much later, the evangelical church is necessarily outside the wall, and it is modest in size and décor. In conformity with Protestant aesthetics, it lacks stained glass and ornate decoration. At the time of our visit it served a small and dwindling congregation. We watched and listened as the choir practiced, trying to imagine our father worshipping there.

Aram's son Ernest was born in England in 1889 and raised in the manner of an English gentleman. Like his father, he became a doctor and, after WWI, he joined his father at the hospital in Aleppo. Their families occupied separate floors in a stone house across the street. Among Ernest's friends (in addition to T. E. Lawrence) were the philosopher Robin Collingwood (whose sister he married), and Arthur Ransome, who based the characters in his children's book series, *Swallows and Amazons*, on Ernest's children, who spent much of their youth in England. Anglo-Armenian colonials of high social status, all four of Ernest's children were home-schooled until they were literally shipped off to boarding schools in England.

One of those children, Taqui, born in 1917, became the family historian, writing two memoirs: *In Aleppo Once* (1969) and *Chimes from a Wooden Bell* (1990). (The title of the former, which I have appropriated for this chapter, comes from a line in Othello's final soliloquy.) Her memoirs give a vivid picture of her Anglo-Armenian family life between the world wars. In 1959, however, following the Suez Canal crisis, in which England acted contrary to Arab nationalist interests, the Altounyans were expelled from Syria on short notice. The family's stone house was razed, leaving a gap in the urban fabric that is still visible, and the hospital was converted into a school; the Altounyans' considerable contributions to the health and welfare of Aleppines were ended and their traces erased.

When Taqui visited decades later, she realized how insulated she had been from Arab life while growing up: "Together we formed a tight, self-contained community as though in an island fortress surrounded by the sea, which was Aleppo town" (50). Their Arab servants did errands for them; the children were not allowed to leave the compound unless chauffeured or otherwise chaperoned.

An entirely unexpected payoff for finding *In Aleppo Once* came when I stumbled upon a passage late in the book, in which Taqui quotes from her girlhood diary:

> That autumn there was also Mr. C., a new teacher in the boys' school, who, of course, came under our microscope, or rather, our distorting magnifying glass. [My sister] and I agreed that he was "Abstract noun. Common gender. Objective case. Very intransitive verb. Most passive voice." But he was very probably an ordinary, perhaps rather shy, young man, who was not particularly interested in girls of fourteen and under. My diary is full of scathing remarks about "grown-ups"—the clothes and hats they wore, the things they said. Everyone was either a friend or an enemy, and there were no half-tones. Young men were usually silly, but I was interested in Mr. C., the games master. I could usually catch sight of him in the distance, from our tennis court, drilling the boys in a neighbouring field. My diary is severe: "After the Christmas party charades Mr. C. came out of his shell amazingly. He even dared to bang on the table." Whenever we met I would be aggressive. He did not know how to take me, having no idea what I was feeling. Later I sent him cards from boarding school and he sent me one, which I treasured for a long time. (154-55)

I was startled, spooked, touched, and immensely gratified to come across this reference to my father so serendipitously. While I am relieved that Dad was not interested in a girl ten years his junior, I am glad that he made such an impression on Taqui that she recorded it, endowing him with a kind of encrypted immortality. I only wish he had come across this passage himself. He would have been delighted, and the discovery might have rekindled his interest in Aleppo—and his faith in himself, which was faltering when the book was published in the late '60s.

The Altounyans were generous to include him in their circle. This social outlet beyond the relatively narrow orbit of the school staff helped fill the void created by his absence from his own large family. It must have pleased him that the Altounyans had children the age of his youngest siblings. Being granted admission to their world was quite an honor. To a young man from New Hampshire, their cosmopolitan lives must have seemed very rarefied. And while he might have been initially intimidated, his being an American abroad probably minimized discomfort. In any case, by Taqui's testimony, he eventually came out of his shell. So while the Altounyans may have been insulated from much of Aleppo's vibrant culture, his acquaintance with them gave him a glimpse into a social world different from his humble origins.

At another margin of his small social world was the College's Arabic instructor, a local man of Turkic and Arab descent, Fouad Aintabi. (His name turns up in one of Dad's final inventories of people he admired.) Surprisingly, Dad reports that Aintabi's uncle had been commander of the Ottoman army in the Caucasus during the war, a connection one would think would not endear him to Armenian students. In any case, a visit to his house afforded Dad a glimpse of

> the home of one of the best and oldest families in Aleppo. . . They have a fine,
> old Arab house in which they have lived for years. From the outside one can
> get no idea of the charm of such a house built around a spacious open court-
> yard with pool and orange trees in the center. The outside aspect is simply a
> part of the continuous wall of the alley-like streets, with low, heavily studded
> iron doors at intervals. (24 January 1932)

When Jane and I visited Aleppo, we stayed in a house of just this type, which had been converted into a boutique hotel by two brothers. Such houses are ingeniously designed to be comfortable in a harsh climate. To step into the courtyard, with a fountain burbling and trees branching overhead, is to enter a sanctuary from busy streets devoid of vegetation. By a fortunate coincidence, our hosts' father had been educated in the ABCFM schools in Aleppo. When the brothers learned why Jane and I had come to Syria, they introduced us to him. In his eighties, he was still enthusiastic about the schools. "What visionaries!" he would say of the staff and administration. Indeed, he was bitter about the later nationalization of the College, which destroyed its distinctive character.

One morning, over coffee in the courtyard, I showed him a schematic hand-drawn map of the city that Dad had annotated and sent home to orient his family. After studying it for a few minutes, he said, "Follow me." He led us out the hotel door, down a crooked alley to the street, and about seventy-five yards along the street. There he paused, pointed to a handsome stone building, and said, "That is where your father taught. When I was a boy, I attended kindergarten there." Insofar as we were finally standing where Dad had stood some eighty years before, this was the high point of our pilgrimage.

~

When Dad came home in 1933, at the end of his three-year term, he spent the summer in New York, taking graduate courses in education at Columbia. Later on he did some further graduate work, but never got a degree. Nevertheless, his work in Syria functioned as a kind of extra-curricular preparation for teaching in the U.S. Indeed, it's hard to imagine a better qualification for someone teaching high school in the U.S. today. His work, residence, and travels in the Middle East gave him a sense of the variety of human cultures and religions that enriched his teaching throughout his career.

Although he never returned to Aleppo, he kept in touch with the Merrills and the Carletons, who occasionally visited us in Melrose at least twenty years after he left Syria. They would update him on the status of the schools. More important, they put him in touch with some former students who had immigrated to New England. One of my most distinct memories of my boyhood in Manchester is of attending the naturalization of Dr. Paul Hasserjian. His family and other Armenian émigré families became friends we saw at regular intervals in the 1950s and 1960s. In particular, my childhood in Melrose was punctuated by trips back and forth to Belmont to visit with the Parseghian family: Richard, who had been Dad's student at Aleppo College; his wife Angel; and their three children. Richard became a very successful clothier, and the family assimilated well into the American culture of the 1950s. But they belonged to an Armenian Protestant church and had extensive ties to the large Armenian community in the Boston area. In a manner that Jane and I hardly appreciated at the time, they were living examples of the fulfillment of mission of the College.

My sister and I knew that this group consisted of genocide survivors and their children. In researching this chapter, I located Paul Hasserjian's son, Dr. Robert Hasserjian, who told me his father's story. Born in 1914, Paul was only nine months old when his father was removed to a concentration camp in Der Zor, in the Syrian desert, where he (and countless others) later died. Paul and his mother lived secretly with neighbors in Aintab until they were able to flee to Aleppo in 1921. After studying at Aleppo College while Dad was there, Paul went on to the American University of Beirut, to medical school, and became a radiologist. During World War II, his mentor there immigrated to New Hampshire and encouraged Paul to follow, which he did in 1947.

As a result of being in regular contact with Armenian friends, my sister and I grew up with an awareness of the Armenian genocide that was rare for our generation, most of whom associated genocide exclusively with the Holocaust, known to us primarily through *The Diary of Anne Frank*—the book, the play, and the movie. Doing an internet search for Richard Parseghian, I experienced a shock of recognition. A search engine led me to a website called "The Forgotten." There I heard Richard's distinctive, slightly accented voice telling how, as a child, he had watched a Turkish soldier beat his father with a rifle butt. Some ten years after Richard's death, and nearly a century after the events occurred, his testimony was vivid and compelling.

Another, more subtle, legacy of Dad's service in Aleppo was our constant exposure to artifacts from the Near East. Underfoot or hanging on walls were rugs he brought or sent back from Syria. He also had collections of coins and buttons—small, inexpensive, highly portable souvenirs. More precious and fragile are tear bottles. Customarily, mourners would bury these vessels, containing their tears, with the dead; long burial gives them a lustrous opalescence. Stored in the attic were colorful robes, headdresses, and footwear. Although we saw these mostly when we they were lent out as costumes for Christmas pageants, we grew up familiar with Arab garb; it remained exotic to us, but it was not alien. In all of these subtle ways, Jane and I grew up in a household quite different from most in our rather homogeneous suburb. Despite the fact that Dad rarely spoke about this period of his life in a sustained way, then, it was a formative experience not just for him but also, in an indirect way, for me and Jane. While he may have been motivated in the beginning as much by curiosity and a taste for adventure as by any sense of "mission," his letters home suggest that his time in Aleppo engaged him in a serious, even profound way; his developing sense of mission, however, was rooted not so much in faith in God as in faith in liberal education. This faith sustained him throughout his career, I think, though the stakes may have seemed lower in his long state-side career than during his Syrian sojourn. Going to Aleppo, then, both reflected the values that defined him in his early twenties and shaped his view of his profession—and the world—for the rest of his life.

Some of his curiosity about other cultures and his commitment to teaching inevitably rubbed off on his children; Jane and I are beneficiaries of his missionary experience. Only as I reached middle age and the end of my own career as a teacher did I come to appreciate how extraordinary it was for him to take a position in such a distant and alien place. Certainly, in view of recent world-historical events, I find his open-minded curiosity and his nonsectarian stance toward Near Eastern Muslim culture all the more impressive, admirable, memorable, and extraordinary. And his faith in liberal arts education became an important legacy for me as a college professor.

His work in Aleppo, progressive for its time, seems even more remarkably so today, when the United States is embroiled in a world-wide struggle against militant Islamists. Jane and I can view this conflict with some perspective, because Dad's experience in Syria enabled him to introduce Islam to us as a religion worthy of respect. He took us to the mosque at the Islamic Center of Washington, D.C., not long after it opened in 1957. I remember being awed by its vast horizontal space. At the time, the mosque was by far the largest house of worship I had ever seen. It prepared me to appreciate the many finer ancient mosques I have since visited in Istanbul, Damascus, and Aleppo. For all of this, I am immensely grateful.

～

CODA: TRAVELS WITH HENRY

In addition to shaping his later life, and ours, in these subtle, but significant ways, Dad's excursion had a more concrete, immediate payoff for him: during the summer of the following year, 1934, he was hired to chaperone a young man from Manchester on a trip to Germany, Russia, and Finland. As with many other aspects of him early life, I had a vague knowledge of this, but no details. The young man's name was probably bandied around the house when I was small, but because it meant nothing to me, I didn't retain it. After Dad died, however, Jane and I came across dozens of photographs from this trip; they were unlabeled but in some cases unmistakable (e.g., Moscow's Red Square, Berlin's Brandenburg Gate). With my interest aroused, I soon identified this man as Henry Melville Fuller, who was sufficiently prominent to merit an obituary in the *New York Times.*

Born in Manchester in 1914, Henry was descended from two old New England families, the Melvilles and the Fullers. His great-grandfather was one of the original Manchester entrepreneurs and investors; he owned the Manchester Locomotive Works, which produced steam locomotives and fire engines beginning in the mid-nineteenth century. After St. Paul's School in Concord, Henry went on to Harvard, and then transferred to Trinity College in Hartford. Henry became a successful stock broker and investor, making his own fortune. With his vast wealth he collected Hudson River School paintings and glass paperweights, many of which he later donated to Manchester's Currier Art Gallery (where Jane and I took art lessons as children). And when he died in 2003, without survivors—having never married—he gave Trinity the largest gift of any alumnus.

For a long time, I wondered how Dad came to chaperone this wealthy heir. The link seems to have been Dad's friend Bob Riedel, who apparently did some money management for the Fullers. In the archives of the Manchester Historical Association I discovered a letter to Henry from his mother, in which she informs him—but advises him to tell no one else—that he is worth "quite a fortune": "Riedel has your and [your sister] Mary's inventories completed and we checked everything over in the bank box. He took stock market prices of March 5th which were pretty high. . . . Your total was 261,317 [dollars] and Mary's slightly less." In 1936, then, at twenty-two, Henry was worth the equivalent of $4,500,000 in 2017.

Not surprisingly, the Fullers' life style was deluxe—even during the Depression—and their letters casually reflect it. They had a summer house on the seacoast at Rye. When Henry's mother praised his skill at "hawking," she was describing his talents as a sportsman, not as a salesman. A casual mention of "Chickie" was a reference to Chick Austin, the director of Hartford's Wadsworth Atheneum from 1927 to 1944 and founder of the Fine Arts Department at Trinity College. Similarly, sister Mary mentions that she had

met Katherine Hepburn (who was raised in Hartford). Henry *was* a bit
spoiled: at Trinity his mother sent him regular care packages from S.S.
Pierce, the renowned Boston purveyor of fine foods. At the same time, however, she complained that he sent too many sheets home for laundering and
advised him to shift the top sheet to the bottom weekly—Yankee thrift.

It may not be surprising, then—but it does seem precocious—that as a
young man Henry became fascinated with Russian aristocracy. In pursuit of
this passion, he amassed a valuable collection of books about Old Russia. He
was particularly interested in Anna Vyrubova, a confidante of the Tsarina
and supposedly the person who introduced Rasputin to the royal family.
Henry was determined to meet her.

Somehow, through Bob, Dad was introduced to Henry, and travel arrangements were made. In the summer of 1934, they set off for Europe. They
took an ocean liner to Bremen, Germany, flew to Moscow, traveled to St.
Petersburg, then flew to Finland and back to Germany, returning to the
United States by ship. (My camp footlocker sported travel stickers from this
trip.) Among Dad's souvenirs are photographs of Moscow, St. Petersburg, a
collective farm, some industrial sites, and German buildings ominously
draped with Nazi banners. The side trip to Finland enabled Henry to meet
Vyrubova, who had fled there during the Revolution.

I was not initially sure that this short discrete episode of Dad's life warranted inclusion here, in part because its minimal documentation makes it
hard for me to read his sense of its significance. But his one surviving letter
yields some insight into that. According to this letter, written on the stationery of the Hotel Knut Posse in Viborg, Finland, Dad was acutely aware of the
class divide between him and his young charge:

> Henry spent most of his time indulging his hobby on imperial Russia and the
> decadent Tsarist regime, while I observed contemporary life. . . . Hotel accom-
> modations were very good; at least they appeared so to me with my democratic
> bringing-up plus experience with the Near East, but I had a time getting Henry
> accustomed to them without complaining. I think he would have been glad to
> leave Moscow the first night. (1 September 1934)

Dad's acquaintance with Henry and the Fullers was the second instance—
and probably the last—of his close contact with the rich and privileged. The
Altounyans had apparently welcomed him into their circle without condes-
cension or prejudice; his being an American far from home probably helped
to ease class consciousness. But Henry was from his home town; though
younger than Dad, and in his custody on this trip, he was, in effect, his
employer. It must have been much harder to overlook the class difference
between them: Dad was the son of a factory overseer, Henry the scion of one
of the founding families. As far as they ventured from Manchester, the class
consciousness of the mill town must have reminded Dad of his place.

So, although he followed Henry's career thereafter, it is perhaps not surprising that the two seem to have had no subsequent contact. There is probably nothing to regret about that. But it's a shame that Dad was not to return to Europe again until we took a grand tour as a family in 1961. Through Henry, he got a taste of what it was like to travel first class, literally. He flew for the first time, and well before many of his peers. He did not fly again commercially until the 1960s, but perhaps this experience of aviation stimulated him to get his pilot's license a few years after this trip.

This trip does not seem to have gratified him like his travels with Bob, who was after all a close friend. But his acquaintance with Henry provided insight into how the other half lived—even, or especially, during the Depression. And visiting Russia in quest of traces of the lives of the aristocracy couldn't have been more different from his sojourn in Aleppo. Traveling with Henry on the heels of his time in Syria further expanded his metaphorical as well as literary horizons and sharpened his sense of social and economic inequality.

Chapter Nine

First Love

Rody

As rich as I find Dad's experience in Aleppo, what I've divulged so far is not the whole story of his life in the early thirties. Far from it. I have limited myself thus far to documents addressed to his parents (and possibly his congregation); hence the formality and the relative impersonality of his tone. What about his inner life? His emotional well-being? Other documents in his archive give intriguing glimpses of these aspects of his early manhood.

∾

The father I knew growing up was, of course, married to my mother; I knew him only as her partner. Like lots of children, then, I had little sense of my father's life as a single man, and since Dad married quite late, at 35, his bachelorhood was relatively long. Unbeknownst to me, his single life was quite rich in romance. In fact, his archive revealed a long-term relationship with a woman named Rody—and several romantic friendships with men. The father I never knew was evidently quite attractive to, and possibly attracted to, members of both sexes.

Despite the obvious lure of travel, I have wondered why a handsome twenty-something male would want to relocate to Aleppo, where the number of available women would be limited. The Aleppo Girls' School did have female teachers, and there were unattached women around, but none gets more than passing mention in his letters. Rather, Dad's correspondence reveals that his real love interests during this period were back in the States: two women—Rody and Lena—and three men, Bob, Edgar, and George. I'm impressed by his ability to attract such affection across gender lines. But I suspect he found it difficult to manage all these overlapping relationships at this juncture in his life.

Each had its own inherent complication. Rody was more in love with him than he was with her. The attraction between him and Lena was evidently mutual, but taboo: Lena was married and a mother. Bob, with whom he lived his first year out of college, was evidently gay. His other two male friends, Edgar and George, were also gay.

In addition, some of these relationships conflicted with others. This is most obvious in the case of Rody and Lena, who competed unwittingly for Dad's love. But his somewhat tortured relationship with Lena was further complicated by the fact that she was the sister of his closest friend, Bob Riedel. Moreover, his relationship with Edgar may have made Bob jealous.

~

When I first perused his papers, I was disappointed to find no letters from Mum. But, because they met as colleagues at Manchester's Central High School, that was not surprising. Seeing her every day at work, he had no need to write to her until they were separated by the War early in their marriage. I was surprised and tantalized, however, to find a set of love letters from another woman, Rody (or Rhody). The name meant nothing to me. Naturally, unlike the names of other friends, colleagues, or correspondents, I hadn't heard her name around the house. Since I knew nothing about Rody, and her letters did not provide much biographical information, I regarded the correspondence as a mere curiosity, a dead end. With lots of other documents to sort through and digest, I put Rody's letters aside and out of mind. Rereading them thirty years later, however, I have been able to make more sense of them. My new understanding of the correspondence is partly a function of simply paying closer attention. It was one thing to read through the letters for the first time, hastily, when I was still dazed by Dad's death; it was quite another to return to them with the idea of reconstructing his life.

On my first perusal of the letters, the signature "Rody" baffled me. But it turned out that Rody had been hidden in plain sight all along. Paging through Dad's high school yearbook one day, I noticed the profile of a classmate, Rosalind Parker:

Closer inspection revealed that Dad and Rosalind Parker both appeared in the photos of the school newspaper staff, the yearbook staff, and the cast of the senior play. Conclusive evidence that "Rody" was Rosalind Parker is that her letters refer to her home as "the Parker House." So it appears that Rody was a high school classmate well known to Dad. If they were high school and college sweethearts, this relationship lasted even longer than the six-year duration of their correspondence—well over a decade in all.

Touching to read, Rody's letters portray a smart, romantic, and somewhat frustrated young woman attracted to an elusive young bachelor. Altogether,

ROSALIND PARKER.

"RHODY," "BUNNY."

"A daughter of the gods, divinely tall and most divinely fair."

It is thought that "Rhody" is endowed by divinities, for she is the envied possessor of a pair of merry brown eyes, flaxen hair, and a most alluring personality, which has won her many friends. It is a difficult task to summarize all her talents and it is no use trying to cover her scholastic points.

Figure 9.1. Rody's Central High School yearbook profile, 1923.

Dad retained about two dozen items of correspondence from Rody from the years 1928 to 1934—a long duration for an emotional relationship that did not culminate in marriage. Some are mere notes. Some are barely even that—mere annotated scraps of poetry. One annotates some news clippings. Another consists in its enigmatic entirety of the sestet of a rather gloomy Edna St. Vincent Millay sonnet (XXXV), with the added comment, "à propos—mais non?" It is dated "the same day. This evening alone—chez moi"—apparently after the two had spent some precious time together. Yet another accompanied the gift of a plant Rody calls an "Amoretta" (a miniature amaryllis).

Rody may have chosen the plant partly for its name, a female diminutive of the Italian word for love. More than that, I take her characterization of the flower to be a sly, playful, even suggestive self-portrait: "very active even without sunlight . . . forever posturing." To this, she added a plea for company: "When are we to have a few hours alone?" With the clippings, she added: "For me last evening was a dream. No nightmare, I assure you. Ask the whippoorwill. He knows the answer. Evidently you and I do not." There is always a personal element that qualifies even these scraps as love notes. Their brevity implies a shared context; Rody is confident that Dad will understand her meaning. She *knows* him.

The best adjective for these letters is "lyrical." They are first and foremost love letters, written mainly, usually solely, to express emotion—longing for Dad. As a result, they convey very little information about either of them or their lives. They do refer to others—her family members, his family members, and a few common friends and acquaintances—but only occasionally and only in passing. In a way, then, they are frustrating to a memoirist; they don't provide much in the way of specifics of Dad's lifes. But their biographical significance may lie precisely in their neglect of the mundane. Rody craved Dad's companionship and affection; she wrote him to express her devotion—and to bind him to her. Her writing to him over such a long period of time is a testament to the depth, as well as the duration, of her affection. So the letters' existence is a major biographical datum for both of them. I wonder whether, later in life, he ever took them out of the box to reminisce. Whether he did or not, the fact that he kept them suggests that he maintained an emotional investment in this relationship long after it ended and he had married Mum and become my father.

~

Unlike the letters he received from Edgar and George, none of these missives is more than a few hundred words long. Whether brief or extended, they are relatively formal in tone and always correct in language, rarely slangy or colloquial. But neither are they flowery or trite. After lying boxed and unread for so many years in my attic, they still sound fresh and vital to me. I can see why he kept them as reminders of an early love affair, evidently his first. They must have been very gratifying to receive; reading them reminds me of how exciting it was to get love letters when I was young. In some ways, love letters can be better than the presence of the beloved; they may voice sentiments more directly, reflectively, and articulately than when lovers are face to face. But reading Rody's letters in long retrospect, I find them rather sad, as well. They provide a record of a passionate, quite mature young woman's devotion to my father, but they also trace a verbal courtship that ultimately failed. Affecting as I find them (and as I assume Dad did), the letters themselves may indicate why they failed, why the relationship did not take hold the way Rody wanted it to.

The first item of this correspondence is a letter dated January 17, 1928, when Rody was a senior at Smith College. Her having gone to Smith may shed some light on a puzzling event in my father's life: his transfer from the

University of New Hampshire to Wesleyan College after his freshman year. As it happened, during his year in Durham, she was not far away, at a finishing school in Lowell, Massachusetts. And when she entered Smith, he transferred to Wesleyan in Middletown, Connecticut, about 50 miles south of Northampton, Massachusetts, in the Connecticut River Valley. I doubt that Dad would have justified his transfer in terms of proximity to a girlfriend. But it may have been an important benefit of a move that could be warranted on more substantial grounds, such as the academic superiority of Wesleyan to UNH. The two must have dated while Dad was at Wesleyan, even though no letters from that period survive.

This first letter, addressed simply to "My dear," was sent to him in mid-January, after Rody had returned to campus for the exam period. (Because of her year in Lowell, Dad had graduated a year earlier, in 1927, and was working at the YMCA in Manchester.) They had seen each other over the holidays, and he had written her afterward. She quotes a bit of a romantic poem she had found in the *Yale Review*, then revels in the afterglow of reading his letter:

> I'm still under the spell of your letter, Griff. And I'm not a laughing girl this moment! I have enough to do to muse on memories I would not lose. . . . It's glorious to be young & beloved—is it not, mon ami? . . . Your letter is [a] nice escape [from reality]. And I find your imagination—your you—a deep but crystal pool of clear sweet water. You are the cool chaste priest of that temple—your mind—but a red rose can melt your heart, I know. You need to be more earthy—more wanton, more nonchalant before your sympathies will be all-embracing. . . . Why do I venture all this? Partly to repossess my self—so take my ravings with a smile, Griff. No more!

What a letter! None of my college girlfriends wrote me such romantic, literate, and literary love letters. Dad comes across as a bit of an emotional tease ("cool chaste priest") and a heartbreaker. Perhaps Rody should have known better than to pursue him. But I'm glad she did, and by epistolary means. I admit to a kind of voyeuristic gratification in reading these letters: envy of him, in fact, as the object of her admiration, adoration, and supplication.

Her next letter, a month later, inquires about his state of mind in the absence of any word from him, for which she chides him gently but hyperbolically: "I have the enormous disappointment to know that your pen has gone rusty & that you haven't the energy or inclination or vulgarity to lick a stamp." She then immediately apologizes for "that despicable note I sent to you. . . . I sent you a hasty note to get some action! I failed. . . . One instant I humbly beg your pardon but the next you infuriate me & I indulge in much too much profanity for one who considers herself a lady!" How he provoked her.

She looks forward to a spring dance, at which "Howard"—a mutual friend—is to be her date. This news is passed on matter-of-factly, as though it would not surprise him or hurt his feelings, but she may have hoped it would make him just a wee bit jealous. She also says that having failed to get a response from him with her "despicable note," she "wrote a page to Howard about you . . . You would be too flattered to know what I said." More teasing. Rody functions—of necessity—as a kind of provocateur, striving to get a response from a man who seems to withhold something she desires and needs. She then encourages him to ask when she would be coming home. "Really, it's surprising what a failure I am—at long distance. If I were home—I wouldn't even be hurt—but I would probably hurt you more, dear." And she closes: "Please, a letter!"

Rody's last letter from Smith was written in late March from the infirmary, where she was recovering from a sore throat. The letter begins with a Latin lamentation: "*Lacrimae rerum*! [a classics major, Dad would have known this means "tears for things"]—& several big sighs were my reactions to your last letter, Grif." Obviously, then, despite some delays or omissions, he did return her letters while she was at college. Indeed, according to her, the balance of the correspondence is actually in his favor at this point, in quality if not quantity: "Your letters are exquisite—lovely & what I write is nil. But if that pleases you—I'm happy."

⌒⌒

In an undated letter written after her graduation, she expresses her hope that he will be part of her future.

> Yes, my dear. I'm free & ready for work—hard work that will consume my energy, take over my mind & make my spirit live & grow. I must find work to lose myself, to forget myself & to find myself & oh, how I wish & pray that you could be one to help me—the one for me—we two together—sharing, living, being everything to each other.

This is perhaps the most direct appeal in her letters; here, she declares her love—and her availability for committed partnership—directly and unequivocally at a key juncture in her life. Was he gratified, I wonder, by this overt offer? Or was it perhaps a bit too forward, a bit intimidating? He was still quite young for such a commitment to monogamy, especially if they'd been a couple since high school.

It can be frustrating to read collected correspondence when one has only one side of it. But having only Rody's letters to Dad is less of a disadvantage than it might seem. For one thing, with Rody, it's obvious that he was not writing as often or as passionately as she desired; the actual correspondence was lopsided. For another, it's somewhat surprising that so much correspondence exists at all, for most of the items in his archive were written when the two were not separated geographically but living in the same small city and seeing each other regularly. So having only "half" the correspondence is less misleading than it might be. Rather, it may reveal something important about the dynamics of the relationship. Rody is typically the initiator of contact or the proposer of plans; he then responds, or doesn't. He was evidently a somewhat passive partner. For all of her good humor about this asymmetry, there is an undercurrent of frustration at his emotional, and perhaps sexual, restraint: "You need to be more earthy—more wanton, more nonchalant before your sympathies will be all-embracing. . . ." She is the wooer—open, passionate—while he seems recessive and unpredictable, if not coy. He comes across as attractive but not fully available. On the other hand, for her to pursue him in this fashion for so long, she must have been getting something in return: articulate notes and letters, pleasant company, flattering attention, some degree of physical intimacy, perhaps more. I wish I knew.

Although telephones had long existed, two young people of his generation would not have used them for casual conversation, much less for lengthy flirtation. Living in a boarding house, he would not have had a private line, and living at home Rody didn't have one, either. They probably used the telephone to make arrangements or inform one another of their whereabouts rather than as a medium of romantic communication. Hence the hand-delivered notes, which would arrive faster than postal delivery. Written notes would also allow for more private, intimate communication than phone messages left with family members or fellow tenants. Rody's hand delivery conveyed its own message about proximity, availability, and urgency.

The letter is its own medium, and Rody seems to have used it to say things that she might not have wanted to say in person or telephonically; it also allowed her to communicate intimately and immediately without violating his privacy. She probably knew him well enough, too, to know that one reliable way to his heart was through carefully chosen words. More than Mum, and rather like his older friend Edgar, Rody seemed to have wooed Dad with words. The letters are thus not merely a supplement to this relationship. To a large extent, they enact it. In having the letters, and saving them, Dad may have felt he could retain the best of this relationship in perpetuity.

He didn't hold on to Rody, but he held on to her letters.

The fact that so many of the notes were hand-delivered to his post-Aleppo address in Manchester suggests that they lived not far apart, and one confirms that. (On a research trip to Manchester, Jane and I located the Parker house and Dad's boarding house; they were mere blocks apart.) In this note, written at midnight on a Saturday, Rody suggests a dinner date (an all too typical gesture):

> Please, my dear, could not we have supper together tomorrow night (I
> work all day & would enjoy even a little while with you) or Monday night or
> even Tuesday night—
>   I would like to have the joy of anticipating your arrival—even though I
> love to be pleasantly surprised. Am I asking too much?
>   This was a long week for me until Friday, you won't make me wait until
> this coming Friday, will you?

They had recently had some sort of date; Rody seems to want more than
weekly contact. Such pressure may have been counterproductive. But I am
touched by her pleasure in both anticipation and surprise. In any case, she
goes on:

> Very late (Ha! Ha!) tonight I had an errand at the drug store for "pills"—
> & I drove by to pay my respects to your lamp light—it was burning & it
> blinked for me.
>   Darling—I know I'm a fool to write you all this. Please telephone me at
> home tomorrow evening—or be there. I do so want to be sure everything is
> right with you—as it is with me when you are with me.

The errand for "pills" may have been a pretext to borrow the family car
and drive by Dad's home, paying him a virtual visit, unseen. Interestingly,
she wrote and delivered the note later, not wanting to impose in real time on
his solitude. She respected his boundaries.

∿

Once Rody graduated from college, she returned to Manchester and began working as a nurse at the Elliot Hospital. With Dad teaching and living in
Concord for the two years preceding his Aleppo stint, they would have
needed to correspond at least in part by mail. A few of the letters seem to
have been written then. One was written from up-country, where Rody was
visiting. It mentions the imminent beginning of deer season. She reassures
him that "the deer will not call—they know even before the gun-play starts &
they are off into the depths of the virgin timber. The leprechauns warn
[them]." She continues with career news, which would be of obvious interest
to him. She had turned down a job as a school nurse in Connecticut; thus,
they would continue to be living in close proximity. She tells him that she
had exchanged waves with his friend Edgar Hawthorne (whose antique shop
was right on Concord's Main Street) on her way north, although she couldn't
be sure he recognized her, and that she intends to "call at Concord" (presumably to see Dad) on her way home. She closes, "Even though you arrange
your time so closely, so carefully—that my name is seldom on your calendar—still—I shall love thee."

This letter, from the last day of July (probably 1929), may best express the bittersweet nature of this relationship.

> Darling—
> Yesterday was heavenly.
> Why did I cry before prayers last night—
> Not because I was happy—I was disturbed—perturbed—Troubled.
> Love you more—
> Rosalind
> [The only time she signed her full name]
> If you are busy tonight, I will understand.
> If you are free, please come see me @ 8:30.

"Love you more" was probably intended as an endearment, but it reads now like a sad admission that her affection was greater than his.

∼

It seems odd that no letters from Rody to Dad survive from his three years in Aleppo. After all, he saved a newsy note from her mother that implies that he and Rody were still on good terms. This letter, of November 1932, begins with best wishes for the upcoming holidays, then offers news of various common acquaintances, beginning with fellow church members. It mentions Rody only to say that she should graduate soon from nursing school in New York. But the letter is full of the news of marriages of their contemporaries: the subtext seems clear enough.

Maybe too clear.

∼

The next letter I have from Rody to Dad comes in 1933, after his return from Aleppo. Still interested in him, she must have looked forward to the resumption of close contact. He spent his first summer back in the States, however, doing graduate work in education at Teacher's College of Columbia University. Rody was obviously disappointed. Fortunately for my purposes, though, his being away was reason for her to continue writing him. And she did so, addressing this first letter to him at Columbia; unstamped, it was apparently delivered by his friend Bob Riedel, who, she says, had "just left me to be with you—how I envy him."

Whatever had been the state of this relationship during the Aleppo years, it seems to be very affectionate at this point: she addresses him as "My darling." She expresses the ardent wish to go to the beach with him again— "take me Dover-way to the sea & into the salty spray. Make it soon, dear. Another such day for us." To console herself, she apparently went riding alone. Oddly, but charmingly, she presents herself not as the rider but as the horse. "I must to horse & away into the woods and fields. . . . Dad knows I have the urge to chew grass so he promises to drive me into a meadow & leave me with the buttercups and field mice before sunset this afternoon."

Bob seems to have gone to New York to fetch Dad home; Rody certainly seems to expect him imminently. She is quite keyed up and expresses a desire for a picnic supper with him and his brother Tom; more significantly, she hopes, and expects, to meet the rest of his family: "When am I to meet your family. . . . I like to think about meeting them in the near future. I will be patient, Grif. But I am impatient to be with you." She signs off, "Devotedly yours."

In the summer of 1933, Dad and Rody were ten years out of high school and more than five years out of college; they had known each other for well over a decade and had been romantically involved for much of that time. The Parkers evidently knew him quite well from his visits to their home in Manchester, but Rody had still not met Dad's parents or any siblings other than Tom. Granted, the Cousers had moved from Manchester to Dover before his senior year in high school, leaving Dad behind. But the distance from Manchester to Dover (about forty miles) is not sufficient to account for Rody's never having met his folks. To a woman in her late twenties, the significance of not having been introduced to her lover's family should have been clear; to continue to believe that the relationship was a serious one would involve a degree of self-deception and denial.

Since love letters shuttle back and forth between absent partners, perhaps it is their nature to dwell in memory and anticipation, but that seems to be especially the case with Rody's. In a letter written in late August of 1933, addressed to him at the family home in Dover, she simply *yearns* for him. This is a characteristic mood of her short letters: they are typically composed almost entirely of reminiscences of their moments together or pleas for more time with him, or both.

> The moon is bright—so full of light tonight—and I wanted to drag you away from your desk (you were probably engaged, being entertained by someone else) any how—my impulse to invite you to enjoy a short drive was soon stifled and here am I—after a hot bath in bed—& lonely. I felt free to go to you. I'd ask you to run out—for a smoke in the moonlight—promise I would have returned you to your labors pronto. But Saturday night is for fun—joy—entertainment—someone was fortunate to have you—but having seen you just Thursday past—I thought better of it—& did not intrude—except—this way to tell you of it now—my simple wish denied.
>
> Life is not a song—& I need you so desperately—your heart—your mind—the very essence of you. You may stay away 24 hours—four days—a fortnight—a month—two months in South America—three more years abroad —*I shall never love again as I do now.* (emphasis added)

She then chides herself for complaining and begs forgiveness "for spilling over to you."

I find this letter somewhat painful to read because of its sense of unrequited love, of conflicted emotions about Dad's frustrating aloofness: she forgives it but clearly resents it. The imbalance in the relationship has turned pleasure to pain for her.

The apogee of the relationship may have passed at some point in the early fall of 1933, after the initial joy of their reunion. Dad had begun teaching English at their alma mater, Central High. By early November of 1933, Rody sounds frustrated, and her tone is occasionally accusatory. According to one letter, the two of them had seen the movie of Hemingway's *A Farewell to Arms* (with Gary Cooper and Helen Hayes)—appropriately, a love story with a sad ending—but since then "you and I have not had a single evening— alone together."

Ironically, when Dad returned to Manchester from Aleppo, his former roommate Bob Riedel was rooming with the Parkers; in one letter, Rody speaks of being up late one night playing bridge with him and her parents. Bob provided a handy conduit for news and messages, and his presence at the Parkers was also apparently occasion for visits from Dad. But as Rody points out, this is hardly ideal from her point of view. She characterizes the ménage as excluding her:

> My family and Bob, who is one of the family—are conveniently to hand. I want you to know that I am aware of these two facts, but what concerns me most of all is this—you yourself have made no attempt to have a date with me. To be sure I have enjoyed having you with others here at the Parker House. Perhaps I've a queer slant on certain situations, but your deliberate neglect of me after the understanding we had about our friendship & my dependence upon you—hurts.
>
> I hoped you would follow up my suggestion about [an excursion to] Concord & Edgar Hawthorne—but not a word from you—as yet.

Obviously, the relationship has not become what she hoped it would, and her disappointment is understandable, especially considering that she put her love life on hold for three years in her mid-twenties. The references to "the understanding we had about our friendship" and to her dependence on Dad are difficult to parse. On the one hand, to call his relationship a "friendship" would seem to concede that they were no longer lovers. And this letter is addressed simply, and curtly, to "Grif." No "dear," no "Darling"—much less the possessive "my." On the other hand, she refers to a recent movie date and looks forward to more. So it's not clear what their understanding is; what is clear is that she feels that "deliberate neglect" is not just inconsistent with their "arrangement" but unacceptable. It is not surprising that she has been hurt. Once again, she finds herself having to take the initiative in the relationship—in this case to raise it as an issue and comment on it. At some point, one would think the asymmetry of the relationship would have affected her self-respect, but she ends by swallowing her pride: "Oh, my dear, don't you care about us. Don't you want to be a `jolly good fellow' as I want to be. I so care."

Around year's end Dad seems to have made at least partial amends with a small gift. The next document in the correspondence is a short note from her, dated January 14, 1934; she thanks him for the "curio," "the little stamp box," and inquires "who carved it so beautifully and from whence it came." (I inherited one just like it, bronze incised with arabesque patterns and lined with wood.) She closes by suggesting that she and he and Bob and Milly "chase up" to Concord to see the new George Cukor movie *Dinner at Eight*. She is evidently willing to double-date as a way to see him. Her sign-off is curt and seems to convey residual hurt: "Sorry, but I'll always love you."

During the following summer, the two seem to have been briefly on better terms. At least that is the implication of a letter Rody sent him care of his parents in Dover, in July. It contained a clipping about a young man who came to appreciate life by letting his boat drift away from him while swimming and having to struggle to save himself. She comments, "To struggle to the point of exhaustion against death. . . . Grand words. How many of us are struggling to the point of exhaustion against Life?" There's more than a hint here of a depressive personality. And I take that as a significant clue as to what held the relationship together and to why it foundered.

She then segues into a proposition:

> My dear, are you game for a picnic supper on a hilltop with me this week? Name the night. I shall wear red trousers & turn cartwheels on the green. . . . Your family or Henry Fuller or Bob have first choice, I grant you – but I so do want to sprawl beneath the stars. . . . One small evening is not too much to ask, now, is it? I like to plan ahead once in a while—just to look forward to the date—rather than an empty week.

I am charmed by Rody's image of turning cartwheels in red trousers on the greensward. It suggests an appealing abandonment. But I wince at her acknowledgment that she ranks below Bob—and even Henry—in his social register; I wonder what such an admission cost her. In offering her company under these circumstances, was she being brave, or pathetic? I find the final tone a bit *too* pleading, and the mention of the "empty week" verges on pathos. I can sense why Dad may have wished to keep Rody at some distance. She was very needy. To have someone depend so much on one's company can be off-putting. For one thing, it sets the stakes too high: to decline her invitations is to hurt her. For another, to be characterized as the alternative to an otherwise empty week is not entirely flattering. The effect can make you feel called upon to supply too much to the other's existence.

Too, Dad may have sensed that her neediness was a function of her depressiveness, a trait he shared.

By that fall, the distance between them seems to have grown, but Rody still had not given up hope for his company, if not his devotion. In November, she began a short letter to "my dear Grif" this way: "Why are the Parkers on your 'blacklist'? Mother & Dad are asking me what I've done to offend you. Perhaps you know the answer. I'm professing my innocence. I'm not asking Bob what you are doing—for his answer would only be that you were 'busy keeping busy'." At this point, she seems reconciled to being just friends; indeed, she advises Dad, with some edge, "I have purposely kept my fingers off to prove to you that I can keep my promise—never to get in your way again. Fear not, courageous one, I have no designs on you." She closes by assuring him that if he "will come," she'll forgive him.

One of the short letters from Rody to Dad accompanied a book she had intended for him to take on his travels to Russia with Henry Fuller. For whatever reason, she did not give it to him before his departure. Rather, she sent it just before Christmas, 1934, with this curt and telling remark: "I can't bear having it on my desk any longer."

The note, the last of their correspondence to my knowledge, opens with a comment on their lack of recent contact: "We seem to be 'missing trains'— Perhaps I shall see more of you by leaving you to your own devices." And it ends with her reminding him that she "never could stop caring and bothering about you and all that envelops you and entices you - no matter how crude or lovely the net." What a dig there at any potential successors! She closes with an enigmatic (to me) quotation from R. H. Bruce Lockhart's recent best-selling *Memoirs of a British Agent* (perhaps they both read it): "'Weak, but not weak enough—, strong, but not strong enough—, clever, but not clever enough.' I love, my friend Grif."

～

I find myself utterly charmed by Rody's prose. Even now, it gives me goose-bumps. In fact, reading her notes and letters, I find myself rooting for her to succeed in winning Dad over. But then I catch myself, thinking it's disloyal to Mum, who won him in the end. For that matter, in some sense to root for Rody is to root not just against Mum but against myself. Who would I be, if I'd been Rody's son? It's dizzying to contemplate this counterfactual scenario. But Rody had a romantic side, a sensitivity, and a gift for written expression that were not so apparent in Mum. I think Rody would have been an interesting woman to know.

I find myself wondering whether Dad ever reread her letters, and if so, how often? More to the point, to what end, and with what emotion? To remind himself of a woman who adored him but whom he finally rejected? More than rejected: let down, after leading her on for a long time. In my first perusals of the letters I found myself thinking how gratifying they might have been for him to retain and how flattering to reread. But the more I consider them, the more I find in them an indictment; it's hard to see how he could reread them without feeling some measure of regret and even guilt for his treatment of Rody.

⌒⌒

But soon there was another woman in Dad's life. After teaching English in Danielson, Connecticut, and New London, New Hampshire, my mother, Ann Van Stelten, returned to her hometown and joined the Manchester Central High English department in 1937. Like most children, I have little sense of what sparked the original attraction between my parents. My sense is that although Rody was quite attractive—judging from her yearbook photos—Mum was prettier and more womanly. Mum was probably also more vivacious and outgoing. So, although I cannot imagine Mum writing such charming romantic notes and letters, I can see why she might have had more appeal to Dad in the flesh.

I am not speaking just of sex appeal. Mum was a focused and determined woman. More important, whereas Rody's father was a mill superintendent, Mum's parents were lower-middle class Dutch immigrants: her mother a nurse, her father a cigar-maker. Her background was like Dad's. For these reasons and more, she may have had a greater sense of her own worth and value independent of male attention.

I find Rody's prose and her written self-presentation so charming that it is hard to imagine Dad's not reciprocating her affection. But her correspondence may have conveyed a sense that she was treading water in her own life, depending too much on him to provide her with company and stimulation. (She rarely refers to friends of her own, college classmates, or colleagues.) If the correspondence between him and Rody ends in the mid-thirties, it may have been because she was eclipsed by a woman who was more self-sufficient and confident, even if not so adoring as Rody.

To me, the saddest thing about this relationship is that Rody seems to have deserved better. In 1934, when their correspondence ceased, Rody would have been approaching thirty. She seems to have invested her emotions exclusively in Dad as a romantic partner for roughly a decade, a decade in which many of her peers married and had children.

⌒⌒

When I first drafted this chapter, I assumed Rody had never married. This supposition reflected my sense of her exclusive devotion to Dad. Just he continued to invest emotionally in her by retaining her letters, so did I by relishing them.

Rody may have continued to pine for Dad, but not as a single woman.

In attempting to trace her, I obtained copies of her college yearbook photo and obituary from Smith College. In the picture she is seen in profile, with short, wavy brown hair and a scarf around her neck. I would describe her expression as wistful, but that may be projection. According to her obituary, she not only married, she married well: her husband, George N. Barry, was a physician she met when he was practicing near Manchester in 1934 or 1935, about the time her relationship with Dad had fizzled out. In March of 1935, Rody's father died of heart disease; she married a year later, well before Dad and Mum married in 1941. She then moved to her husband's native Oklahoma, where she spent the rest of her life. In 1938, she had a son, George Barry, Junior, who, like his father, became a doctor. Though "active in [Episcopal] church and community life," she apparently did not work as a nurse. She died in 1970, about five years before Dad and Mum.

I was gratified, mostly, to learn that Rody did marry, have a child, and a life. In a way, learning this eased my sense that Dad had monopolized her love life during the period of her greatest marriageability without commitment to her or even full reciprocation of her devotion. At the same time, I confess that I was not wholly pleased by this discovery. It took me a while to understand this. Why would I not be entirely happy to learn that Rody had moved on? I suppose because—irrationally, I admit—I had become invested in the idea of her pining for Dad forever after. Oddly, I was taking her at her word that she would always love him. Dad evidently didn't deserve that sort of devotion, and I certainly had no right to wish it from her. But I was vicariously gratified that she might have carried the torch for him and him alone, forever.

It would make a better story.

Better for him and me perhaps, but not for her. She deserved more, and she apparently found it. Good for her, I thought, after reading the Smith obituary.

~

But later I learned that that wasn't the whole story, either. With her obituary I was able to identify her descendants—the son and three granddaughters listed as survivors. I hoped to contact them, partly to alert them to my possession of her letters, partly in hope that they might have the other side of the correspondence. In the spring of 2012, an internet search turned up an obituary for her son, who had died only months earlier. But that led me to his daughters, one of whom graciously provided me with photos and additional information about their grandmother, whom her granddaughters had barely known: they were very young when Rody died. Her granddaughter supplied this bittersweet capsule portrait of Rody after Grif:

I have been told that my grandparents were respectful and affectionate, but not "madly in love." It was probably more like a happy arranged marriage. . . . They had a 2nd son 5 years after my father was born in 1938, but the baby was born 2 months early and died of prematurity. She was very sad after that and was probably a closet drinker with hidden alcoholism, according to my mother. She was a very attentive grandmother and showered love on me and my sisters, I am told.

I am struck by Rody's apparent depression and alcoholism, which parallel Dad's. I don't attribute her sadness to heartbreak over the end of the relationship; no doubt it had more to do with the loss of her second child. But I wonder whether their relationship was built, and eventually foundered, on their kinship as romantics who were never quite satisfied with what life offered them. It may be that, as appealing as Rody was, Dad sensed he could not afford commitment to such a vulnerable soul; instead, he chose a more self-assured and optimistic woman—one on whom he became pathologically dependent in late life.

I am also led to wonder, however, whether Rody's plaintive claim—"I shall never love again as I do now"—may have proved true in the end, and, indeed, whether—despite the strength of his love for Mum and hers for him—he may never have been loved later as he was then, by Rody, his first love.

Chapter Ten

Illicit Love

Lena

In the late 1920s, even as Dad held Rody at arm's length, he was drawn to a woman he knew well but who was unavailable: Lena Inglis (pronounced Ingles), a married woman with a young son. It was not only her status as a married mother that was an issue; she was also the older sister of his closest friend, Bob Riedel. Because Dad and Bob continued to be friends until Bob died, I do remember hearing Lena's name, unlike Rody's, around the house in Manchester when I was a small child.

So even as Bob, living with the Parkers after Dad's return from Aleppo, served as an unofficial (and probably reluctant) liaison between Dad and Rody, he also served as a link between Dad and Lena, to whom Dad was more attracted. The situation must have been very awkward. I doubt that Dad confided this attraction to Bob, but I imagine Bob must have sensed it nevertheless.

Dad never addresses this situation in his letters; each set involved a different correspondent, and while he might refer to other correspondents, he didn't confide his emotional conflicts to any of them (aside from George, as we'll see later). Only someone with access to all the correspondence can grasp the complexity of Dad's love life. Thanks to his archive, I occupy that privileged—indeed, panoptic—vantage. It gives me extraordinary access to the web of relationships in which he was embedded and thus invaluable insight into the father I never knew.

As important as Dad's professional work in Aleppo was to him, much of his emotional life was necessarily carried on solely through correspondence—with family, friends, and lovers back home. Indeed, these existing relationships may have been more important than any he formed in Aleppo;

his stint there, while formative, was quite brief. From my standpoint, it appears that—whatever his conscious reasons for going there—Aleppo provided perspective from which Dad could sort out his feelings for two women who were strongly attracted to him—and also for his friends Bob and Edgar, who may also have competed for his affection. His geographical isolation could also allow *their* feelings to settle. So this sojourn functioned as an emotional moratorium in his conflicted romantic life.

~

Biographical details about Lena in the letters are scant, but according to census records she was about eleven years older than Dad, and she and her husband William (Billie, to her) had a son, Russell, born in 1921. The Riedel family origins were in Bohemia, where her mother Rose and six of her eight children were born; only Bob and Lena were born in New Hampshire. Although Rody's mother seems to have been very fond of Dad, he may have felt more comfortable with the Riedels than with the Parkers, who were native born, relatively affluent and even, according to Rody's marriage announcement, "socially prominent." Dad, Bob, and Lena came from more similar backgrounds—immigrant families with lots of children.

His relationship with Bob was fraught on its own terms, as we'll see in the next chapter. They were close in age and lived together the year after Dad graduated from college, when he worked at the Manchester YMCA (where I assume they first met). Of his seven siblings, Bob seems to have been closest to Lena, and through his friendship with Bob, Dad had access to her household and got to know her well. Indeed, he became a confidant, privy to her predicament: too late, after the birth of their son, she came to regret her marriage to Billie, a carpenter. As a considerably older sister, Lena may have been a maternal figure for her somewhat fragile brother Bob. I suspect Lena's maturity and her concern for Bob were part of her appeal to Dad, whose own mother was reserved, even remote. But he was also attracted by a romantic streak in Lena akin to his own.

There is very little in the way of correspondence between these two; since they saw each other regularly, there was no need for any until he went to Aleppo. Part of what I know about this relationship I infer from remarks about Lena in letters Dad wrote to Bob from there. Oddly, when it comes to letters between Dad and Lena, I have only his side of the correspondence; no letters from Lena survive, although I know she wrote him at least one. In letters Dad wrote to Bob from Aleppo he sometimes mentioned that he was including notes to Lena—presumably sealed. I don't have any of these or letters he sent her directly. What I do have are drafts of letters to her. This is significant, because he only saved drafts of important letters. In fact, he may have only *made* drafts of important letters. As it happens, the surviving drafts of letters to Lena often contain cross-outs and revisions. He was obviously very careful in his communication with her.

The document that sheds most light on his relationship with Lena is unique: a diary-like account of separate interactions with her and Bob on a single remarkable day. In it he refers to both Bob and Lena in the third person, not the second, as would be the case if he were addressing either. Moreover, given its content, I can't imagine he would have shared it with anyone, certainly not either of them. It seems to have been written for his private consumption and contemplation—even commemoration.

It is dated January 24. No year is given, but it evidently dates from the two-year period. 1928-1930, when he was living and teaching in Concord before he went to Aleppo. Like his correspondence with Rody, this document may shed some light on his decision to go to Syria. For while he may not have gone to Aleppo in order to distance himself from Rody and Lena, his relationships with both seem to have reached awkward impasses in 1930.

Here is part of his account of that significant day in January:

> Came to Manchester [from Concord] with Miss Knox [an older colleague at Concord High School] and found in [Bob's] room a note saying that he had gone to Boston in accordance with my request. I called Lena and took the trolley over [to her house on Manchester's west side]. She merely asked was I coming over. I said I wished to. Mary [Lena's older sister] was not there—we had supper, three of us [Dad, Lena, and her son]. Lena and I did the dishes, talking the while. The "Bent Twig" was one topic of conversation.
>
> After that we sat and talked by the fireplace. I gave the boy a business letter form for a letter he was writing.
>
> Lena once said, laughingly, "What shall I do when my husband gets back and I can't talk to you any longer. I shall have to close up this little chamber in my heart & lock it forever."
>
> We joked and laughed thinking of Mary's remarks made when she returned, as we took care of the furnace.
>
> We were laughing about something as I left (was it the smell of garlic on my breath) and Lena brushed her hand across my cheek and chin as if in fun but it seemed that we both felt there was deeper feeling under that mask of fun.
>
> For minutes I stood motionless facing the house when I reached the [trolley] car stop. I felt as if I had, as we parted, rather weakly evaded my feelings. I thot then that I wanted to say "Would there be any harm in my kissing you. I want to awfully."

Evidently, Dad had casual access to Lena's household; indeed, he seems to have been a fixture there—on this occasion spending consecutive weekend evenings there. Billie seems to have been away; in any case, Dad and Lena were enjoying rare intimacy. As is obvious here, each was attracted to the other. The crucial moment is ambiguous; Lena may have been encouraging further physical contact, if only in the form of a goodbye kiss, and he seems to have felt he had missed an opportunity to act on his attraction to her. His account is slightly self-dramatizing, but I can well believe that he might have stared back at the house from the trolley stop, wondering what had just happened.

Or hadn't.

Overall, the account is quite restrained in its language. But it hints at strong emotional undercurrents—highlighted by the reference to *The Bent Twig*. This is no idle allusion. The title is that of a 1915 novel by Dorothy Canfield that dramatized the progressive values of Montessori education. Its protagonist is described on the Ohio University Press website as "a compelling figure [who] resists efforts to mold her with every rebellious fiber of her independent nature."

His purpose in writing this vignette is obscure. It obviously recounts a significant moment, and he may just have wanted to make his own record of it, as in a diary. Or he may have wanted to replay it in his mind, not just to savor it, but to weigh his own feelings. How strong was his attraction to Lena? Hers to him? What was the meaning of her gesture? Had he missed an opportunity? Or had he resisted a temptation?

Other documents he left behind reinforce the impression that they were attracted to each other and that both felt that that attraction threatened her marriage. The chief of these documents is a draft of a letter evidently intended for Lena, written in Aleppo. The tone is formal and the rhetoric hortatory, with many verbs in the imperative mood. In that regard it is quite exceptional in his correspondence.

Dad opens by counseling her to (re)invest her emotions in her family—in her son's future, if not in her husband's companionship. Much of the advice, about taking the high road, may of course have been intended as much for himself as for poor, trapped Lena.

> You must choose between the good and the pleasurable. You have your boy—find joy in him. He is raw material for your hands. If you were childless I should pity you so. Let your happiness be in giving him what you could not have.
>
> Cultivate in him high ideals. Do not tell him to do right because God will find him out if he does wrong. Tell him to act honorably because of the respect it will give him for himself.
>
> What a happiness there will be in helping him avoid the mistakes you made.

Thus far, he focuses on how she should find consolation in doing the right thing. But here it becomes clear that their mutual attraction, rather than being a matter of idle pleasure, could put the marriage at risk:

The things that marriage has to offer are permanent. As mature persons in a grown-up world we can't drift with every passion.

It is not a choice between two men but between two modes of life, between the glitter of a temporary presence or a permanent absorption in husband, son, and home.

If it could come to a choice you know you would not make the rebellious one.

What could I offer you that is permanent? It would be impossible for me even to support you.

Evidently, then, Billie was a good provider, whereas Dad would not have been able to support Lena, let alone her and her son, on his teacher's salary. So doing the right thing was also doing the practical thing. Both of them may have admired the rebellious Sylvia of *The Bent Twig*, but they knew that Lena could not emulate her. Real life is not a novel.

Then comes more consolation, in looking down upon the simple-mindedly happy:

Few people know real peace or contentment. Those who do are probably rather stupid. Just because we have insurgent desires is no license that we can immediately gratify them.

Loyalty to the good demands certain sufferings and sacrifices made for it. With faith in the way of conduct you have chosen and in your own creative imagination you may create in your own life a more beautiful loveliness than this temporary ecstasy you have found by fleeing from reality.

His reference to "temporary ecstasy" took me by surprise when I first read it, and it intrigues me still, as it—along with "insurgent desires" and "license"—suggests more in the way of expressed passion than is implied by his description of quiet evenings with Lena—one more indication of a complex and unconventional love life. There is a striking tension between his mostly detached tone and abstract terms, on the one hand, and the recognition of strong erotic urges on the other. I wonder how much this reveals about his character and his life: the more I know about him, the more I sense the cost of repression. The adventure of traveling to Aleppo may have been the alternative to a sexual adventure he feared would end badly and ruin lives. He confined that adventure to his (and Lena's) fantasy life. Perhaps by writing this vignette, he asserted some control over it, savoring its possibility without acting it out—and, not incidentally, holding on to it forever.

Next he offers Lena advice on how to reconcile herself to her marriage—not by self-sacrifice but by educating her husband to her needs: "You must teach [Billie] to recognize your desire for wider boundaries. If he cannot sympathize with them, he will respect them." (Even allowing for his self-interest in deflecting her attention, this seems progressive as counsel to an unhappily married woman.) Last, but hardly least, he asks what renunciation

of their passion—the decision *not* to have an irresponsible selfish affair—
means for the future of their relationship:

> Because of the difficulty of carrying out your efforts do you wish it to
> preclude our friendship. If not entirely, how near may I exist?
> Could it be so without causing you pain, I would wish it to be the warmest
> kind, a close and trusting friendship. We shall ride together but not be bound
> together.
> We shall look at each other earnestly without feeling that we must avoid
> observation. We shall not hide our friendship. There will be nothing furtive or
> secretive about it.
> There is so much we can give each other in the way of stimulation &
> interest. It will be a fine companionship centering about those things.
> However we will need to be careful, to be in full control at all times.
> We might fall in love.

Well, it would appear that they already had fallen in love, more or less,
and perhaps acted on their attraction to each other; I'd love to know the
details of "this temporary ecstasy." But Dad withheld them (and presumably
Lena knew them.) What he proposes is a modus vivendi, a resolution to be
close friends, but only friends. At the same time that he declares that there
should be nothing furtive about their relationship, he acknowledges the danger of their continuing to see each other. Obviously, this had become a
delicate situation for both, but he was loath to give up Lena's company as
there was more to their friendship than sexual desire.

What Bob knew, or sensed, of this is far from clear. But as I said at the
outset, the fact that the married woman to whom Dad was attracted was
Bob's sister surely complicated both relationships. For Dad to act on his
attraction to Lena would of course hurt her husband and presumably her son.
Billie and Russell really don't seem to factor into the ethical calculus, however. Rather, Dad seems to be concerned that Lena could not afford to lose
Billie's financial support and assistance in raising Russell. But to act on his
impulses might also have been to betray Bob's confidence. After all, Bob
must have introduced them to each other, and apparently the three enjoyed
each other's company. An intimate relationship between Dad and Lena could
not be concealed from Bob indefinitely, and it would put him in a very
awkward position. Bob might worry that he was a means of access to Lena.
He might feel a traitor to his brother-in-law and nephew. He might feel
distanced from Lena, no longer first in her affections. If Lena divorced Billie
and married Dad, of course, Dad would become Bob's brother-in-law, which
might have been gratifying to both. But it is difficult to imagine how the
three of them could have carried on their warm friendship in the event of an
affair. And they did remain friends, even into the 1950s, when Dad had been
married for ten years and had two small children of his own.

~

The last surviving document I have from this relationship may well be the last letter between Dad and Lena. It is a draft of a long letter to Lena, posted from Aleppo, apparently in the fall of 1930, not long after he arrived there. It is remarkable in its length (nearly 1,000 words) and its inspirational tone.

Dear Lena,

You have waited long for this letter, perhaps continually puzzled about its not coming, perhaps thinking after a time that you understood my silence. Whatever the case I know the difficulty and pain there has been for you. Whether or not I should have written I do not know, nor did I know when first asking myself that question – one cannot always feel convinced that he is doing the right thing but some principle has to be formed. That this principle should be the right I most earnestly hoped. It was imperative I felt that my conduct in this should be wise above all else. Wisdom is sometimes a greater virtue than charity. But please don't think that all the charity[,] all the tenderness has gone out of me. Rather, think of me as trying to direct my conduct by what seems wise and good. One would have so much less to regret if always a stern consciousness as to what was good and wise had controlled his actions.

Your letters have been a joy and an eager study to me. I have studied them for the indications of your health, mental and physical, that they reveal. I have found joy in them because they have told me the story of a body and spirit that is mending. Even your first letter was brave with the will to mend that it told me of. That letter was one of those waiting for me when I reached Aleppo. I could hardly tell you such an encouragement it was to know that you were mustering heart again and building up your will for a sure tough slow recovery. I have followed the working of your will to recover, knowing that the will was half the battle won, and have seen it go ahead surefootedly. Your first letter finished on a note that was a great spur to me. There was never anything quavery about my will to come to Aleppo but I must confess to certain trembling regarding the situation I might find myself in. But after I read this letter I felt that no situation could be too diff[icult], no adjustment too great with the example before me of your besieged but courageous spirit.

And your other letters have made your example even more shining. As I read, it seemed as if everything said "look up and ahead" in your story of meeting the little squirrel, the partridges, and other birds on your walk at the farm. I think I unconsciously exclaimed aloud, Bravo, Lena. Not only was it happiness that your spirit had led you to interpret it so but it was the indication that your eyes were not focused inward but were being drawn to the world outside you. It was a satisfaction to know that soon the glorious pageant of autumn would come and call to you.

My hopes in that were granted and proven to me when I read—the hills are so beautiful, one can just feel one's soul expand—you see the old ecstasy is returning—Bravo, Bravo, bravo, Lena!

How filled I was with admiration. There was before my eyes the picture of your face at that moment, a glow, uplifted, and your figure pressing forward like a very Samothracian victory. For any other mortal to have had a part in that achievement would have been to rob you of something you will treasure as infinitely precious because it came independently.

You have been called up to make a very great adjustment and you have had the highness of heart to make it. You will, I think, look back upon it as the greatest achievement of your life. You have made a virtue of a necessity which you could have existed with by reacting to it second- or third-ratedly. That you have reached this point all as an independent accomplishment will have done something to your fiber, to your very soul that will be as sword and buckler to you for the winning of battles ahead.

It seems to me each of us has begun something very like a new period in our lives. Shall we not make them periods of zealous loyalty to the good and the noble. Loyalty to the good and noble demands certain sufferings & sacrifices made for it with unflagging faith in the way of conduct we have chosen. But we're ready for anything, aren't we, Lena?

There are other things I'd like to say. They are difficult to say. About the great grief you have faced. [crossed out]

You have asked about Aleppo, about my work & surroundings. I hope Bob let you read a certain quite lengthy letter I wrote him. I'm so anxious to have a letter from him written since he reached home because I haven't so far. He will have heard from me by now. I do hope nothing has happened to my letters. The lengthy one I spoke of was registered but one can't even be sure of registered mail here.

But I shall trust it reached Manchester & gave you something of a background for imagining what Aleppo is like. Certainly much must remain to the imagination because the city is quite beyond description.

Regarding this less personal type of subj. I'm going to ask may I write to you & Bob together. My time is so limited. You'll not mind, will you? And since I'm sending this care of Bob I'll enclose a few pages of general talk.

As I close this I reckon it will be very near Xmas when you receive [it]. I confess the time seems longer than I realized it would be.

But may this carry to you all my wishes for a beautiful & serene Xmas. You will be making others happy I know & that will bring you happiness, too.

As this letter was written during his first year at Aleppo, it helps to date the documents already discussed to earlier the same year. Interestingly, unlike Bob, Lena has been sending Dad letters all along during that fall of 1930. And in those letters, she has evidently referred to some great personal sadness or disappointment, some grief from which she is mending. But Dad has not written back; this letter comes as an apologetic, belated response.

This is not the longest letter I found among Dad's papers, but it may be the longest of its sort, a letter totally devoted to advice, commentary, and outright exhortation. His epistolary tone is often quite formal by today's standards, but this letter is unusual in sustaining its lofty tone for its entirety. There's much talk of the good, the noble, and the brave—even imagery of heroism in battle ("sword and buckler"). I don't mean to belittle this—although at times Dad seems to be trying a bit too hard—merely to point out this letter represents one of his modes at its extreme: he pulls out all the rhetorical stops.

Much is mysterious here because it is frustratingly unspecified. The central question, of course, is: What has Lena disclosed to him? What is the grief, the setback that she is facing so bravely? Initially I thought it might refer to a death in the family, but that seemed unlikely (or Bob would have shared the grief). Moreover, a letter of condolence would have been much easier to write and more transparent in its message; Dad would not have waited so long to fulfill that duty to her.

I also considered the possibility that Lena had "lost" her husband in some way, though not to death. Had he left her, or she him? Neither seems likely given the ethos of the day. A stay-at-home mother, Lena could hardly have afforded to leave him. Her family was far from wealthy. According to census records, most of her siblings (aside from Bob, who seems to have worked in finance) worked in the mills, and her sister Mary lived with Lena, Billie, and her son. In any case, the end of her marriage would have been a financial disaster, rather than an emotional one, not requiring the tact and delicacy of his response.

It is no doubt significant both that Dad does not name the tragic event and that he took so long to respond to it. The loss must have been one Lena suffered privately. I think he deferred his response—even after receiving several letters from her—and phrased it at once delicately (not specifying the loss) and inspirationally because he felt implicated in it. For a time I was utterly stumped by this letter. But with some prodding from two friends (perhaps not coincidentally female), I have come to the conclusion—which now seems obvious to me—that the loss Dad consoled Lena for was the loss of himself—the renunciation of the idea of consummating their love for one another. His going to Aleppo would of course have prevented any such affair in the immediate future. But she, and he, might have clung to the fantasy at long distance and in fact intensified their feelings for each other through correspondence. Perhaps, then, the solution to this enigma was hidden in plain sight all along: the cause of Lena's grief may have been his first letter to her, which I quoted earlier. If that is the case, it must have been written before his departure for Aleppo, because her response was waiting for him when he arrived.

That letter begins, "You must choose between the good and the pleasurable." Putting it that way, of course, does not lay out two equal alternatives; it points to one, "the good." If there were any doubt, the next line would resolve it, with its shift from the declarative to the imperative mood and from an unavailable object of affection (Dad) to a more proper one (her son, not her husband): "You have your boy—find joy in him."

I doubt that the obstacle to an affair with Lena was his feeling for Rody; rather, it was his sense that an affair could only be temporary and that it would be very costly to Lena. On rereading the first letter with new eyes, I believe that in it he was trying let Lena down very gently. Indeed, he did it so subtly that I missed his drift initially. But Lena, clearly, did not.

So the underlying reason for Dad's slowness to respond to Lena's letters and for his fulsome encouragement was his sense of implication in her sadness. In short, what Lena had lost was Dad as her lover; he was the cause of her desolation. Grif was her grief. And that recognition made it awkward for him to console her, even from a safe distance. In fact, as one friend pointed out, he tends to shirk responsibility for her grief, shifting responsibility from his agency in the breakup to her heroic response.

He was trying to put the best face on a very delicate situation, emphasizing how much he admired Lena's resolution to make the best of marriage and maternity, while also signaling her that they must not carry on a furtive relationship, even in correspondence. Going forward, he would address his letters to Bob and Lena together. She would be part of a dual audience, rather than the addressee of letters that might be misconstrued. He thus put rhetorical as well as geographical distance between them in the hope of protecting against any expression of inappropriate emotion, no matter how welcome it might have been.

$\sim$

As I review Dad's letters, then, it appears that the six months preceding Dad's departure for Aleppo had been particularly eventful, stimulating, and emotionally rich—but also stressful. There had been Rody's persistent entreaties for attention and companionship. There had been—as we'll see—the inauguration of his friendship with Edgar, which in some way may have competed with his relationship with Bob. There had been the day described above, when the attraction between him and Lena seems to have become undeniable to both. And there had been a crisis with Bob, which led him to threaten to stay behind, rather than accompany Dad on his trip east. Dad was caught up in a vortex of emotions. Professional or missionary motives aside, traveling to Aleppo must have appealed to him as a respite from a very complicated love life—one which came as a total surprise to me as his son.

$\sim$

When he died in 1953, Bob's modest obituary in the Manchester *Union Leader* noted that he died "at the home of his sister `Mrs.' Lena Inglis, of 56 Plymouth Street." I ascribe no significance to the quotation marks around Lena's title, but the obituary does not mention in-laws among survivors, so there is no indication of whether she and Billie were still together. In doing leg-work for the memoir, I located this address; it proved to be right around the corner from the house where Dad visited Lena on that fateful day in

January 1930 (and—small world, Manchester—not far from my mother's childhood home on Manchester's West Side).

I know that Dad visited Bob regularly during his final illness, so he and Lena must have been in touch with each other for the duration of Bob's life, and every visit must have reminded him of that earlier encounter in the same neighborhood. If, as seems likely, Bob's funeral was the last time Dad saw Lena (who died at age 81 in 1976, a year after Dad), then that event marked the end of two complicated, but important, relationships in his early adulthood, both of which continued well into his life as a husband and father.

Chapter Eleven

Manly Love

Bob and the YMCA

In addition to his correspondence with Rody and Lena, Dad's archive contained correspondence with the three men who were his closest friends in his twenties and beyond: Bob Riedel, Edgar Hawthorne, and George Saylor. His letters from George are affectionate; those from Edgar and Bob are full of longing, and their topic is often the relationship between correspondents. They are starkly different from letters I exchanged with male friends as a young man. In my correspondence, there was always a clear gender line: love letters for women; newsy letters for men. But Dad's archive contains love letters from men, as well as from women. One of the striking revelations yielded by his archive, then, was that my father had had romantic relationships with other men.

I had no idea.

What makes this more intriguing and provocative is that all three of these close male friends seem to have been gay. Together, these relationships reveal unsuspected dimensions of Dad's early life and character. Evidently, my father's romantic life was even more complex than his correspondence with Rody and Lena has shown it to be. Each new set of letters I examined complicated my understanding of him.

~

His emotional intimacy with these three men raises obvious questions about Dad's sexuality. Were any of these relationships consummated? Was he secretly gay? Bisexual? Bi-curious?

Certainly, the father I knew—in his forties, fifties, and sixties—seemed resolutely heterosexual. He was attractive to women and apparently attracted to them. But the evidence of his letters is that he was attractive to gay men, as well. And possibly attracted to them.

Ultimately, I am not as concerned with what, if anything, "happened" between Dad and these friends sexually (which I can never know for sure) as with the intensity and dynamics of these significant relationships. At the very least, for an apparently straight man of his generation, he seems to have had an unusual degree of familiarity with gay life. I find that intriguing, even admirable. In fact, I resent that he didn't share it with me. As with so many other dimensions of his early life, he was quite reticent about this. Without meaning any harm, he deprived me of the benefit of his broad experience. All too typically, we missed connecting.

~

The discovery of these love letters from men sent me to historians for perspective. According to social and cultural historians, same-sex romantic friendships were quite common among middle-class American men, as well as women, in the nineteenth century, especially in the Northeastern states, before dating became customary—facilitated, if not transformed, by the automobile.[1] Such friendships allowed people to try out intimate relationships without the prospect of life-long commitment. Evidence of their ordinariness is that same-sex romantic friendships were a staple of late nineteenth-century American fiction by writers such as William Dean Howells, Thomas Bailey Aldrich, Mark Twain, Bret Harte, and "the master" himself, Henry James. Such friendships would have been familiar to readers of Dad's generation.

The major difference between male and female romantic friendships in the Victorian era was that male friendships tended to end when the men married, whereas female friendships might be sustained for life in place of heterosexual unions.

As sexuality was medicalized in the late nineteenth century, however, homosexuality was stigmatized; what had been considered wholesome in the 19th century was increasingly regarded as deviant after the turn of the 20th. Accordingly, male romantic friendships died out. So historians say. If this is true, Dad's were unusual in being formed so late, in the 1920s, and sustained for so long; he maintained all of these friendships well after he married. Jane and I remember childhood visits to Edgar's antique shop in Concord, George's visits to our home in Melrose, and Dad's grief when Bob died. His sustaining these relationships suggests that he felt no need to dissemble or hide them from Mum.

Going to Aleppo entailed a long absence from all three men, as well as from Lena and Rody. This was not an issue for George, who was not living in New England at the time, but it was for Edgar, whom Dad had just met while teaching in Concord, and for Bob, who'd been his roommate immediately after college. Although Edgar seemed to have resigned himself to it, Dad's departure created something of a crisis for Bob. Whatever Dad's intentions, going to Aleppo afforded him some insulation from two men (as well as two women) who were strongly attracted to him. Marrying at the end of his thirties finally relieved him of the stress of juggling these sometimes intense relationships.

~

Bob Riedel was evidently Dad's closest friend. Having grown up and attended school on Manchester's west side, he was not a high-school mate, but he and Dad both belonged to the Franklin Street Congregational Church and the Manchester YMCA. They probably met at the Y during high school. They were literally closest when Dad roomed with Bob in Manchester after he graduated from Wesleyan in 1927. Indeed, for a year they were colleagues as well as roommates; Dad was the membership secretary of the Y, Bob its treasurer.

Dad's life-long association with this institution is intriguing in this respect, for the Y has been associated with gay subculture since the late nineteenth century. A number of this homosocial institution's features were conducive to gay cruising. In the late 19th century, to reach beyond its middle-class clientele to working class youths, it shifted its emphasis from Christianity to physical culture—gymnastics, body-building, swimming, and indoor sports. By that time YMCAs were likely to occupy their own buildings, complete with gymnasia, pools, locker rooms, and steam rooms. To house rural youths arriving in the city, the Y incorporated dormitories as well. The emphasis on physical culture allowed men to examine one another's bodies in a non-threatening way. Dormitories provided close private quarters. Moreover, because of its association with Christianity, the Y was largely exempt from police scrutiny. By the turn of the century, it had become a notorious site for cruising. Indeed, in 1912 the exposure of homosexual activity at the Y in Portland, Oregon, made national news.

What this indicates about my father's sexuality is of course beyond my ability to know. My sense of the man I knew is that he was exclusively heterosexual. But if there was a gay scene at the Manchester Y, he must have known of it. It's possible that he dabbled in same-sex activity there. As historians have observed, the Y provides a place where homosexual relations may happen without one's having to admit to seeking them—or that such relations define one's sexual identity.

I have no reason to think that Dad indulged in same-sex acts. But it wouldn't embarrass me to know that he did. After all, he was a very attractive man, and he might well have been propositioned, or made a pass himself. I find myself rather titillated by that possibility. More than the possibility of his having been sexually involved with other men, though, what interests me is that he seems to have grown up with knowledge of, and close friendships with, gay men and probably with up-close awareness of a cruising scene. I find myself envious of this aspect of his life, as contrasted with my own cluelessness as an adolescent and a young man. I was not a member, much less a habitué, of the Melrose Y, but I did attend a single-sex college. And I know now that some of my classmates and fraternity brothers were closeted gay men. I wish I'd been more attuned to their situation, so that they might have felt comfortable confiding in me. But the times militated against that kind of openness.

~

The best evidence that Bob was gay lies in a single document, the one in which Dad revealed his feelings for his sister Lena. In it, he recounts coming to Manchester from Concord and finding Bob absent: "Came to Manchester with Miss Knox and found in [Bob's] room a note saying that he had gone to Boston *in accordance with my request.*" [emphasis added] Dad then went to Lena's. After nearly kissing her on his departure, he took the trolley back to Bob's.

> He was home when I reached the room. *I was much encouraged in his telling about it—that it had been good advice. He seemed like one unburdened. Said he had told me more than he should have and as regards instructions I would see by his actions what else he had been told.*
>
> *Then came the disap. like a slap in the face. Not a complete case—only partial & curable. To take treatments once a week indefinitely. The night acutely miserable to me.* Completely fatigued as I was from an enervating week. Had planned on bed at 7:30 or 8.
>
> He seemed not to be able to understand my impatience the next morning. . . .
>
> During the P.M. when I stopped in the store he asked what the matter was. I said I was tired & sleepy. Asked if it was his fault. I could not deny it. He said he was sorry but little sat. to me. *I could not but feel that it would happen soon again.* [emphasis added]

On this extraordinary day (in 1929 or 1930), then, Dad recorded two revealing encounters, one with Lena, and one with Bob. It's far from clear what Bob was doing while Dad was at Lena's. But he seems to have gone to Boston on Dad's recommendation, and his reference to weekly treatments indicates that he saw someone about a medical problem of some sort: hence his report that Dad's advice had been valuable. Dad evidently knew, or suspected, what the issue was. What points to something very private is that Bob "seemed like one unburdened," even as he remained ambivalent about having disclosed the issue to Dad: "He had told me more than he should have."

But the real enigma in this passage lies in Dad's reaction to Bob's announcement of his diagnosis: "then came the disap. like a slap in the face."

Why would it be a *disappointment* to Dad that Bob's affliction was *not* "a complete case—only partial & curable." Surely, Dad would not have wished Bob harm—a total, incurable case of any serious illness. I can think of only two possibilities: alcoholism and homosexuality. In the former case, he might have hoped that Bob would be advised to give up drinking completely, rather than try to control the problem—only to have him relapse immediately: "I could not but feel that it would happen soon again." If Bob was struggling with alcohol, this would be an interesting backstory for Dad's own late-life struggle, of course. But the fact of Bob's going out of town for a formal diagnosis and coming home feeling "unburdened" doesn't seem to fit alcoholism. That wouldn't have been such a big deal or a hard call.

My best guess is that Bob's problematic condition was his sexual orientation. Perhaps he had disclosed to Dad (what he probably already sensed) that he was attracted to men (and perhaps was acting on his impulses, possibly at the Y). Dad might well have thought that a therapist might help, and Bob might be better off going out of town for the sake of privacy. Here's the most interesting part to me: Dad's response to Bob's report suggests that he hoped that a diagnosis would reconcile Bob to his homosexuality: you're gay, get over it. Homosexuality is the only condition that seems to explain his reaction, that Bob's having a partial, "curable" case was *bad* news—insofar as he seems to have been advised to undergo weekly treatments indefinitely to "cure him" or at least tamp down his urges, further torment, and inner conflict.

I admit this is speculative, but if I'm right, then Dad was remarkably accepting of Bob's sexuality. Indeed, he seems to have been far more comfortable with Bob's sexuality than Bob was, and that seems admirable to me. His advice may have backfired somewhat, but Dad seems to have offered a supportive response to an issue that must have complicated his relationship with Bob. Did Bob ever come on to Dad, I wonder, when they were rooming together? All of this is intriguing. I'm not surprised Dad didn't share all this with me. But I feel entitled here to indulge the fantasy of what I might have learned from Dad, had he disclosed his interesting past. He could have helped me mature in this regard; I might have been a better friend to closeted gay men I knew.

~

The other document pertinent here is one of only a few surviving letters from Bob. It's surprising that so few survive, as I know that Dad and he corresponded while Dad was in Aleppo. But the one letter that does survive, written *before* his departure, conveys much about their relationship, which came to some kind of crisis at the beginning of the summer of 1930.

It appears that, as Dad's departure approached, he gave Bob the impression that he did not value their friendship very much. However he conveyed that, it wounded Bob to the core—so much that Bob wrote Dad an anguished letter seeking reassurance.

In recognition of his mission to Aleppo Dad received a formal sendoff from his church on June 29, 1930. Bob's letter was sent to him in the immediate aftermath of this event, which he attended.

> Dear Grif,
>
> Having hoped that you would awaken me when you came to the room, I was quite disappointed to find you had gone. I did want to see your family and wish [your brother] Tom luck in his new adventure. I also had numerous things I wanted to say to you.
>
> I hope you don't feel offended if I write frankly, as I can't help expressing what has been in my heart these last few days. I had continually hoped that in my direst moment of the need of sympathy and comfort you would fill that place faithfully regardless of disappointing surfaces. I still have a soft and yielding heart with all my troubles and faults. I have always felt that both of us considering unfortunate happenings would always be ready to help when most needed. I think I tried to fill that bill. Perhaps in your mind I have failed you in that respect, too.
>
> I did wish that Saturday afternoon you would come to the house with me so I could talk and was quite sorry that you were so aloof. Naturally I felt shy and heartsick and tired, I just couldn't break the ice. That is when I needed you most. At times you made me feel that you didn't much care one way or the other and I really felt that now you didn't need me anymore so why worry about him. If I am too severe, I am sorry but I must let you know how I felt.
>
> Last night over the telephone when you said, "Don't go to church on my account," I was almost convinced that such was the case. You made me feel and almost realize that you didn't want to feel that you owed me anything and certainly nothing in the way of gratitude or of an obligatory manner. How could I feel otherwise?
>
> Some things are to be, and our unfortunate relationship is undoubtedly one of them. I have tried but perhaps not hard enough. I was quite happy to be in church today and will always remember that you stood up there with the determined expression and hopes that nothing or nobody would daunt you in your attempts. *Certainly I must wish that we two could have felt and looked at each other differently than we did and not have to keep the shame of pretense aglow amongst our other friends who were there.*
>
> As you prepare to leave for Aleppo I want you to feel that my real feelings of friendliness and love have not waned in the least. Also feel assured that my haunting ghost is slowly disappearing and my real feeling of regard and affection of the highest type and moral is reappearing.
>
> That will have to be proven, I know, and before you go you will feel skeptical as to how strong and substantial the foundation is. Be that as it may: I nevertheless feel that it will be lasting. At least I hope and pray that it will. I still feel that it is best for you that I stay here and let you be quite sure that nothing stands in your way of happiness and contentment.
>
> Affectionately, Bob

P.S. You left your slicker in my closet. I will send it to you if you like.
[emphasis mine]

The letter is intriguing in its references to an "unfortunate" relationship, to Bob's "haunting ghost," and to "the shame of pretense," but its declaration of affection is quite direct and forward: it is explicitly and unabashedly a love letter. Indeed, among all of the surviving letters from Dad's three male friends, it alone contains the word "love." Bob admits to some failings as a friend, but he has been deeply hurt by Dad's apparent indifference to his presence at the ceremony. Bob obviously wanted to be recognized as a special friend. More important, he seems to have wanted some sign from Dad that their relationship had a future, that he would not be ignored or forgotten when Dad was away. He didn't want to be just another well-wisher in the congregation.

Although Bob's reference to "the shame of pretense" may seem to hint at an illicit dimension of their relationship, I construe the phrase not as a reference to homoerotic love but rather to their pretending to be on better terms than Bob felt really obtained. Bob was ashamed, I think, that the two men had to pretend that everything was fine between them when he felt so hurt. Evidently the relationship—perhaps already strained by Bob's attraction to Dad—had become further stressed by Bob's anxiety about Dad's impending absence.

This is not to deny any homoerotic dimension in this relationship; I suspect that Bob was sexually attracted to Dad, and it pained him that his love for Dad was not requited. Evidence in other letters suggests that Bob was a somewhat troubled young man—unhappy, insecure, a bit fragile, and depressive. (While Dad was away, people would apprise him of Bob's state of mind, which suggests that it was a source of worry. And Dad's letters to Bob reiterate his worry about Bob's epistolary silence.) I take Bob's reference to his "haunting ghost" as a reference either to his depressive side or to a tendency to depend on Dad in a way that made Dad uncomfortable.

That dependency may have included or sublimated a desire for physical intimacy. In any case, Bob tries to put a good front on his state of mind, reassuring Dad that his "haunting ghost" is fading and being replaced by a more wholesome affection ("of the highest type and moral"). The latter phrase could also, obviously, refer to a desire untainted by any sexual dimension. Clearly, Bob's feelings toward Dad were complicated. And Bob evidently was even more in need of reassurance than Rody, who expressed her desires in writing with far more nuance, wit, and self-awareness than he did.

Happily, the crisis passed. Bob did come to the ceremony. More important, his poignant entreaty seems to have had the desired effect: later that summer he accompanied Dad as far as Istanbul. So the two of them evidently patched up their relationship, and Bob did not have to stand by his offer to stay behind so "that nothing stands in your way of happiness and content-ment." Both of them must have decided that Bob would be good company, and he went along on a journey that had very different significance for each of him.

I read this letter, then, as a testament to the depth, complexity, and fragil-ity of one of Dad's important friendships. It also suggests that at a critical moment in his life this relationship may have threatened to exceed the bounds of what Dad wanted from it. So I interpret his aloofness as a (prob-ably) unconscious emotional withdrawal that might prepare them both for a long separation. His insecure friend seems to have interpreted this as a lack of feeling, when it may have actually reflected an excess of feeling—a form of denial, in fact. The upshot seems to have been that the extent and nature of

Figure 11.1. Dad and Bob in the Swiss alps, 1930.

this relationship were negotiated so that it satisfied both men, more or less. (And Bob's letter—the explicit written assertion of his need—was instrumental in this reconciliation.)

∼

This important friendship endured until Bob died of a brain tumor. Bob's obituary in the Manchester *Union Leader* of December 2, 1953, is disappointingly brief for a man who seemed to be so much a part of the city community:

> Robert A. Riedel, well-known local resident, died Monday evening at the home of his sister, "Mrs." Lena Inglis of 50 Plymouth Street.
>
> He was a member of the Franklin Street Congregational Church and at one time served as church treasurer. He was past president of the YMCA, past member of Lafayette Lodge [of Masons] . . .
>
> Mr. Riedel was a native of this city and resided here all his life.
>
> He is survived by three sisters, . . . four brothers, . . . and by four nephews.

The obituary does not indicate his age, but he was only in his late forties when he died. The significant biographical detail is that he died at Lena's home. She and Bob seem to have remained very close.

The effect of his death on my father, whom I saw bereft for the first time, probably constituted my first intimations of mortality. More to the point, here, perhaps, it was also a powerful example of the grief one man could feel for another. Married at the time, Dad was unlikely ever to make another such close male friend, and I think he never did. I sometimes wonder what his later life might have been like had Bob lived on. Certainly, after Mum died, he would have benefitted from having a friend as devoted as Bob. But that was not to be.

Chapter Twelve

Edgar

"To you, I shall return a Prodigal"

When my father left for Aleppo in 1930, he had known Bob for several years and been his roommate for one, 1927-1928. In contrast, his relationship with Edgar was very new. Although the two had met about a year earlier, they grew close only in the spring of 1930, in the months preceding Dad's departure. The timing of this makes me wonder whether Bob saw Edgar as a rival. If Dad was suddenly spending time with a new friend in Concord as his departure date approached, Bob, isolated in Manchester, may have felt threatened. This may have precipitated the crisis between him and Dad. Bob and Edgar may have competed for Dad's time, attention, and affection. But as the older, more sophisticated man—and, important in what was to be for three years an epistolary relationship, much the better writer—Edgar had clear advantages in this competition.

Thanks to scraps of autobiography scattered throughout his letters, I know more about Edgar's life than I do about Bob's. Born in 1883 in rural Maine, he was more than twenty years older than Dad—old enough to be his father. Edgar's early family life had been unhappy. His mother died when he was only two; he says that his father might as well have, which suggests a profound rift between them.

At some point, the Hawthornes moved to New Hampshire; after graduating from grammar school in 1898, Edgar worked for three years as a mill greaser, taking time off to study bookkeeping. He found his vocation when, as a teenager, he began working in a book and art store in Concord. Although Edgar apparently never left the United States (or even New England), he learned a good deal about European culture from customers who brought in works for framing that they had bought abroad. Edgar seems to have cultivated a group of young men in Concord who thought of themselves as more refined than the townspeople of this provincial state capital. This was, after all, the era of Sinclair Lewis's Babbitt, and "Rotarian" is a common term of disparagement in Edgar's letters. He appreciated, but was not overtly envious of, Dad's opportunity for travel. He seemed content to enjoy it vicariously; when he knew Dad's itinerary, he liked to trace his movements on a map and accompany him in his imagination.

∼

Although I have (with minor, but important exceptions) only Edgar's side of the correspondence, Dad seem to have saved every one of Edgar's letters, and the sequence permits quite a full reconstruction of this relationship during Dad's time in Syria, when it was at its most intense. Edgar wrote regularly and lengthily throughout Dad's absence; he was probably Dad's most devoted correspondent. In all, he sent him more than two dozen letters in less than three years, some well over a thousand words long. Perhaps as significant as their quantity is the care with which they were composed; despite a limited formal education, Edgar was Dad's equal as a stylist, and the correspondence seems to have given both of them a good deal of aesthetic pleasure.

In their more objective mode, Edgar's letters convey news of, and sometimes acerbic commentary on, mutual acquaintances and local "culture"; accounts of his travels through rural New Hampshire in search of antiques, including descriptions of his finds; and instructions to Dad on what sort of objects to send home to be sold. Dad served Edgar as a kind of long-range "picker." A couple of letters are devoted to discerning appraisals (aesthetic and monetary) of objects Dad sent him. Edgar advises him that there is no market for Roman coins and offers this advice: "Never buy anything no matter how old it may be or seem unless it is DIRT CHEAP. If it proves unmarketable then it is but a minor loss; if it is saleable, then there will be a good percentage of profit."

The vast majority of the correspondence, however, is decidedly subjective and intimate in tone. Each of the men says that the other is often in his thoughts and that the letters represent only their verbal communion. For example, Edgar takes a line from one of Dad's letters—"Often it's part of an experience at even the oddest time or place to think of you"—as the springboard for an excursus on his almost hallucinatory sense of their presence to one another:

> Frequently . . . my mind has been instantaneously directed to thoughts of you. Again I would be surprised to hear myself speak your name and my mind would then carry on a sort of conversational monologue. At other times I have had the impression of hearing my name spoken. . . . Through these experiences

I feel that we can have moments together without the stimulus of a stated schedule of letters on your part.

Dad shared Edgar's sense of this transcontinental non-verbal communication. Below Edgar's signature on one letter appears the following in Dad's handwriting: "Spring days in Concord. It was you who took me away. Such days they were—like the appeal of love." There's the word "love" again, this time in Dad's hand.

In a sense, the letters represent only the occasional verbal distillate of a relationship that was of constant concern to both. But in another sense, the letters *constitute* the friendship: for the duration of Dad's time in Aleppo, they were the medium through which this friendship was sustained and developed. Though they have nothing to do with me, having been written more than a decade before I was born, they make me feel present in Dad's early life. Of course there's a voyeuristic element to this, but it doesn't trouble me much: I am immensely grateful for such entrée to his life.

Edgar was as appreciative of natural as of artistic beauty, and his letters often contain lyrical descriptions of New England scenery in changing seasons, which he knew Dad would miss. His prose is romantic but never cloying or clichéd. Two letters contained actual bits of nature: a pressed bit of vetch, which survives; and a milkweed seed, which Edgar suggested Dad should "try out in the sunlight" (i.e., toss in the air on a sunny day) as Edgar had done. Indeed, his description of the seed makes it a metaphor for their correspondence:

> The floating, irised threads of gossamer resemble the fanciful thoughts and desires we have that are unutterable; the little brown seed seemed like the word we attach to that thought or wish.
> And now, Goodnight, Grif, with all the wishes that you know that I have for you.

The best example of Edgar's nature writing comes in a letter written early in Dad's absence. Edgar devotes several hundred words to a meteorological event he witnessed while driving through the New Hampshire countryside, a thunderstorm followed by a rainbow:

> This in itself [the rainbow's emergence] was well worth stopping to see, but did you ever see a rainbow travel? This one began to glow more brightly and gradually receded and climbed the nearby, low hills. The northern end of the hills was covered with maples and birches. These drank up some of its vivid coloring. To the south the hills were grown to pine and their darkness intensified the colors. I could almost feel the slow motion of the rainbow as it scaled these low hills and then stepped over to the higher range. The southern end seemed entangled in the pines of the low hills as though they were unwilling for this color to leave their darkened depths. . . . Almost as though it had

snapped from some rooting, the southern end appeared on the top of the far away hills and both ends were resting on the rim of the hills. The color was then more vivid as though it were glorying in its achievement or possibly it saw something in the East to excite it, something that called it from a drab America to a colorful shore.

Only after I'd read this letter a number of times did it occur to me that the final touch could be an allusion to Dad's being "called" to Syria, or perhaps to his calling to Edgar from Syria. Conversely, these descriptions of nature may have functioned—have even been intended—to make Dad homesick, to lure him home.

However miscellaneous the letters may seem on the surface, their ground bass is always Edgar's affection and longing for Dad. Most of the letters were typed on flimsy air-mail stationery, but the very first one was hand-written on sturdy stock. Composed soon after Dad's departure, it was timed to precede him to his new surroundings and be there to welcome him:

> Dear Grif:-
> I want a few words from me to be here in Aleppo, waiting to greet you upon your arrival. . . .
> I have trailed you across the "Big Pond." You must have had some wonderful moonlight nights. The first few evenings after you had sailed, I saw the moon come up out of the East and wondered if recently you had been appreciating it. . . . In your mail you will find this "God Bless You" from me—not in stentorian bass but whispered like the last, soft mute of the organ.
> And now good night,
> Edgar

I like "here in Aleppo": if Edgar couldn't be there in the flesh, he'd be there in his prose, a thoughtful gesture of self-projection, virtual travel. I'm sure it comforted Dad to have this letter waiting, even as it may have aroused some homesickness.

Edgar's next letter opens with a poignant account of the arrival of Dad's first letter:

> There has been a particular sweetness in the past few days. It will linger for days to come. Your letter brought it. It seems to have lessened this line called "distance" that you have drawn across a few short years or so. I could only see a hard, straight line but now it is an arc instead and that denotes the circle. When you have traveled the circumference of that circle what things you will have seen and experienced to tell me about!
> Your letter! I have read it many times. The first few times—yes, through tears—with an ache to see you mixed with the joy of having you talk with me.

The joy that Dad's letters brought Edgar becomes a theme of the correspondence. For example, he recalls surveying a batch of mail at the end of a discouraging day. At first, he thinks it is all junk mail, but "Then I saw the foreign stamps . . . . O, Grif, it was no longer a wobbly world." Edgar clearly hungered for and reveled in correspondence from Dad: "Your letters will always be eagerly awaited." At the same time, Edgar knew that Dad needed to write home regularly and report periodically to his church. So he declined to plead for mail: "You may recall, in none of my letters have I importuned you to write. To my mind that would be obligating you, and obligation is our form of tyranny." No doubt Edgar was sincere, but his very reiteration of this lack of obligation may have been a way to elevate his relationship above the mundane and familial.

A confirmed bachelor, Edgar writes amusingly of fending off invitations to Thanksgiving and Christmas dinners: "I refused three invitations to join three family circles. Nothing doing—I preferred to be the paying guest at the Cinderella, where I could have my own thoughts for company. I gave the toast to you. It was a splendid dinner and a far more pleasing thing to do than being obliged to adapt myself to the laws, in-laws and out-laws of my would-be hosts and hostesses." This letter does not seem quite so amusing to me since I learned, from his obituary, that Edgar had a married sister who also lived in Concord. Evidently, he was not welcome at her house—or he declined to go there—on holidays. I count this, and his alienation from his father, as evidence of his homosexuality—and of its cost to him.

Further evidence lies in the fact that he speaks only of male friends and acquaintances, typically much younger men. In contrast to these casual friendships are some serious past relationships; in one letter he refers to Dad as the latest and most promising of a series of close friends. It is an artfully composed passage. Dad had sailed to Europe on the "SS California," and Edgar makes a sad joke out of the fact that his previous male friends had all been lost to California. First

> George Farnum, my earliest friend of my own age went out there for his health. Subsequently, Redfield Anderson, a friend of twelve years standing, went to California; after ten years there, he came east for one winter, only to return to Napa and [take] unto himself a wife. Finis. Then toward the first of the present year [1930] I met an acquaintance of about a year's standing. I came to know him better and then better still. He discounted [i.e., surpassed] everyone I had ever known. Each meeting was some new discovery. He sailed to the other side of the globe on a boat named "California."
> Do you wonder that I consider California my jinx?

This passage is all the more significant in the light of a passage in another letter, which implies that meeting Dad revived Edgar's capacity for love: "A few years back I dug great ditches and until recently thought I had thoroughly drained the bog of my emotions. I have been quite vain of my dusty desert." This implication is spelled out in a later letter in which he recounts the development of their friendship. Edgar's sense of inferiority about his background and education made him self-conscious, and he assumed he had been a "flop" on his first evening with Dad. But meeting him by chance later, he decided that Dad was, though a pedagogue, not a pedant—able to see that Edgar was "neither a moron nor a Rotarian." This serendipitous meeting, Edgar says, brought him back from a decade-long withdrawal from serious involvement with another man:

> My code of so far and no farther had always been efficient until a year ago. I fought to maintain my tradition but I encountered something that was stronger than I was. I am glad that I did. . . . Although I revealed but little of my world to you, it was more than I had ever revealed before. There were many doors that I would gladly have opened, but what was beyond them might have seemed a queer assortment of junk. My reluctance was occasioned purely to protect you from a possible boredom if from nothing worse.

Edgar goes on in a confessional mode to try to say how important Dad's letters are, how much he appreciates his devotion of time in a very busy schedule (which Edgar describes sardonically as "such an one as only a CHRISTIAN INSTITUTION could be capable of expecting of one").

At the beginning of Dad's summer break in 1931, Edgar resigned himself to Dad's spending at least another year in Aleppo, but at the end of a letter otherwise devoted to appraising things Dad had sent, Edgar proposes this: "I am going to suggest that 1933 will be your sabbatical year. Why not plan to spend it with me? I think we could knock out some sort of a living together. . . . This would not probably mean to spend it in Concord by any means." The implication is that the two could become professional partners, at least for a short time. I take the offer of a professional partnership to be a pretext, however, for an emotional commitment as well. Marks of the romantic friendship in the correspondence (if we needed any more) are that Edgar almost always notes the anniversaries of getting to know Dad and of his departure and that he counts down to the date of Dad's eagerly anticipated return.

In 1930, Dad evidently had a habit of dropping by Edgar's shop after work. In this letter, written on the anniversary of his departure, Edgar assures Dad that he misses him even more than he had at first:

> It is over a year since the High School days and those early hours of evening that we had together. Often each day I recall them, and, Grif, I would like to have you know that I mind the interruption of them more deeply than I did then. There is sometimes a numbness that attends the initial period of submission and when that has worn away the senses are more acute.

Similarly, on the second anniversary of getting to know Dad well, he writes: "Another reason for a letter now is that two years ago about this time there began a series of days in which there were a few too short hours that I shall always cherish and for which I have you to thank. . . . I am not going to say more about them for there are no words for them. . . I have relived them many times."

When, in his next letter, he announces a move to a new apartment, he notes that one of his regrets is that he must leave a place redolent of Dad and to which Dad had a key, which Edgar promises to replace with a key to his new home. Visiting Concord to research Dad's life there, Jane and I located the handsome brick block on Main Street in which Edgar lived when the two met. His original shop, also on Main Street, had been razed and replaced with an ugly commercial building. Still standing, however, was the large Victorian house and barn a few blocks away, to which Edgar eventually relocated his shop and his home—the site we knew as Edgar's shop when we were children.

⟨~⟩

Although Edgar was circumspect in his writing, the depth of his affection for Dad is clear. Perhaps significantly, Edgar was at pains to assure Dad that his letters were for Edgar's eyes only. Stamp collectors importuned him for the stamps on Dad's letters. Although he admits he has parted with some of these, he assures Dad that the correspondence itself "is not lying around promiscuously but is under lock and key with instructions for disposal unread in case of an erasure of yours truly." In researching my memoir, I visited the New Hampshire Historical Society Library in Concord in the hope that its archives might hold Edgar's papers. The librarian's answer was affirmative, and when the archivist brought me a thick file, my heart raced at the prospect of finding Dad's letters to him. But Edgar's file contained no personal papers, only a batch of receipts. Edgar seems to have been true to his word, alas.

Again and again, Edgar's letters allude to the depth of his emotion, but he always stops short of expressing it explicitly:

> It is always difficult to write to you for with my post-Victorian background, I sometimes hesitate to express my thoughts to you on paper. I have wanted you to know the depths of my regard for you. I think you are aware of it. . . . That you may know that it is the deepest regard, I am asking you if you recall one evening early in our acquaintance. At that time you asked if there should not be some one of whom one could ask everything. Do you remember?—At that time I was laboring under a mistaken sense of loyalty, obligation or what you may term it. I have cancelled that indefinable something. When you return, Grif, if you care to, I offer you the freedom to ask anything. Need I say more?

Edgar is so oblique that I can't be quite sure quite what he is offering, or requesting. He seems to be saying that he is available, emotionally at least, in a way that he was not when the subject was first broached. In any case, he follows up in a typically self-effacing way: "This note calls for no recognition and for no remembrance of it after it is read, if it is your wish. If it is something to be dismissed from your mind, there will be no embarrassment because of it when we are together again." But there is no doubt that Edgar had in some sense "proposed" here to Dad. He obviously wished that they could become closer emotionally, and possibly physically, after Dad returned from Syria. It was a big step for a man who'd apparently renounced romance years earlier.

～

The correspondence draws toward a close in the spring of 1933 with a series of letters that anticipate Dad's return. In April, Edgar writes to say that he had deliberately not written while Dad was deciding whether to stay for an additional year. This prospect was obviously distressing to Edgar, but he studiously avoided making his feelings a consideration: "I did not feel that I should inflict the weight of my hopes and fears upon you. I did not wish them to have even a slight pressure or be a disturbing element to your decision."

As for Dad's side of the correspondence, only one letter and scraps of a draft survive.

The only surviving letter from Dad to Edgar is a brief but significant note announcing that he would, after all, return as scheduled at the end of his third year. It concludes, "To you, I shall return a Prodigal," and is signed, "Your worthless, Grif." The biblical allusion was presumably meant as an apology for having been a neglectful correspondent. In his response, Edgar assures Dad, "If there were anything to forgive, Grif, you would be freely forgiven. There is nothing that needs forgiveness: so let your soul be at rest. . . ." He goes on, "Grif, there is no way to tell you what joy it is to know that you will soon be home! . . . If you have nothing better to do why not come in with me and we will eke a living (or a starving) together? At least there would be the happiness of going places and doing things together. . . . What boat? And When? A happy landing, Grif!" In a later welcoming note, Edgar also offers to share his small apartment with Dad: "If there is no summer school for you, plan to spend the summer or more here! I'll promise you what solitude you wish."

After some vacillation, however, Dad spent the summer doing graduate work in education at Teacher's College of Columbia University in New York. He had mentioned this possibility in letters to Edgar before he left Aleppo, but he seems to have made up his mind only when he arrived home; he apparently delivered the news to Edgar in a phone call. To soften the blow, he invited him to Dover to dine with the family, an occasion that would be their only contact before Dad left for New York. So their reunion occurred not at Edgar's home in Concord but at the Couser homestead. What, I wonder, did Dad's family know, or make, of Edgar and his relationship with Dad?

Certainly, in Edgar's eyes, the meeting did not go well. Exactly what happened is not clear, but Edgar felt he behaved badly, sufficiently so that— fortunately for me—he wrote, rather than phoned, to apologize. The letter is long and uncharacteristically abject in tone:

> Dear Grif;-
>
> I owe you something of an explanation and feel that I must lay some of my cards on the table at this time that I may more clearly convey my meaning to you.
>
> I think I made a reference the other day to having had much trouble from nerves. Directly after your telephone call, according to provincial terminology, "I went to pieces." For such occasions Dr. McIvor gave me some little to pills to take as needed. (Incidently it is not a drug [dope] habit formula.) At the time I know I doubled and think I trebled the dose to get myself in hand. I had rather a rough passage to Dover and drew up by the side of the road twice for rest. I was quite late arriving at your home.
>
> The next phase you already know—that I was not myself. I am sorry.
>
> I have been much upset since I returned over my whole behavior at the time. If I had been normal, I should not have inflicted myself upon you for more than the hour or two after supper—at another time a longer visit would have been quite all right but not at the time when you had so recently returned and with so brief a time at home. It was more than selfish and thoughtless of me. Will you overlook it?
>
> I do appreciate more than I can tell you all of your goodness to me and your patience with me. I am grateful.
>
> In spite of my disgust with myself there is so much that is particularly pleasant to recall of my visit. I would like to come again. I would like to know all your family better. They were so nice to Grif's friend that I would like also to be their friend.
>
> The things that I said and did that should not have been and those that should have been said and done that were not, will you also overlook?
>
> Can I anticipate seeing you again when you get back from Summer School or are you too disgusted?
>
> I am not going to attempt to say anything about how good it was to see you again even though I was only in a semi-rational state.
>
> Among the things undone, I know there were the wishes for you at Columbia – is it too late to offer them now?
>
> Edgar

Keyed up for their long anticipated reunion, Edgar was evidently crushed by Dad's decision to prolong their separation just as it seemed to be ending. The prospect of being reunited with Dad in the presence of his large family must have been a mixed blessing at best, but he could not turn down the invitation. He tried, unsuccessfully, to pull himself together for what must have been a daunting scenario: at once a reunion with Dad and an introduction to the rather staid Couser household. Having to restrain his feelings for Dad in such circumstances must have been hard; at the same time, he must have felt a need to make a favorable impression on Dad's family—six strangers, if all were present. Afterward, Edgar apparently felt he had not had his feelings under control and had overstayed his welcome—in short, had failed his audition.

Hence his plea for forgiveness. Continuing to fear that his behavior had alarmed or upset Dad, he wrote him at Columbia to reassure him: "Yes, I am tired, but you will learn by all of this that I am much better and more master of myself than when you saw me a few weeks ago. I am much better, thank you! I am really in fine fettle to greet you when you get back and am looking forward to seeing you soon. Come over as soon as you can and as often as possible."

Upon Dad's eventual return to New Hampshire, Edgar wrote again, welcoming Dad home once more and expressing his eagerness to see him, while trying not to importune. In addition to his letter, the envelope contained that key to his new apartment:

> It seems good to think of you again as only a few miles away [Manchester now, however, rather than Concord]. I feel that it is the me you knew who is writing this and saying "Welcome!"
>
> The lock to my door has been changed since you were here and this one is now the key to my castle. Keep it against any time you may feel the urge to come in. You know how welcome you will be!
>
> This is not an S. O. S. For I anticipate you have various and many people to re-connect with but I wanted you to know that I was waiting against your good time to greet you here. . . .

All credit to Edgar for his sensitivity to Dad's need to reconnect with others. Reading this, I wonder how Dad finessed his many reunions and resumed his complicated relationships with Rody, with Lena, and with Bob. But I am touched by this letter's tacit acknowledgment that Dad and Edgar would not be living together, even for the summer. That must have been a great disappointment to Edgar. And I wince at Edgar's obvious hurt that Dad had not hastened to rejoin him.

In the only complete letter I have from Dad to Edgar, he apologized for his failings as a friend in anticipation of his return to the States. I also have several drafts of a letter in which Dad struggled to articulate his feelings after he had settled in to his new life in Aleppo. The very existence of these drafts suggests how important Edgar was to Dad, in two ways. First, the multiple drafts show that Dad took great pains with this correspondence. He seem to have agonized over this letter especially, seeking not only to find les mots justes—a matter of style—but also, apparently, to calibrate the nature and the degree of his emotion—a matter of self-examination. Second, his retaining the drafts suggests how precious the correspondence—and the relationship—was to him. Perhaps the key to the entire correspondence as biographical evidence about Dad is that his side of it remains either entirely inaccessible or hard to read. Even when, as here, there is explicit emotion, the text is literally fragmentary—full of false starts, cross-outs, and dead ends. Moreover, just when it appears that Dad will deliver something direct and confessional, the letter takes a new direction.

It begins by mirroring several of Edgar's letters to Dad in commenting on how valuable the correspondence has been: "When I returned home this afternoon having thought of you often on the way, I read again your last letter. And very poignantly there rose again the sweet feeling that came with the first reading of your letter." He continues,

> Often I wish that I might get to an absolute knowledge of what causes my wishes and my happinesses. . . . I [have not been] the friend I might have been. It's my turn to be confessional. You will not do me the injustice of thinking me homesick, will you? The truth is I am happy here. It's devilishly hard to get this out, Edgar. It's just that I am not the same, and just how that is true is more than I can say. Though not because I am unwilling to tell you. If we could have a talk, but because a letter . . .

This is one of the few points in Dad's correspondence at which I find him inarticulate, and it frustrates me to have to guess at his meaning. There is no way to know what he was about to, or trying to, say when the letter trails off. Partly, he seems to be saying that he feels he has not deserved Edgar's outpouring of emotion. And while he may seem to be indicating that he does not reciprocate it, I think rather that he is trying to suggest that, though he very much appreciates Edgar's affection, his stint in Aleppo has affected him in ways that may necessarily alter their relationship when it is resumed face to face. He may be trying to lower Edgar's emotional expectations in anticipation of their eventual reunion.

In another attempt at the same letter, Dad reiterated his bittersweet pleasure in rereading Edgar's letter, then went on, "there is so much to say to you." But rather than saying whatever that was, he changed course and gave Edgar a description of the Arab custom of burying tear bottles in the graves of loved ones. (This by way of explaining a tear bottle that he was sending along to Edgar, not to sell, but as a gift.) He struggled to communicate the "almost ecstatic sense of being satisfied" that he experienced on first seeing the bottle in the bazaar. The point of this is partly that he knew how very much Edgar would have enjoyed that experience and partly that Dad would have enjoyed sharing it with him. The letter and the gift are a way of simulating that experience, bridging the gap in time and space between them. But the gift also functions as an objective correlative of his emotions toward Edgar. Not that he mourns Edgar. Although he misses him, the two are apparently in some sense present to each other despite their physical separation. Rather, the object must convey what is so hard to express verbally. Instead of communicating his emotion in words, then, he sent to Edgar a physical surrogate (suitably antique): an opalescent but opaque container, in which, perhaps, Edgar might capture tears generated by Dad's absence. This may have been the most precious artifact Dad sent Edgar; in any case, it is an overtly romantic gesture. In also helps me better appreciate the tear bottles that Jane and I inherited when Dad died. They have become not merely heirlooms or mementos but symbolic vessels for our grief.

~

Dad's relationship with Edgar continued after his return but was, predictably, attenuated. After spending the summer in New York, Dad took up residence not in Edgar's home town, Concord, but in his own, Manchester, where he had obtained a teaching position at his alma mater, Central High School. Rather than moving back in with Bob, however, he got his own place. He resumed seeing Rody—however infrequently—and he eventually met Mum when she joined his department in the late 1930s. In the meantime, he presumably visited Edgar at the shop and his new apartment.

With his return, and the two living much less far apart, there was less need for epistolary communication, and I have no further letters between them. The relationship becomes impossible to trace. But it must have been clear to Edgar that Dad was not going to be the partner he yearned for: his remark about California being his jinx proved sadly true once more. The relationship that had been intensified by Dad's departure on the "California" subsided in intensity after his return, despite—or perhaps because of—their relative geographical proximity. Up close again, Dad was probably not able, and perhaps not eager, to continue the friendship at the same romantic pitch.

~

Born in the mid-1940s, Jane and I both fondly remember visits to Edgar's shop, not just while we were living in Manchester but even after we moved to Melrose in 1954. By that time, he had consolidated his business and his residence in the large Victorian house on Jackson Street, off Concord's main street. There he carried on his business for nearly the rest of his life. According to townspeople, he had a reputation in the state as a reliable middle-tier antique dealer and "picker"—someone who seeks out valuable antiques in unlikely places and passes them on to specialty dealers in Boston. Jane and I remember that house well. In addition to the adjoining barn, Edgar used rooms on the first floor as shop space, so to enter his home was to enter his showroom; curiosities were everywhere. On our visits, we'd be allowed to pick out little knickknacks for ourselves. Jane still has a few of hers.

Reading Edgar's letters, I became very fond of him. Like Rody, he sensed and responded to something aesthetic and romantic in Dad's character that he had difficulty expressing with others. Given the age difference between them, I think that Edgar served as a kind of surrogate father for Dad; he certainly offered an emotional openness and an interest in beauty that Isaac seemed to lack. So Edgar was a particularly valuable, as well as a dear, friend.

Given his self-narrated romantic history, it was probably somewhat painful for Edgar to see Dad marry and have children, even if Dad did continue to drop by the shop periodically, on his own or with family in tow. Edgar's later life may have been rather lonely and not entirely fulfilling—like his earlier life by his own testimony. I wonder how much affection and support Dad was able to give him in his post-Concord years. Probably very little.

∿

Still, it's quite remarkable that such an intense friendship developed over the period of a few months in 1930 and then was sustained at a high pitch over their three-year separation. Unlike Bob, Edgar seems to have been quite accepting of his sexuality. For Edgar, I think the problem was not self-acceptance but lack of tolerance on the part of others—beginning with his family—and his failure to find a worthy long-term partner. Without a sympathetic family and a partner, it must have been hard for him to live a gratifying life as a gay man in conservative Concord.

∿

While I find Rody's letters touching, I find Edgar's very moving. In the early stages of writing this memoir, I discussed its genesis at an international gathering of scholars in the field of life writing. At one point, while quoting one of Edgar's letters to Dad, I suddenly utterly lost my composure, sobbing audibly. As the audience averted its eyes and I struggled to regain control of my voice, I blurted out, "Why does this happen?"—meaning, why should I break down while reading one of *Edgar's* letters? Without thinking, I answered my own question: "Because I never wrote my father such a loving letter."

I had been moved to tears by Edgar's ability to express his love for my father so openly whereas I, his only son, had bottled up my feelings for years. (I have since referred to this moment, only half-facetiously, as self-administered psychotherapy as performance art.) Edgar's letter somehow penetrated my emotional defenses and helped me understand one source of my unresolved grief. For that reason, I treasure this correspondence. I admire Edgar for his candor as well as his tact in reaching out to Dad in a non-threatening way. I think his friendship awakened and gratified needs in Dad that no other relationship did, including his marriage. I'm thankful for his friendship and his letters. Through them I've come to know more of Dad's early love life and indeed to love him more fully myself.

❧

Partly out of concern about my right to quote Edgar's letters, I searched for any descendants. Not knowing when Edgar had died, I was initially unable to find even an obituary. Fortunately, the town of Concord has a cemetery administrator; she quickly located his burial records, which led me to his obituary—and to his grave. Edgar died at the age of 79 in 1963, about ten years after we moved to Melrose. The obituary, though brief, provided some information about his family—including the existence of the married sister who lived in Concord. Like him, she had no children, so there were no descendants to reckon with.

A poignant revelation came, however, when I visited the Hawthorne family plot. Edgar was buried with the rest of his family only in a nominal sense. Edgar's father, mother, sister, and brother-in-law are buried in side-by-side vaults in front of a single upright HAWTHORNE headstone; each grave has its own horizontal marker. Parallel with the headstone but in the very corner of the plot—and facing the opposite way from the other graves—is a stone marking the location of Edgar's cremated remains. Thus, in death as in life, Edgar is marginalized, at odds with his closest relatives. His sister, who survived him, was presumably responsible for this arrangement. Family plot, indeed.

On my visit, I knelt, whispered my appreciation to Edgar for having been Dad's friend, and placed a small stone on his grave as a token of my gratitude and a trace of my private pilgrimage.

Chapter Thirteen

George Saylor

Gay Blade

Bob seems to have been ambivalent about his sexuality; Edgar was accepting of his, but lonely and emotionally frustrated without a partner. Only George seems to have embraced his sexuality and the world it opened up to him. George's sexual orientation is not conjecture on my part; he addressed it explicitly in an important letter. If he was Dad's gayest friend, he was also the least attached to Dad; this was least romantic of these friendships. But George alone was in a position to give Dad access to the gay culture of the day. And he did, which speaks of his trust in Dad.

In reconstructing my father's complex emotional life, I have had to wonder about his sexual orientation, of course. While I can never know for sure whether he was sexually attracted to these friends or had physical relationships with any of them, I have to take into account the times he was living in. Gender and sexuality were not the same then as now. According to George Chauncy's *Gay New York*, sexual identity was understood very differently in the twenties and thirties.

> Particularly in working-class culture, homosexual behavior per se became the primary basis for the labeling and self-identification of men as "queer" only around the middle of the twentieth century; before then, most men were so labeled only if they displayed a much broader inversion of their ascribed gender status by assuming the sexual and other cultural roles ascribed to women. The abnormality (or "queerness") of the "fairy," that is, was defined as much by his "womanlike" character or "effeminacy" as his solicitation of male sexual partners; the "man" who responded to his solicitations—no matter how often—was not considered abnormal, a "homosexual," so long as he abided by masculine gender conventions. . . .

> Only in the 1930s, 1940s, and 1950s did the now-conventional division of
> men into "homosexuals" and "heterosexuals," based on the sex of their sexual
> partners, replace the division of men into "fairies" and "normal men" on the
> basis of their imaginary gender status as the hegemonic way of understanding
> sexuality.[1]

So when Dad was young, men who had sex with other men could interpret that not as a function of their *gender* (their identity) which they considered "normal" (i.e., masculine), but only of their *sexuality* (their behavior).
That began to change in the decade when Dad met and married Mum.

Chauncy goes on to note, however, that the paradigm shift occurred perhaps a generation earlier among middle-class males,[2] among which I would
count my father and his friends. As middle-class labor became de-masculi-
nized and women entered the work force (especially during and after WWII),
it became more important for middle-class men to define their gender identity differently: by their sexual partners. Middle-class men whose work required them to submit to male superiors (and work side by side with women,
in some professions, like teaching) could reassure themselves that they were
normal, masculine, if they had sex with women and not with other men.
Romantic friendships declined as homosexuality was stigmatized and medicalized.[3] Given this chronology, Dad's relationship romantic friendships
were cultural throwbacks.

Chauncy's work has important implications for my sense of this dimension of Dad's life. The first is that if he had sex with any of these friends (or
any other man), he could have done so without thinking of himself as what
we would call gay or homosexual. Dad was certainly "a conventionally masculine man," and so were his friends; none of them assumed "the sexual and
other cultural roles ascribed to women." His friends may have been homosexual, but they were not fairies.

Chauncy also helps me understand gay subculture in Dad's era: "The gay
world that flourished before World War II has been almost entirely forgotten
in popular memory and overlooked by professional historians. It is not supposed to have existed."[4] As a corrective, Chauncy documents not merely the
existence, but the visibility, of gay life in that era: "Gay men were highly
visible figures in early-twentieth-century New York, in part because gay life
was more integrated into the everyday life of the city in the prewar decades
than it would be after World War II."[5] Gay subculture was hidden in plain
sight, at least in some urban centers: "Many New Yorkers viewed the gay
subculture's most dramatic manifestations as part of the spectacle that defined the distinctive character of their city. Tourists visited the Bowery, the
Village, and Harlem in part to view gay men's haunts."[6]

～

George's letters to Dad corroborate Chauncy by testifying to the vitality of gay culture. If Edgar gave Dad access to the world of gay esthetes, George was his conduit to the world of gays in entertainment and theater. In particular, George brought him to gay New York hotspots—especially Times Square and the theater district. The return addresses on George's letters locate him in or near gay neighborhoods, first in the West Forties, then the East Forties—in proximity to gay hotels, rooming houses, restaurants, clubs, and speakeasies.

Dad's visits to New York before his departure for Aleppo brought him there at the height of what Chauncy calls the Pansy Craze, when gay men

> acquired unprecedented prominence throughout the city, taking a central place in its culture. As a "pansy craze" swept through New York, they became the subject of newspaper headlines, Broadway dramas, films, and novels. The drag balls they organized attracted thousands of spectators, and the nightclubs where they performed became the most popular in the city. Visible gay life moved from the margins of the city—from the waterfront and the Bowery, Harlem, and Greenwich Village—into Times Square, the city's most prestigious cultural center. [7]

Thanks to George, Dad had privileged access to gay culture when it was flourishing more openly than at any previous time in American history. And he seemed to relish it. George seems to have been roughly Dad's age, but the two of them had quite different temperaments and orientations. Their only obvious common interest was in theater, but what was for Dad largely a curricular concern (as an English teacher) was for George a passion and a profession. As with Edgar, Bob, and Rody, he retained George's letters for the rest of his life—a sign that the relationship continued to be meaningful for him.

Dad brought George home to Dover at least once: his youngest brother, Ken, remembers George dancing up and down the stairs. I wonder what Dad's parents, sober Northern Irish Presbyterians, thought of that spectacle. Whatever their reaction, I'm glad Dad had the audacity to produce it and George the pluck to perform it. Like Dad's sojourn in Aleppo, this aspect of his life seems beyond his parents' ken and well outside their comfort zone. My father somehow transcended the culture in which he was raised, but apparently without hurting feelings or becoming distant from his nuclear family.

Like the other friendships, this one continued after he married and had children. Jane and I remember George visiting our home in Melrose in the 1950s; we recall a slender, dapper, dark-haired, and high-spirited man with a pencil mustache, whom both Dad and Mum greatly enjoyed. We would be

sent to bed early, and from our respective bedrooms would strain to eaves-
drop on the three adults as they reminisced and traded off-color jokes over
drinks in the living room. Was it from George that Dad picked up that party
trick in which he pretended to be a one-armed, cane-carrying pan-handler? It
embarrasses me to remember it—and he was a bit shy about sharing it with
us—but at the time I thought it was hilarious. He hid his "missing" arm
inside his clothes; when he needed to reach for a handout, he transferred his
cane from his hand to a forefinger extended, obscenely, out of his fly.

Dad's correspondence with George is quite extensive: his archive contained nearly a dozen substantial letters from George to him and two from
him to George between 1929 and 1934. It is not just Dad's being in Aleppo,
however, that required the two to keep in touch by mail; George's career in
show business took him away from New Hampshire. During this time, as he
pursued opportunity in theater and radio, he wrote to Dad from Baltimore,
New York, Des Moines, Altoona, and Chicago.

Although Dad and George were very close, this relationship was not as
complicated as Dad's relationship with Bob nor as romantic as that with
Edgar; George seems to treat him like a younger, inhibited brother who
needed to loosen up. It can be a relief to read these letters after the intensity
of Edgar's and Bob's. George's tone is generally much lighter than Bob's
and less formal than Edgar's. He addresses Dad as "Dear Griff old boy,"
"Griff Dear Pal," "Swell Fella," "Old Pot," or just "Kiddo." This informality,
however, masks deeper feeling; there are moments when both men acknowledge emotions that were difficult to articulate in person *or* in writing.

Dad greatly valued having a close friend in show business who could
relay gossip about, or insight into, theater celebrities. George never made it
big, but he did appear in a Broadway show during the period of his correspondence; later he had a modest career in radio, and he wound up in Holly-
wood. But while Dad may have vicariously enjoyed George's work, George
had a hard time empathizing with the struggles of a young English teacher in
Concord, New Hampshire—let alone in Syria. He might have been more
supportive if Dad had seemed to enjoy his first job. When this correspondence begins, however, Dad seems to have complained about it. Even allowing for some exaggeration on his part and some projection on George's, I am
taken aback to find George advising Dad to give up teaching, which George
thinks he does solely out of a sense of mission. As a lifelong teacher myself, I
read these letters in a different context: memories of the frustrations of the
first years of my career. These come with the territory and are not necessarily
a sign of a mismatch of talents and vocation.

George's first letter was sent to Dad's Concord rooming house from
Baltimore, where his show was in tryouts. He was delighted to announce that
the show was to move to the Shubert Theater in New York. It was not just
any show: knowing the date and the venue, I was able to identify it as *The*

Street Singer, a musical comedy produced and directed by Busby Berkeley shortly before his celebrated Depression-era musical films, *42ⁿᵈ Street*, *Gold Diggers of 1933*, and *Footlight Parade*. Although George was merely a member of the chorus, it must have been exciting for him to work for this renowned artist—and for Dad to claim him as a friend.

The bulk of the letter consists of inspirational advice to Dad:

> I am so sorry for you, Griff—to think you are apparently wasting the best time of your life doing the things that seem to depress you so. . . . Can't you break away and seek a position somewhere where the atmosphere will be brighter—I know you'd be a different person . . . . One day you will find years have passed and you've been living in a small little world of what might have been, but what never did afford you the freedom and joys of living as you would have liked to. . . . You make yourself believe you must do just the thing you're doing—you're trained for it and now must go through with it if it kills you—so—you've settled down to it—inwardly beating your own head for the desires you try to suppress.

George compares Dad invidiously to himself, a man who was pursuing his passion.

This indirect evidence of job dissatisfaction may help to illuminate Dad's decision to go to Aleppo, which otherwise might seem to come out of the blue. It may seem odd that a man who was manifestly unhappy in his first teaching job would choose to teach so far from home, but he may have sensed that it would be more gratifying in an unfamiliar setting and with higher stakes. And so it proved. Rather than abandoning teaching, then, he upped the ante. While "the work" in Aleppo was demanding and all-consuming, it was very rewarding. What may have been a gamble paid off richly, cementing his devotion to his chosen profession, which he pursued for the rest of his working life. Dad literally decided there was "a better place for" him and determined to go there. And it did work out, as George was so sure it would.

From my current perspective, however, I am interested in the suggestion that Dad may have been depressed in his twenties; perhaps his late-life depression was in part an exacerbation of a long lasting, deep-seated condition, rather than the sudden collapse it seemed to us at the time. Dad certainly did not believe in the power of positive thinking—George was a Christian Scientist—but he may have liked having a friend who encouraged him to hope for and seek out happiness. Bob was too troubled to do so, and Edgar wanted him to remain close by. Part of George's appeal may have been the sunniness of his temperament. But it's possible, too, that he sensed that Dad had desires, vocational or otherwise, that he suppressed in favor of a practical career. More suggestive evidence of self-sacrifice or repression.

After *The Street Singer* closed, George wrote from Chicago. That letter includes a long excursus about how much he cherishes this friendship. He encourages Dad to unburden himself further than he had been willing to do in his last letter:

> You speak of our friendship—you compare me to others—you would hold me above others in your confidence—There are things you would tell me—the truth of matters bothering you—maybe bothering only because you can't tell them—would we could be alone. . . . I'm proud that you are placing me in that category. I want you to feel that way about me—as the feeling is quite mutual I assure you, old pal. New friends cannot impair old friendships. I wonder sometimes if that has ever come into your mind.

The reference to new friends may be an acknowledgment of George's relationship with a man he refers to as Add (for Addison), apparently a musician in show business. George and Add lived together, but at this point George assures Dad that Add is no competition, "for you don't know how deep a love I have for you both." He concludes by asking Dad to "pretend we're together and write me some of those things you would say. Please."

In July of 1930, Dad wrote to George from Dover, where he was spending a precious final interlude with his family before his departure for Europe and beyond: "It fills me with sadness when I think of leaving them. I sometimes wonder if ever again there will be moments like these. But you will think me sentimental . . . ." George was back in New York City with Addison; Dad had apparently visited them there and hoped to do so again before boarding his ship: "My days in N.Y. with you & Add made a very happy [time] & I cannot tell you how happy I am to be seeing you before leaving. . . . And here I come to an added reason for wishing to stay a bit with you before I go. In that little time I must absorb years of being with you, enough to recreate later, as many times as I'll wish the illusion of your presence." I like this romantic notion of Dad's, that experience of others, once absorbed, or distilled, in their presence, can be reconstituted at will in their absence. It seems to have eased his apprehension about being so far for so long from his loved ones, and he tried to make it console them as well.

～

He and George continued to correspond during Dad's time abroad, but not frequently or regularly. Still in New York the following January (Dad's first winter in Aleppo), George sent a long letter to "Dear Mr. W. G. Couser, Esq: Old Pot, etc." George had not heard from him, and he asks for "all the dirt, big boy." Here I sense a difference between their sensibilities. George could not appreciate what a teacher's life was all about. He proffers his sympathy to "a poor pal o' mine stranded way over in those greasy countries somewhere—livin on salami and trusting himself to the mercy of those greesy Greek chefs.—Woe is he—ah, woe. . . . Nevertheless—you have savages to play with—maybe you get nothing but Turkish coffee." Even allowing for rather awkward attempts at humor, here George seems utterly clueless about what Dad's life was like in Aleppo—not to mention Aleppo's location and rich culture.

Perhaps because of the Depression, George's career slumped. For regular income he continued to sing in shows, but Add began to mock him for resigning himself to lowly roles—to the point that George considered leaving him. Here the roles are reversed between him and Dad: Dad had found gratifying work, while George was doing things he didn't believe in to pay the rent while waiting for a break. He confesses that he's been unhappy and frustrated and hints that he's even considered suicide:

> I am not myself at all. I used to be the happy-go-lucky fool but was at least happy. I can't say that anymore and I'm afraid it shows on me too. . . . I had reached the point of doing silly desperate things a time ago and had I not a sweet mother to think of I'm afraid to say what I might have done but the folly of such an attitude makes me ashamed to speak of it now. Please think nothing of that any more. After all I wouldn't be worth knowing to anyone had I not more courage and determination to make the grade in spite of all this. I'll make it—I'm fully determined—more than ever before.

Another year passed. Dad returned to the United States. He spent his first summer stateside in New York, taking education courses at Teacher's College. George was in Iowa, but Dad saw some of his New York friends. George apparently had many gay and lesbian friends in the theater world, and he was happy to introduce Dad to them, even from afar. From Altoona, he reports being pleased that Dad had met an actress called "Sunny," and he tells Dad of her family's revulsion from her sexuality:

> She is still a virgin—just as fine as they come, and the greatest tragedy in her life has been the loss of one friendship which she cherished above everything else excepting "loyalty" to her mother.
>
> This was as sweet a friendship and as necessary to Sunny as one could possibly conceive. It lasted over a period of a few years and was broken up by her mother in a jealous frenzy during which Sunny was brought out on the carpet unsuspectingly and before all her relatives she was held up against the wall by her very manly brother and openly denounced by both mother and brother as a "dirty little Lesbian"—each relative in turn took a dig at her and left her crying alone and frightened to death at this awful surprise party so stealthily planned for her. . . . Sunny was made to choose her future path—remain at home and "do her duty and support her family as a loyal child should do"—or—get out and remain friendly with this "low creature." Sunny's greatest mistake was in promising not to see that girl, in promising to kick her out of their home where she had lived for a couple of years and had worked hard to help support that mother of Sunny's. She was the means of the only bit of

sunshine that kid ever knew. She is the only one Sunny has ever known who has given her a real genuine affection. . . . Sunny never had this from any one of her own family—never in all her life—can she be condemned for reciprocating? There is a great difference [between] degeneracy and homosexualism.

Given the sympathetic view of lesbianism expressed in the letter, the last phrase seems not only surprising but a bit mystifying. But George seems to want to distinguish same-sex relationships that are affectionate, mutually respectful, and enduring (homosexualism) from same-sex relations that are merely erotic, transitory, or exploitative (degeneracy)—that is, those based in love from those driven by lust.

He then relates Sunny's experience to his own and expresses his theory of love, sex, and happiness. He recounts how he came to accept his own erotic desires and thus his sexual orientation:

Griff, I am being frank and open. I am laying bare my own theory because my own life has taught me to face things squarely. . . . It is possible to go all the way through life sacrificing the things one feels he needs or wants when they are right within his reach if he has the courage to reach out to grasp them. Well, I never had the courage and maybe I never knew what I wanted in this blamed old existence until I saw something of life. Saw it in many of its fazes, laughed at much I saw—ridiculed much I saw—pitied and even feared it. Experience was lacking. I learned and became broadened to the facts as I saw them first without an actual affair or any experience other than observation. I never did fully realize the depth, the sincerity, the profound joy, in this thing called love myself—but when someone else showed me the way—someone I regarded so highly it just couldn't be helped—I found happiness such as I have never known. I have found the majority of people are either wise to the true facts of life and live accordingly or they are blind and can't even see or appreciate what the others . . . can see.

This seems to expand on, and explain, his distinction between degeneracy and homosexualism. George himself had apparently been repulsed by, or fearful of, what he had seen of gay life until he was initiated by someone he esteemed; when his sexual desires were directed toward someone he appreciated as a person and not just as a sex partner, he was able to come to terms with his orientation. Being "wise to the true facts of life" seems to mean accepting gay relationships as every bit as deep and committed as heterosexual ones.

He then goes on to lament that fact some of his good New York friends are *not* wise in this way. He then turns to Dad's status in this regard, with reference to a gay friend he had apparently arranged for Dad to meet in New York that summer:

Ernest asked me the very first thing if you were "wise" or not. I suppose simply so that he could tell whether or not we were all at liberty to say whatever popped into the mind. I am afraid I did the wisest thing by saying "OH SURE" but poor Griff may have little desire to be wise. It seemed best to me but I should have told you something of this before. I just couldn't, Grif. Oh how I wish I were there to go and do the things you should do for laughs and an incite into the side of life you have never seen from my angle I know.

Here George seems to mean that he has been assuming Dad's awareness of his homosexuality and tolerance of gay life in general (and assuring others, like Ernest, of that) without having formally broached the subject or being entirely sure where Dad stood. And he wishes he had been on hand to further initiate Dad into New York's gay scene:

I was not wrong in introducing you to the kids and saying my pal was wise to all the facts of life. He really is—after a fashion. So I did not lie. They knew that you meant more to me than just another friend—you will mean more to them partly for that reason and again because they liked you anyway. Do call them sometime before you return to N.H. anyway.

Ernest is really fond of you too and I know if you called him he would ask you out to a speak[easy] for dinner or drinks. His only trouble is in picking up with others if he has too much under his belt. He treats them all to drink after drink. One night he dragged four others back with us to Mike's apt. We didn't even know them although it turned out rather amusing.

Here he seems to suggest that Dad's gay cred lies not so much in specific knowledge of gay life as in his respectful relationship with George. That is, Dad was "wise" insofar as he knew George was gay and his friendship with him takes that into account, going beyond conventional camaraderie. All of this must have been immensely flattering to Dad, whose family background seems to have been not just straight but quite narrow. He took pleasure and pride in his sophistication in matters cultural, intellectual, and here sexual.

Having exhausted this side of the topic, homosexual desire and love, George segues to heterosexual love and Dad's predicament with regard to Rody. Presumably responding to Dad's epistolary testimony, George summarizes it thus: "No I'm not in love, George." "But Rody is, etc." George then assumes the role of homosexual confidant to a heterosexual man seeking romantic advice. At first, his counsel is clear and forthright: tell the truth: "She could be told of your sincere regard for her. She should likewise be told as sweetly as possible that you are not in love and cannot say so. It would not be fair." But then he adds, "If necessary there can always be another." That is, George seems to be saying that, to soften the blow, he could tell Rody that he was interested in another woman.

He even nominates a candidate: "Sunny would be a swell colleague . . . who would cooperate whenever needed. It would not even be a lie now would it? You are *interested* at least—you need not say love." Mostly, though, he advocates candor: "To be frank as possible is always so much more successful in the long run." He also suggests seeing Rody less frequently. Dad seems to have taken George's advice, or perhaps he arrived independently at the same conclusion: he distanced himself from Rody, insisting on being only a friend. As we've seen, however, Rody had trouble letting go.

Then things become more complex and more interesting: Dad's lack of desire for Rody has troubled him. Perhaps, despite his attraction to Lena, he feared he was incapable of a fully requited romantic relationship with a woman. George reassures him:

> No, I don't think there is necessarily anything the matter with you. Wrong, you say. Not wrong anyway. You are to me so fine—so good and real—that I would even like to see you break loose one day and give vent to your innermost emotions—do you think that would change you any? Mm—Mm—no—but it would do something for you you need, fellow.
> There will be a day when you will do that—and I hope I am present Grif. Present—and very close to you.

George seems to feel there's nothing *fundamentally* wrong with Dad; he is capable of love and heterosexual desire. But George finds him repressed, unable or unwilling to give full expression to his emotions. So did Rody, of course; they were no doubt right.

At the same time, George acknowledges never previously having been so frank and confessional with Dad: "Oh how frank and open I have been in this letter." And he expresses the hope that this relationship can continue in this new vein, despite, or perhaps because of, his geographical distance:

> Please understand me—confide in me—write to me as you might wish to speak to me—let me do that too. Perhaps I can with much more courage than I've had in our presence. I am ashamed to say that, but fear of being misunderstood has always gripped me and as a result I have had to be happy just being with you without saying much that I desire to each time that we have had the good fortune to meet.
> That is all over—nobody else is as close to me inside somewhere—why should I have to restrain myself. I can't do it.

Here George seems to be confessing to having strong emotions toward Dad but having not expressed them, out of fear of being misunderstood—perhaps as erotic in nature. He now pledges a new phase in his relationship: "That is all over."

In subsequent letters he keeps Dad posted on plans but spends a great deal of space on how much he misses regular communication, which is in turn a poor substitute for Dad's company. He then fantasizes about a road trip:

Someday I'm going to be able to drive to New Hampshire—swoop you up— "during a lull" and whisk you off on a swell trip somewhere with nothing to think about but fun and laughs. I've never had your companionship for long— when there weren't so many obstacles that it was only to result in heartache at saying au-revoir. Well, "my fran," don't get your nose so buried in books that you'll forget this "apple." Honest I've written you more often than you know—a sweet thing to admit but I have truly—a long letter was typed in answer to your last one . . . . The subtlety of my remarks, Oh, Gee—I wrote and wrote—and then some—but wrote too much to send on to you—I know that that kind of letter is the one I should send yet it sounds so silly somehow after reading it over. Oh, well. I'm sorry my buddy—skip it for now! I put so much in that letter—I kept it. It may prove a menace to me but one day I'll hand it to you. It expresses me better than I'd be able to do so in person.

How I'd love to have that letter, had he had the nerve to send it.

In another letter, he reiterates his desire for private time with my father: "Wish we—you and I—could be together Grif. I'd be happy then. Don't criticize me for saying this—I mean it. Sometime I'm going to manage somehow so that an age-old desire will be realized—You and I may then break out—do things, go places, enjoy that swell opportunity—together!"

I am struck by an echo in this letter of one of Rody's in which she too suggests that Dad is somehow not allowing himself full expression of his emotion. But I sense that his upbringing was part of that: his teetotaling Protestant parents did not encourage sheer fun, mindless pleasure, or any kind of self-indulgence. He was tempted from various sides to cut loose. Both Rody and George seem to have sensed the cost to Dad of this habitual self-repression. But George seems to have had a very different fantasy in mind—one involving male camaraderie, or more.

On May 17, 1933, as his time in Aleppo was ending, Dad at last wrote to George, laying out, somewhat defensively, his philosophy of nonverbal communication. (Fortunately for me, he retained a carbon copy.)

I manage ordinarily not to miss letters, thinking them unrequired in the community of spirit in which friends live. That is a conception that I have followed quite earnestly, and have even advocated, as you may have noticed in other letters. It has a strong intellectual appeal, the idea of thinking yourself never very far away from your friends, that although you are here and he is there physically, that we are going in the same direction though by slightly different paths, thinking often similar thoughts, even at times seeming to catch a glimpse of the other's eye and sending a smile of understanding, while both know all the time that if they are in difficulty or trouble, they have a sure comforter and ally in the other. For one who is removed from his friends, it is a conception that does, I think, help one to live better, more constantly conscious of his kinship with his friends. I do not mean that writing letters has not its good place, but for me it requires a quiet and apartness that I have very little of here, but it can be a part of everyday existence, even in the midst of work, to

think of this or that friend as familiarly as if we had met on the street. Such a
philosophy requires keeping alive and living at one's best.

This romantic notion of friendship seems consistent with the idea expressed above about absorbing experience of friends and saving it for later
reconstitution. It seems altogether wholesome and appealing (and sincere) to
me. But of course, as George is not shy to say, it is no substitute for actual
letters, and he complains now of the lopsidedness of their correspondence:
"Philosophy is okay—and even though it may be thoroughly understood, it is
still my great delight to hear from you often—Grif—there is no one person I
care more for than this boy to whom I am now writing—that you may well
understand the satisfaction given me when word comes from you."

Like Edgar, George hungered for words from my father's pen, and the
irony of Dad's philosophy of correspondence may be that he was such a good
writer that in his case the kind of spiritual communion he likes to imagine
may have been less satisfying than it might have been for someone less deft
with words. The very letters in which he minimized the need for literal
correspondence were so flattering and articulate that they were in a sense
self-defeating. They just made his correspondents hunger for more. At face
value, this affirmation of spiritual kinship may have been gratifying to
George, but I wonder whether it also struck him as a bit impersonal. It is
certainly in a very different register from George's effusions. Dad could have
said—indeed, did say—pretty much the same thing to other correspondents,
male and female. George might have relished more in the way of epistolary
intimacy.

In any case, it is clear that George felt great affection for Dad, and very
likely erotic attraction as well. Hence his repeated references to letters he had
written but not sent, to emotions too strong to be communicated directly.
And I am left to wonder to what extent Dad felt a mutual attraction.

∽

At this point, the correspondence comes to an end—at least, as far as I can
tell: no later letters survive. Perhaps George returned to New Hampshire for a
while, and letters were not necessary. Even if the correspondence ceased, or
dwindled, the relationship did not. The two stayed in touch well into my
lifetime. But in the mid-thirties, Dad met and fell in love with Mum; that
relationship and his marriage must have occupied the foreground of his life
and consigned his relationships with his male friends to the periphery. Certainly, his marriage would have put a damper on Edgar's fantasy that he two
might live together and George's that the two might hit the road together.
Although his friendships with Bob, Edgar, and George continued long
enough for Mum, me, and Jane to be introduced to all three, his priorities in
affectional—and perhaps sexual—matters obviously changed at this time.

Nevertheless, Dad gained from these relationships a strong sense of what it was like to be gay in an increasingly heteronormative culture; he attained real insight into the lives of men whose sexuality had to be concealed, at least some of the time.

∽

I only wish that he had given me the advantage of his advantage in this. My new understanding of his romantic friendships makes me feel that by comparison, I grew up very innocent forty years later. On the one hand, I grew up with no parental model of homophobia; homosexuality was certainly not demonized or ridiculed in our household. On the other hand, the lack of recognition of homosexuality left me open to the mild homophobia characteristic of male adolescents. I'm grateful Dad didn't in any way reinforce my garden-variety adolescent prejudice but sorry he didn't expose it for what it was (if, indeed, he even noticed it). Had he confided in me, shared these letters with me, I might have been more alert to and appreciative of those around me who were in the closet in high school, college, and beyond.

The irony of Dad's interesting life as a friend to other men is that it bound him to *them* but not in any way to *me*.

Chapter Fourteen

Marriage, War, and Family

As a boy, I certainly knew my father had been in the Navy during World War II. His Bronze Star and its citation—framed in red, white, and blue—hung on my bedroom wall in Melrose. (It now decorates my home office.)

His service in the Navy was the one phase of his pre-marital life about which I was curious as a child. But I actually knew very little about his experience of the War. Like most veterans, Dad didn't talk much about it. Not because it involved witnessing unspeakable horrors; as far as I know, he was spared that. But rather because he had relatively little to report in the way of drama, and because, by the time I was old enough to be interested, the War was a decade in the past. At any rate, as with so much of his life, he conveyed little to me directly about his experience.

What I learned about Navy life came instead from indirect sources. My Cub Scout and Boy Scout troops toured Navy vessels—both surface and submarine—at nearby bases. And I remember Dad taking me to visit a British warship docked in Boston Harbor. So I had a sense of what ships looked and felt like—their dimensions, their confines—admittedly, while secure in port. There was also *Navy Log*, a half-hour dramatic TV series that aired in the 1950s, one of the few TV shows I was allowed to watch. Its sound track featured the Navy Hymn ("Eternal Father, strong to save"), which I still find stirring. What little I learned about naval warfare in WWII, then, I picked up by osmosis, so to speak.

I was excited, then, to find in Dad's archive his military records and a set of letters he had written home to Mum from the Pacific Theater of Operations (PTO), where he served late in the War. Along with them I came across a seven-by-ten inch sheet of sturdy stock embossed with a gold spread-eagle Navy seal and the words "United States Navy." As it happened, though, this documented not his military career but his family life. Or rather, both at

once; the two—the martial and the marital—began almost simultaneously,
and this document cleverly conflated them. It looked like this:

Lt. and Mrs. W.G. Couser, U.S.N.R.

announce

the launching of the

U.S.S.

Jane Leida Griffith Couser

on

June 28, 1944

Characteristics

First of its class. Displacement 8 ½ pounds. Overall length 19 inches. Beam 5
inches. Speed and range unknown. Equipped with fog whistle. Camouflaged
by jury-rigged white awning over fantail. May be inspected in drydock at
Christine Parker House, Manchester, New Hampshire. S.O.P.A. feeling fine
and elated over her new command.

In Naval parlance "S.O.P.A." ("Senior Officer Present Afloat") refers to
the highest ranking officer aboard a ship at any particular moment. Here, of
course, it refers to my mother, vested with the command of the newly
launched *U.S.S. Jane Leida Griffith Couser*. That was only fair, and a sweet
tribute, since Mum had to raise Jane mostly single-handedly for the duration
of the War.

Whether or not it was original with him, this clever metaphor suggests
how closely Dad identified with his naval role. And despite his taciturnity
about the War, it was clear to me that his service was—and remained—a
highlight of his life. For him, as for many of his generation, World War II
was "the good war," and he was unreservedly proud of his role in it. Indeed,
he seems to have been somewhat reluctant to put it completely behind him.
When he died thirty years later, I came across neatly pressed dress uniforms
in a trunk in the basement—as though he might be called back to active
service at any moment.

But this birth announcement may also represent the paradox of this phase
of his life. On the one hand, it was the one period of his life when he was
directly engaged in events of world historical significance. On the other, his
archive tends to highlight the private and familial even during this era. I find
myself alternately frustrated and heartened by this. I'd like to know more of
what he did in the War, but his letters tell me a lot about life on the home
front. Ironically, his going to war has given me rare and privileged access to
his relationship with Mum before I was born.

∾

Dad met Mum in 1937, when she joined the English Department at Central High School in Manchester, where he'd been teaching since his return

Figure 14.1. Dad and Mum on wedding day, August 1941.

from Aleppo. I know little of the courtship, except that Mum's younger brother John used to refer to her new beau, Grif Couser, as "Rip Trouser." I find that funny. Dad may not have, but the two men got along well. Dad and Mum married in Manchester in August 1941.

World War II began well before their wedding, and although the attack on Pearl Harbor came as a shock, it had been widely assumed that the United States would eventually enter the War. Only from my posthumous discovery of his archive, though, did I learn that Dad sought to get involved ahead of his country. Among the surprises in his papers was his student pilot's license, issued in November of 1940. I had no idea he knew how to fly: evidently, his adventurousness was not limited to the geographical (Aleppo) and the romantic (Lena, Bob, and Edgar). Even more surprising, there was a letter from a recruiting office in Montreal, dated May 1, 1941, specifying the documents needed to file to complete Dad's application to the Royal Canadian Air Force. Since he had no other reason to learn to fly—he was in no position to own a plane—he must have aspired to become an air force pilot and fight for the Allies, whether or not the U.S. entered the War.

He did not follow through, however. Presumably, Mum had other ideas.

Pearl Harbor changed everything—for Dad, for Mum, and for their families. Already in his mid-thirties and college educated, Dad was in little danger of becoming cannon fodder. Along with his three brothers and his sister's husband, he joined the Navy. We have a photo of the officers in spanking new dress whites in the yard of the family home in Dover. In a companion photo, their wives jauntily sport their caps. The pictures must date from the spring of 1942, before the men dispersed to their various assignments..

In the grand scheme of this truly global war, the American experience was exceptional. Among the estimated 50 million people who died in the War, fewer than 1 percent were American. After all, most of those killed world-wide were civilians, and the continental United States was never a war zone. But war is experienced on an intimate scale. And in the Couser/Van Stelten context, it consumed an entire generation for its duration. The mood in the Dover pictures is upbeat, even celebratory, but my father's parents had an enormous stake in the War: four sons and a son-in-law in the Navy. Fortunately, all those in the service survived, but it must have been an anxious time for all: the servicemen, their wives, and their parents.

Three of my cousins were born before the War; Jane is one of three born during it. Having married in their thirties, Dad and Mum may not have wanted to risk waiting until the war's end to reproduce. Nevertheless, it impresses me that these couples began to procreate with the knowledge that their early married years would involve separation and risk of death for the male partners. I suppose that Dad and his siblings just assumed they would survive. As it happened, all of them did. Making war did not prevent them from creating families. On the contrary, doing so may have been one way of addressing their mortality. If the men did not survive, at least they would leave progeny behind. In this, they were typical of their generation: after declining during the Depression, the American birth rate actually rose in the first few years of the 1940s. (I am one of five cousins born immediately after the War, the leading edge of the baby-boom generation.)

～

On January 5 of 1942, a month after Pearl Harbor, and only six months after his wedding, Dad began military service—one of 15,000,000 men inducted into the U. S. armed forces during the War. After emerging from Midshipman School at the Boston Section Base as an ensign in the Navy Reserve—a "ninety-day wonder"—he was assigned to the National Local Defense Forces in Portsmouth, New Hampshire. This was a convenient posting: the Portsmouth Base was close to the Couser home in Dover (a mere ten miles) and to the Van Stelten family in Manchester (about thirty-five miles). In fact, when Dad was sent to the Pacific in 1944, Mum moved in with her mother in Manchester.

Exactly how or when Dad got to Pearl Harbor I have been unable to determine; presumably he sailed through the Panama Canal. If so, he followed the itinerary traced in *To the War*, a memoir by Robert Edson Lee, whose rank and assignments paralleled Dad's. Reading it, I imagined Dad on that 9,000-mile sea voyage, over five or six weeks, with resupply stops in San Pedro and San Francisco.

Dad was in San Francisco long enough to rendezvous with Mum, who left baby Jane in the care of her mother and sister. Aside from that second honeymoon, he and Mum were separated for the rest of the War—indeed, until the fall of 1945. Mum was then truly in sole command of her infant daughter (insofar as a mother can be in command of an infant). And Dad's duties and regimen were completely different from those in Portsmouth.

The separation must have been difficult for them as relative newlyweds and new parents, but it is fortunate for me, for it meant that they could communicate only by mail—with the rare exception of a pre-scheduled phone call. When I first came across Dad's letter to Mum, I was thrilled, thinking of them as the "war letters." I looked forward to learning what ships Dad had been on, where and when they sailed. And so on.

My initial response to *reading* these letters, however, was disappointment: they contained very little information about the War. They did not provide the long-deferred answer to my question: "What did you do in the War, Dad?" For one thing, the correspondence is not complete; I know this because Dad numbered the letters as he wrote them, and there are breaks in the sequence. Much to my annoyance, I discovered that he had told Mum that she need not keep all of his letters: "P.S. Subject is saving my letters. Most of them certainly not. But if you think they have any diary quality of my life in the Pacific, you might save those particular ones. Not that I shall ever use them, but that I am a natural accumulator of records." Dad certainly was a "natural accumulator of records," and I am grateful for that. (Without them no memoir.) But unfortunately, Mum seems to have taken him at his word. In any case, he never did use the ones she saved, and I'm sorry for that. I'd love to have his own account of his Navy service. Instead, I've had to go to some lengths to construct one on my own.

～

The first of the ten surviving letters is dated February 5, 1945; the last, June 19, 1945. Dad seems to have written Mum nearly every other day (he also corresponded, less frequently, with his parents), and his letters were quite long, averaging almost 1,000 words each. The first to survive is— alas—the seventeenth letter he sent her. (Damn it, Mum!) And ten letters over a five-month period do not constitute a very full record. But those are the months I am most curious about—the period of his active service in a war theater.

Far more frustrating than the gaps between them is their vagueness about his duties. This is primarily a function of censorship. For fear that mail would be intercepted and used by the enemy, service members were forbidden to reveal details of their whereabouts and activities. This was not left up to the correspondents; letters were screened to be sure they were discreet. So Dad's would have vetted mail sent home by those of lower ranks; in turn, his letters would have been read by someone of higher rank. At least in principle, the military hierarchy functioned as a tiered system of surveillance.

Dad chafed a bit under the constraints on correspondence. In mid-February, he wrote: "At sea again and en route to my original destination (getting tired of that phrase—wish censorship would allow me to vary it)." Apparently, not only did censorship preclude naming his destination; he was supposed to use a stock phrase for it (so as to defeat attempts to disclose it in a code, I suppose). His destination was apparently Pearl Harbor, where Dad was stationed for the next few months, and I suspect that Mum knew that, too, having just seen him in San Francisco. But censorship makes it difficult to discover much about his actions, his exact role in the War.

Sadly, none of Mum's letters to him have survived. One reason may be that the military discouraged combatants from keeping received correspondence to prevent personal data from being used coercively in case of capture. This seems pretty unlikely in the case of seagoing personnel. But that was the policy. Regardless, I find it difficult to believe that Dad didn't save Mum's letters initially; he was after all a "natural accumulator of records," and the letters would have been especially precious to him under the circumstances. But they did not survive.

～

For reasons I've already suggested, his letters to Mum do not constitute a war diary. Nor could they have. After my initial disappointment, however, I have come to value them for what they are: a moving testament of his love for her (and for my new-born sister) and to the happiness of the early years of marriage, during which they began to create the family I was to join soon after the War ended. The letters were a means of engaging vicariously with his distant wife and child and a medium for shaping the relationship from afar.

Despite—or perhaps because of—the fact that his correspondence is one-sided, we need to acknowledge Mum's role in it. For one thing, in effect, she set the letters' agendas. Dad kept track of, and responded to, questions she asked and issues she raised: "In my queer methodical way I check the remarks I wish to comment on and feel that this must be done before I put your letters away. Later I review" (June 18, 1945). So his letters can be read, in part, as a palimpsest of hers. For another thing, he wrote as he did because he wrote to *her*; the letters were composed with her alone as their audience. Moreover, having been told she didn't need to save them all, perhaps she saved only the ones that meant most to her. In all these ways she shaped the correspondence that survives.

For me—a secondary and unanticipated audience—the letters offer invaluable insight into my family before I joined it and especially into the relation that engendered me. Reading them, then, is an odd experience. Insofar as the letters are intimate and not intended for me, reading them feels a bit voyeuristic. Insofar as they are very much concerned with the advent and infancy of my older sister, reading them might also arouse envy or jealousy of the attention lavished on her as the "first of her class." But I relish my access to the domestic circle, which would be utterly hidden from me but for the War, which separated him and Mum.

~

The War figures importantly, of course, in several ways, from the mundane to the most serious. There is mention of how Dad's pay is to be transferred to Mum. There are hints—but only hints—of his whereabouts and duties. There is an acute awareness of the cost of the War in lives and in grief. In the very first surviving letter, he reflected on the death of someone he and Mum knew, a Marine lost on an island Dad visited (probably Midway Atoll):

> Dear Ann,
> There is a strong urge upon me to talk to you today. Talking would be so much better than just writing. There would be your comments to meet, your mind, your clearness and good sense to steady my own thinking. But there is no help for that so you will have to put up with my soliloquy.
> So near to where Roger died, I cannot help but think much of him these days and of the significance of his death. I have stood on the beach where he fought and looked at the atoll which became ours because he and his fellow Marines gave their lives for it. Physically, it is so little—a few acres of coral sand and broken palms barely rising above the level of the sea. In the strategy of the Pacific war, however, it was very important. Symbolically it may have great and far consequences in the sort of world that will resolve out of this war and the peace to come. That must be so to compensate in any part for the tragic and premature deaths of such men. (February 5, 1945)

Once in the PTO—where I think he always wanted to be—Dad took quite a synoptic view of the War. He commented on its progress—"Actually this is all one American lake now" (February 15, 1945)—and on his hopes for an enduring international order. He took advantage of the military's provision of "pony" editions of major media, like *Time,* to follow what world leaders were doing and saying so as to understand the big picture. In his first letter, he went on at some length about the geopolitics of the War, distinguishing between the military goals and the larger ends of the War:

> We seem to be advancing more rapidly now toward the end of the war. The radio reports are good—our troops close to Manila, the Russians pushing hard at Berlin. We can well be thankful for what a military victory alone will give us. It will have prevented what Germany and Japan would have done to our world—certainly the destruction and disrepute of the best things we believed in—justice, decency and kindness—which at bottom have made our lives so happy and so worth living. But this victory and this kind of survival will serve us no good unless we can put an end to the possibilities of more war.

There are days when one wonders what kind of a show is being put up to win that fight. I came eagerly upon a recent copy of Time (Jan. 22), the latest broad report of news that we have aboard and read with much satisfaction . . . of the heavy persuasion being put upon the President to declare our intentions for international cooperation before the present trend of allied disunity goes any farther. That is good. I am glad that Roosevelt is being pushed. It is his weakness to need to know that he is being supported. . . .

These look like desperate days ahead for all the men who have the making of a fairer world in their hands. It is time for Roosevelt to justify that faith which many have put in him. . . .

And how proud these soldiers and sailors would be to come back home not only with a victory but knowing that their leaders had licked the peace. We shall see.

From today's perspective, Dad's views may seem somewhat naïve, but I admire his idealism about justice and the necessity of international cooperation to guarantee world peace. Indeed, I envy his immersion in a worthwhile mission—so foreign to my generation experience of war.

At the time of writing, he had the luxury of leisure in which to reflect this way: he was traveling to his "undisclosed destination" as a transient officer—in effect, a passenger—aboard a merchant vessel. With no responsibilities, he had time to expatiate on paper. He quickly apologized: "Shall I ask you to forgive me for running on, Ann? It seems to ease my sense of idleness which at present is quite without relief."

He then went on to offer rare details of an actual incident of his Navy life—ironically,

a fishing party that we have had. There was the merchant skipper, a few of his officers, and three of us transient officers. In the ship's big lifeboat, which is a powerboat, we fished with troll lines just outside the break of the surf along the islands of the atoll. You must imagine the white beach, the glassy green and blue water, the white, white foam of the surf, and the brilliant sun. And the excitement of a strike, playing and then landing a ten to twenty pounder with brilliant color to match the coral background of his sea haunt. It could only have been more fun if you had been there. How excited you would have been and how you would have loved it!

While the ship was in motion, he spent a good deal of his time reading and sunbathing—often in the nude:

Like all sea voyages as a passenger it is an existence in limbo, a partial vacuum. From the physical point of view, I am in rugged health and brown all over, even the bottom side. This is altogether a man's world, you see, with no need of one's having [to be] conscious of what he wears or doesn't wear. It's going to be hellish to put clothes on again after so long in this shipboard outfit of shorts and slippers and frequently not even that when one lies in the sun.

Ashore no neckties are worn, sleeves are rolled and khaki shorts are coming in, but even that seems cumbersome.

Dad tells Mum what he's been reading—James Norman Hall's *Lost Island* (a novel written and set during the War on a small Pacific Island)—and asks her to send Christopher La Farge's *East by Southwest: Stories of the Pacific* (1944). The Pacific was new to him, and he tried to gain familiarity with it by reading around.

In researching this chapter, I did the same thing. I started with naval history, in an attempt to locate Dad in the big picture of the War's narrative. But without his particulars I had trouble placing him in the epic sweep of these histories. More useful were personal accounts, memoirs of naval service. I found two especially illuminating because they were written by men of Dad's rank and background who also served in the PTO: Douglas Edward Leach's *Now Hear This: The Memoir of a Junior Naval Officer in the Great Pacific War* (1987) and the aforementioned Robert Edson Lee's *To the War* (1968). These books helped flesh out my sense of shipboard life: the boredom; the routines; the occasional adrenaline rush of danger, real or perceived; the trivial pastimes; the logistics of bunk and mess; the relations between officers and men and between different ranks of officers; the taken-for-granted racial segregation; the nightly films on the fantail while at anchor or in port.

As it happens, Lee's experience seems to have tracked Dad's quite closely. Given that Lee's book was published in the sixties and Leach's in the eighties, one of my responses to discovering them was to wish that Dad had written his own. He had the writing skills and the time—summers off—but lacked the impulse or perhaps the confidence. By leaving his letters behind, however, he has enabled me to convey some sense of his experience and perceptions.

I also made an effort to supplement his letters with naval records that might yield more details, using official and unofficial on-line resources. Indeed, for a time I was mildly obsessed with this endeavor. Any descendant of a veteran can get copies of his military records, and initially I thought Dad's would reveal all of his assignments: what ships he served on, and so on. Armed with that knowledge, I could use standard military histories to track his whereabouts in the PTO.

So I requested his military records from the Navy, using the requisite forms. After a considerable delay, I received a packet of documents.

I opened them with great anticipation.

I perused them with great disappointment.

Most of them were medical records, beginning with Dad's discharge physical and continuing at intervals for ten years. These furnished some useful facts about family medical history—always good to have—but shed no light whatsoever on Dad's actions during the War, since he was never wounded or otherwise injured.

The most promising document was his separation notice. This lists the dates of his entry and separation and the units to which he was assigned. But this alone told me very little. Worse, after my initial excitement, I realized that I'd had this very document all along: being a "natural accumulator of records," he had saved the copy he was given when demobilized. Not one of these documents so much as refers to a particular ship.

From his return addresses, however, I know that when he was transferred from the East Coast to the PTO, Dad was assigned first to Service Squadron 8; later, to Service Squadron 10. As their names suggest, these units served battle squadrons, which did the actual fighting. Service squadrons comprised utilitarian vessels, often converted merchant marine vessels: tankers, oilers, supply ships, refrigerator ships, and repair ships. When Dad was finally assigned to sea duty, he served on one of the latter, known as a destroyer tender. Tenders were huge, slow vessels that served as floating shipyards. Damaged destroyers would tie up to them and undergo repairs without having to travel to distant ports. Destroyer tenders were hardly on the front lines. But the achievements of battle squadrons were not possible without service squadrons. Moreover, an officer serving on such a ship would be in a position to see up close the damage done by enemy mines, shells, torpedoes, and kamikaze planes, and he would no doubt hear stories of action. Dad's early service in Portsmouth put him aboard small vessels, patrol ships and mine-sweepers, but it kept him close to shore and a home port. It wouldn't have seemed as much like the real war as service on a tender in the distant Pacific.

The trajectory of his service seems to have taken him ever closer to the heart of the PTO: from Portsmouth to San Francisco; then to Pearl Harbor, where the Pacific war began. From there it has been harder to trace him, but he seems to have been assigned in the final months of the War to the *USS Hamul*, a tender that supported the invasion of Okinawa, a crucial battle in the final advance on Japan. And I know, from letters sent home by his brother Jim, that both of them were in Tokyo right after the end of the fighting, in time to witness the formal surrender ceremonies.

∽

Life at Pearl Harbor was not as leisurely as the idyll aboard the merchant vessel. Still, Dad managed to swim nearly every day. And he reports being in good health and well-fed:

> No weighing machine is available to me but I feel sure I have added a number of pounds. My face is very much filled out and I think I have perhaps added a little all over. No sign of fat, rather an absence of any hollows. The food, of course, is very good and I eat heartily. Sunday night we actually had T-bone

steaks. Never do I eat steak without thinking of you and having a slight guilty feeling at having it all to myself. (April 9, 1945)

One of the perks of life in Honolulu was the opportunity to make an occasional telephone call home, by prearrangement. Here is his account of an excursion into the city to do that:

> On my way in to Hon yes. p.m. . . . . There are moments of high expectation in life when everything takes on the color of one's mood. Perhaps that is why all Oahu looked so beaut. to me as I rode the bus to town this aft. for my tel. date with you. The island-side view has always drawn my eyes but today it seemed to fall into frame after frame of moving beauty. Back from the thickly built flat land near the sea rise dark red fields of ploughed ground ending suddenly in great up-cropping peaks. Beyond them the clouds—always like our summer clouds to me—had rolled in and were piling up like a huge surf ready to crash over a reef. Here and there where a valley cut through, the clouds sifted down the trough in a dark mist of rain, occasionally glinted with a quick shaft of rainbow.
>
> [The tone and descriptive detail here remind me of Edgar's letters to him.]
>
> Then too all my sensations in these parts are sharpened by a half-sad consc. of your absence, a feeling that I must see them for you. Delightful as they are to me alone, I miss the joy of your experience at those times sharing them.
>
> For you have all the makings of a good traveler. I often think it a pity that some of this opportunity hasn't come to you rather than to me this time since I have had a bit of a chance to look at the faraway places.

We don't associate the old slogan "Join the Navy, See the World" with wartime duty, but Dad appreciated his posting to Pearl Harbor as, among other things, a chance to see an unfamiliar, exotic, and very beautiful part of the world. It is odd to have him lament that this "opportunity" hadn't been Mum's rather than his, but it suggests his awareness of how much more he'd traveled than she had. And it suggests an agenda for their married life, one which having children postponed for decades and which, alas, was never fully realized.

∽

While Dad relished certain features of life in Hawai'i, his letters reveal growing impatience with his duties there, his desire to have a more active role. On March 23, 1945, on the eve of his 39th birthday, he voiced his dissatisfaction:

> For a moment I had a start today as I asked myself, Am I going to be thirty-nine or forty? It is not much comfort but something to be still on the thirty-nine side of forty. . . .

You ask many times how I like what I am doing. The answer is that I don't, Ann. It is tolerable and I am not making myself unhappy, but I do feel wasted in this sort of thing. As I accumulate information I have not been too encouraged about things. When it actually comes to taking action I may find it otherwise, but there is a lot of politics at play here. It is a big organization with all the cross-currents of individual self-aggrandizement and advantage. For an organization of this size there is undoubtedly less of it than in civilian life. I sensed some of this from the beginning and found the lack of it up forward very refreshing.

So I am trying to look the situation over very carefully before I make a move, though my greatest unrest comes from holding back in this way. . . . I haven't spoken very cheerfully about my duty but don't you worry. Things will break right, I know.

Eventually, he requested, and was assigned to, sea duty. One clue is that his return address changed, from Service Squadron 8 in Pearl Harbor, to Service Squadron Ten Rep B thousands of miles to the west. Another clue: in a letter of June 18, he refers explicitly to leaving Oahu and expresses satisfaction at having a more active, risky role as the war winds down. Characteristically, he embeds this sentiment in a concern for Mum's morale:

Most of all it gives me pleasure to find your old spirit, that smiling spirit, in your letters. I hope it is there naturally and not by effort. As sure as I was of having done the right thing in leaving Pearl, I hated to think of your being anxious and unhappy about it. Let any such fears never overtake you again. This work gives me what I wanted; my conscience is at rest.

I believe that this reassignment came in April. One piece of evidence is an extraordinary—indeed, unique—letter, one that stands out from the rest in three ways. First, it is not handwritten but typed, on official navy stationery. Second, it is addressed not to Mum, or to her and Jane (as a few are), but to Jane alone. Third, its tone is entirely unprecedented.

28th April 1945
My very dear Jane,

If so much of my time had not been taken up advising Admiral Nimitz and General McArthur, I would have written you sooner to explain my long absence from home and honorable duties as your father. You have probably missed me at 6:30 in the morning when you had just about given up hope that anybody in the house was ever going to wake up. Perhaps you are having some difficulty with your mother in this respect at present. But about mothers you will soon discover like most wise children that you will have to take them as they are. One mustn't wait too long in life to learn tolerance, you know, and like charity it begins at home.

As for my absence, well, it seems that your rich Uncle Sam, who is sometimes a haughty and provincial [read: isolationist] old codger, decided that the gangs of hoodlum Heinies and Nips who were pushing our neighbors around,

Figure 14.2. Dad aboard ship in the PTO, 1945.

were working up to him as the next victim, and decided to do something about it. He is rather a determined and fierce old guy when his temper is up. So one day he said to me, "You know, it's time we went out and got those guys." It has taken a little longer than we expected so you will have to wait a bit longer for me to come home and tell you how I won the war.

We'll have fun, though, when I do come home, your mother, you and I. Besides, I have been collecting some nice pets for you. Pass the word to your mother that she will have to make room for a tiger and an elephant (just a small elephant). Had rather a rough time talking Rufus (that's the tiger) into coming stateside with me, but when he heard that you were such a nice, smiling little girl and that there were some lady tigers in the U.S., it changed his outlook entirely. He is all for becoming a citizen right away and settling down with us. The two of them will make nice playmates for you, and useful too. On cold nights the tiger can sleep at the bottom of your bed and keep you warm; and if there is ever anything you need to remember, like your mother's birthday, you can always tell it to the elephant because they never forget.

There is also a crusty old parrot with a lot of experience in the Navy who should make a good tutor and confidential advisor for you. He is a real "sea lawyer," has seen an awful lot of life in Navy ports and speaks a colorful language. Perhaps a little too colorful for your mother's taste, but of course your mother has lived a very sheltered life, and for the last four years has been out of the rain entirely.

Then we'll also have a monkey with a little red cap and satchel. If he's a smart one, we can train him to pick pockets and then I won't have to work at all but can stay at home and play with you and your mother and the tiger and the parrot and the monkey and the elephant.

Don't mention it to your mother, as I want to surprise her, but I will also bring home a couple of cute native girls with rings in their noses and grass skirts on their hips. She has always wanted a couple of helpers around the house, and in this way you and I can probably get out of washing the dishes. And for myself I will bring a little Philippine houseboy because I will need someone to keep my dress clothes in order so that I can take your mother out dancing every night.

For ordinary occasions like picnics and trips to the beach, I'll bring home a smart and shiny upholstered station wagon with white-walled tires. Marine General Holland Smith has a nice one that he would swap me for a few of my ideas on licking the Nips, but his license plate has only three stars on it and I am holding out for at least four. We'll want one that will really make an impression on the kids in the neighborhood.

So be a good girl until I come home with all my war trophies, and be sure to keep your mother well-humored. You'll find that a smile and a little Blarney will go a long way. But don't let her begin this business of saying, "I love you still," the way she does. That will put you at a disadvantage from the start.

Your Sea-Daddy

Griffith Couser

P. S. Don't breathe a word about those native girls.

Of course, at this time Jane was years away from being able to read. Dad was having a lot of fun here, imagining an idyllic home life after a hero's return—with a wife he missed hugely and a daughter he barely knew. He was also, I think, hinting at some of the temptations, dangers, and habits of military life that would require adjustment to a domestic regimen. (The only part of this vision that materialized was the station wagon, sans license plate stars, and that took years.) He gently ribbed Mum about her conditional expressions of love, "I love you *still*" (read: nevertheless). I find all of this very charming and affecting—a side of him I rarely saw as his son. This aspect of the letter reflects his confidence that the War will be won in the foreseeable future. He can begin to invest in a vision of a post-war family life that is domestic, but also somehow exotic, stocked with reminders of his far travels and adventures. Indeed, he imagines quite a complex ménage, not to say menagerie.

But the most unusual part of the letter is its mock-boastful rhetoric. On one level, this is clearly facetious. Dad knew he was only a small cog in a large war machine. At the same time, this letter hints, by exaggeration, at his real pride that he was about to assume a more significant role in the real business of the war. Hidden in the mock-heroic rhetoric is his pleasure in having been given a new role, such that after the War, as he said in a later letter, "I know I can look anyone in the face and say that I did my part, that have not avoided what other men have been called upon to do" (June 18, 1945). Evidently, his conscience *had* been bothering him; his new orders were a great relief.

So behind the whimsy, I find evidence that he was about to embark on a more adventurous kind of duty. And his replacement of Nimitz's name with MacArthur's may not be comic bravado but evidence that he knew he would be supporting an important invasion, that of Okinawa. He might still be in a service squadron, but he would be much closer to actual fighting. And, knowing that, he could imagine returning a hero (in his own mind) and enjoying a peace he had helped to bring about. I can sense here his feeling that he will have earned the pleasure of post-war family life.

But I do wonder what the censors made of this fantasy.

⁓

The specifics of his final months in the War have eluded my attempts at research. The last surviving letter was written on June 19th, only a day after the one I have just quoted. It offers some unusual glimpses of his where-abouts and duties. "Have I told you that we are part of [Admiral 'Bull'] Halsey's fleet or had you known it? One gets a kick out of working for a skipper who throws his weight around once in a while."

In any case, the shift from Servron 8 to Servron 10 was momentous. Initially, Pacific operations were conceived and planned at Pearl Harbor, thousands of miles from battle sites. In contrast, Servron 10 was based at Ulithi, an atoll in the Caroline Islands, due south of Japan and thousands of miles from Pearl. There Servron 10 created a naval base from scratch—a floating harbor from which the invasion of Okinawa was launched and man-aged. So the work of the service squadron was crucial to its success. Okina-wa was within the range of B-29 Superfortress bombers and large enough to accommodate the necessary airstrips; the taking of Okinawa was thought necessary to enable air raids on Japan. Dad's transfer to Ulithi put him quite close to the heart of the final assault on Japan.

It was his service at this time that earned Dad that Bronze Medal, as described in his citation: "For meritorious service while serving as operations officer on the staff of the commander Service Division 104 from 20 May 1945 to 15 August 1945. During this period he was charged with the impor-tant and complex task of rendering logistic support to combatant units during the capture and occupation of Okinawa."

In tracing Dad's service during the War, I have benefitted from letters his brother Jim wrote home to his wife Betty in August, September, and October of 1945 after Dad's correspondence lapsed or was lost. Jim's letters nicely complement Dad's, picking up where they leave off. Written in a very different tone—quite jocular—they are fascinating in their own right. For my purposes, though, their value lies in their reference to facts of Dad's Navy history not disclosed in his own letters. (This is largely a function of the easing of censorship in September, after the surrender.) First, Jim reports from Tokyo in August that "Grif is on a swell ship with very comfortable quarters. He's quite a big shot" (August 20). (This is modest of Jim, as he had actually commanded smaller vessels, such as patrol ships and mine-sweepers.)

In a later letter, he explains why Dad was still only a lieutenant:

> You wondered why Grif hadn't made Lt. Cmdr after doing such a good job out here—it seems he had never had a fitness report submitted out here. His last one was from Pearl Harbor where he had very little to do. Grif was on the *Hamul* which is a large destroyer tender. He works aboard but as part of the Admiral's [Halsey] Staff and not part of the ship's company. The Admiral and his staff are aboard only to direct ships under his activity, one of which is the *Hamul*. (September 13)

(At last a reference to a particular ship.) Jim seems to be saying that Dad missed out on promotion because, as a member of Halsey's staff rather than a member of the *Hamul*'s crew, he would not have been reviewed by the ship's captain for promotion.

In the spring of 1945, the *Hamul* was in Eniwetok, supporting the invasion of Iwo Jima; in late March, she sailed to Ulithi, where she serviced ships damaged in the battle of Okinawa—and apparently housed Halsey's staff. After Okinawa was conquered, she sailed there on May 10 and stayed until February, 1946. I believe Dad was aboard her during the battle of Okinawa. But if he was in Tokyo with Jim that summer, then he must have been transferred, with the rest of Halsey's staff, to another vessel, evidently the flagship, the battleship *Missouri*. Jim provides a useful accounting of the final period of Dad's service, which earned him that promotion to Lieutenant Commander at the end of the War, as well as his medal.

This crucial passage helps to fill, and possibly explain, a gap in Dad's letters. He stopped numbering letters in early April. Aside from that singular boastful letter to Jane, no more letters survive until June 18th. This gap, from early April to mid-June, coincides exactly with the 10-week duration of the Battle of Okinawa, the largest amphibious assault and the last major battle of the Pacific War, and the mostly costly in lives. At Okinawa the U. S. Navy experienced its greatest losses in its history: some thirty ships and some 5,000 men—not including the 3,000 Marines lost on land. Aboard ships, casualties were mostly caused by ferocious kamikaze attacks. Ashore, the death toll was high, too. As on Iwo Jima, the Japanese chose not to contest the landing; rather, they allowed the American troops to land and advance miles inland before they launched a devastating counterattack from a complex of caves and tunnels. One has only to read an account of this combat to appreciate the relative safety and security of those on ships, like Dad. The classic account is *With the Old Breed,* by a Marine, E.B. Sledge. A young man at the time of the invasion, Sledge did not produce his memoir until 1981, but he utilized detailed notes he had written immediately after the war, along with historical accounts. His account spares no detail of the horrific conditions. (Published to acclaim, it later served as the basis for an HBO miniseries, *The Pacific.*)

It is a terrible irony, however, that the development and application of the atomic bomb made this entire operation unnecessary, obviating the need for a costly, protracted amphibious invasion of Japan, which was to be launched from Okinawa. Dad's role in supporting this invasion, however peripheral, is the main basis of his pride in his wartime service. The one thing I remember Dad telling me about his naval service was that, although he was not in much danger himself, his duties involved assigning ships to battle patrols. Knowing men on many of the ships, he was acutely aware he had a hand in their fates.

Jim's letters also help to extend the narrative of Dad's service to the War's end. In August, the United States dropped atomic bombs on Hiroshima and Nagasaki; as intended, this precipitated Japan's surrender, announced on August 15, known henceforth as V-J (Victory in Japan) Day. So the War was over when Jim's letters were composed. In those of late August, he is very coy in writing about his duties. He can't tell Betty precisely what he's doing, but he suggests that he doesn't need to: "If you've heard the news these past few days, you may be able to guess what we've been involved in" (August 27). In fact, he had long suspected that he was going to be present at the formal surrender ceremonies. Despite this advance warning, Jim's departure for Tokyo—apparently from Okinawa—was quite sudden:

> We got underway very unexpectedly a few days ago and I didn't even have a change to say "So Long" to Grif. [The two of them had been seeing each other regularly for drinks or dinner, on one's ship or the other's.] He must have got the word we were leaving as he came charging along in a small boat after we were underway. At the time I was so busy it was impossible to do anything but wave. (August 27)

I find this gesture of fraternal loyalty quite remarkable, under the circumstances.

From there, Jim's ship and Dad's sailed to Japan where, reunited, they resumed visiting each other and had what Jim called "ringside seats" for the surrender ceremonies on September 2. (While Dad was on Halsey's staff, Jim's vessel was used as General MacArthur's communications office until a facility could be established on shore.) I certainly wish Dad had confided in me about all of this. I had no idea he'd been at the surrender, for example.

War matters, while interesting to me, account for only a fraction of the contents of the letters. Most letters have to do with keeping in touch with family and friends, and Mum had to serve as the conduit of news in both directions. And, of course, there are housekeeping details. But the letters' main focus is, as I've suggested at the outset, not on the battlefield but on the home front. The letters are a way of maintaining and deepening the relationship that sustained him and of incorporating himself, virtually, into the home from which he was physically absent. He projects an image of a carefree life at home after the War. He also inquires often, and comments on, Jane's development, sometimes vis à vis her slightly older cousin Judy.

> At the moment I am aglow with pride of my daughter—our daughter. She is lovely, Ann. The pictures were delightful. And how she has grown into the little girl age in the last month or so. Everyone seems to agree with my admiration of her. How sunny and blonde she looks, and are her eyes still blue? [Yes] There will be no containing my pride when I can be with you both again. (June 18, 1945)

He reminds Mum of moments shared at home: "While at work the other evening the radio was on. An orchestra suddenly broke into `Love Walked In.' If that happened to you, would you recall our musical breakfasts in Melrose?" (March 23, 1945) He attempts to express the tenor of his love for her, calling on Elizabeth Barrett Browning for help:

> Do you remember times of idle intimacy in our married life when you have laughed a bit at me for fun and said, "How do you love me?" And I was embarrassed and quite without words to answer you. Because I could not answer with real sincerity when cornered, so to speak. If I had had more of a sense of humor I would have given you some foolish answer.
> Asking that question, "How do I love you" of my own accord tonight, may I substitute for my own poor words, which never catch what I feel, the words of E. B. B. who asks the same question in one of the "Sonnets from the Portuguese." And answers it in many ways but let me give you just two lines:
> I love thee to the level of every day's
> Most quiet need, by sun and candle-light.
> That is it. In my great needs, of course, but in all my small and quiet needs, I love you. (March 8, 1945)

And, most lyrically, he projects his idealization of her (and Jane) onto the planetarium of the Pacific sky:

> In one of my earlier letters I mentioned how wonderful these Pacific skies are at night. Even without knowing their individual identity one cannot help but be aware of the stars. When last ashore I picked up a small manual with

some star charts and have spent evenings finding the constellations and naming the brighter stars. Right over my head in the early evening is the constella-
tion of Orion with two lovely stars, red Betelgeuse and blue Rigel. It is good to
see them here as they are stars of an earlier acquaintance which I have often
picked out over our own winter hills and fields.

[here he drew in the constellation]

One star near Orion had a particular attraction from the time I first observed it. Very near to it as if held close in the familiar orbit of the brighter star
is a tiny one, yet bright, positive and clear. Now this will sound like a ridicu-
lous sentiment to you but somehow without knowing how it happened I began
to think of these two stars as representing you and Jane. My chart, at least,
gives them no other names. At the further risk of your taking me to be a bit off
my cracker I could also tell you that I have an awareness of your personalities
in these stars, both as individuals and the joint personality of mother and child.
And also that in their nearness to each other and seeming intimacy with me,
they convey a strange sense of your presence. At their appearance each night
in the sky, it is as if I had myself come home, opened the door and there found
you and Jane.

I suppose it is all my subconscious longing to see you both that stirs up this
high fancy. But don't mistake that I am suffering from any melancholy or
homesickness. If that were the case, my imaginings would be much more
morbid. This one gives me the greatest of pleasure. (February 15, 1945)

Here again, his prose puts me in mind of Edgar's, as does his habit of
seeing the distant beloved in the proximate landscape—or sky.

~

Jane's birth, in June 1944, came a year before Dad's most intense involvement in the War; mine came in September 1946, thirteen months after
V-J Day. Between us, then, our births neatly bracket this period of his life.
And the evidence of the surviving letters is that in the midst of war he was
deeply invested in creating and nurturing life in a peaceful world. As inven-
tive as Jane's birth announcement may have been, mine was even more so.
Dated September 22, 1946, and printed on what appeared to be personal
stationery headed "Jane Leida Couser," it took the form of a confidential
letter from my sister to me:

Dear Brother Tom,

In all the stir and excitement of your arrival into the solar system and the
Couser family, I hope you will find time for this welcome from your sister
Jane. A stupid hospital rule forbids it or I would come in to greet you myself.
Daddy has told me wondrous tales about you, not all of it reliable, I'm afraid,
especially the trailing clouds of glory part. [an allusion to Wordsworth's "Ode:
Intimations of Immortality"]

Your father, incidentally, is that beaming, proudful man who has been
admiring you so earnestly through the hospital glass. Sometimes I think daddy
takes himself and the world too seriously, but we have very good times togeth-

er—best of all during the story time before bed, on trips to the zoo and at the beach. He has great expectations for you, of course. I don't think he will mind if you don't become President but he surely will expect you to be a future swimming champion. It is a great disappointment to him that I still sputter when water gets in my face. Daddy seems to think that his children should inherit a special kind of aquatic instinct like Polynesian babies and be able to swim from the day they are born.

There is no need for me to describe your mother to you. Daddy says that Mummy is a pearl among women and you will undoubtedly grow up adoring her in the same way. Though she says she doesn't, Mummy has a real talent for motherhood. She has read the best books on child study but has too much common sense to be entirely guided by them. One can bother her no end and still be "a good child." But there is one time to beware and that is when she says, "My dear, I love you still."

Like all parents, they are both susceptible to certain wiles. I can teach you some of the tricks, but of course many of mine, especially with Daddy, are strictly feminine technique. There will be times when they will miss the real wit of what you say and misinterpret your intent but on the whole they are very satisfactory as parents. Neither is the kissing type and though they take parenthood very seriously they try not to be intense about it.

Our "dulce decorum," as your father sometimes refers to it, is 90 Cottage Street in Melrose. I think you will find it a rather exciting place to live. There is a large yard, a stand-up-in playhouse, a sand-box, two swings, a fascinating cellar, a cricket in the terrace wall, a mouse, and Glassus. In spite of their efforts to find out, Glassus is still a secret from Daddy and Mummy, so be sure we are well out of ear-shot before you ask about him.

It will be more fun than ever when you are here, so do hurry. I can hardly wait to see you.

Affectionately,
Jane

Well, I hurried to our new home, and our life as a post-war family began.

∾

How I cherish this ghost-written letter, which I was to read only years later. What a wonderful welcome to the world—warm, funny, and wise. If I had to choose one document to memorialize my father, this would be it; it captures his pleasure in fatherhood in a remarkable feat of ventriloquism. I enjoy the paean to Mum. At the same time, I am struck by his self-awareness, which hints at future family tensions. From my current perspective, I see the bit about his taking the world too seriously as not just about his moral character but also as a hint of his depressiveness. (Perhaps it takes one to know one: the same could be said of me.) In the comment that he and Mum are not the "kissing type," he concedes, but defends, his tendency to avoid open displays of affection. Ours was a loving family, but the love was not always readily apparent. Finally, in the mention of his expectations for me, I sense future trouble. It wasn't so much that I failed to fulfill them—though I was never much of a swimmer—as that my fulfillment of them may have created conflicts neither of us fully acknowledged.

I was fortunate in the man who begot me.

He was not just my father but my parent—and a good one. But he was also a far more complicated man than I understood during his life time. I have come to know him well only since his death, in large part thanks to the documents he left behind for me to find.

Epilogue

Grief Interrupted

While my father's archive transformed my understanding of him, it shed little light on the mystery that left me, decades earlier, not only bereft but unable to mourn him properly: the matter of his late-life decline. So even after composing the preceding narrative, I felt stymied, my grief stifled. I remained in some sense at my point of origin, the primal scene of the memoir: my father's messy, sort-of suicide.

But I had not carefully scrutinized the sparsely documented first few years of his life. In doing so, I believe I have found the answer I'd long been seeking.

~

As I've noted earlier, his family's relocation from Ireland to the United States—though not a function of poverty—no doubt took an emotional toll on all its members.

But even before emigration tore my father away from his familiar surroundings and extensive family, he had suffered more significant losses. Ironically, the evidence of this was hidden in plain sight all along—in the family tree, which reveals that my father, whom I knew as the oldest of five siblings, had not been the first child born to his parents.

That child was a girl, Edith Muriel, born in 1903. Dad came next, in 1906. Two years later, a third child, Isaac, was born. But on the very day of Isaac's birth—August 2, 1908—Muriel, as she was known, died at age four. Only four weeks later, Isaac also died. So in a period of a single month, when he was only two, my father lost his only siblings, an older sister and a newborn brother. Moreover, his parents lost two children—one her mother's firstborn, the other his father's namesake. Knowing this, I suspect that the deep impetus for Isaac and Maria's transatlantic relocation was the desire to put an ocean between themselves and the graves of their two infants (which remain unmarked).

Presumably, Dad had no understanding of death at the age of two. But he must have registered the abrupt disappearance of his siblings, and his parents' grief would have marked those losses for him as well. Whatever his level of comprehension, the sudden loss of his two siblings would have utterly transformed his small world. (According to Muriel's brief death notice, "the deceased was well known and liked by the villagers with whom she came in contact.") When he was two, his older sister would have been an important companion; he must have looked up to her literally as well as figuratively.

As Maria's first child and daughter, Muriel would have been especially dear to her mother. Maria's grief must have been palpable to Dad when he, too, was feeling abandoned. But whereas she may have received support from her large family and consolation from her faith, Dad's emotional needs may have been neglected—especially by her. Distracted by grief, she may have withdrawn from him to protect herself against further hurt. He may have withdrawn from her as well, in response. Did he experience survivor's guilt? Did she unconsciously assign him blame for surviving? At the very least, the bond between them must have been complicated by this episode.

For me these losses answer the question that has haunted me since his death: how could such an accomplished man, with so much to live for, lapse into a terminal depression just when he should have been poised to retire in good health and a sense of pride? I believe that this threefold deprivation wounded Dad deeply—indeed, traumatically—but so early in his life as to make it difficult for him to reckon with it later. Giving birth to four more children may have compensated Maria somewhat for her losses. But her dour and distant demeanor when my sister and I knew her suggested lingering pain and sadness. We have no memory of comforting maternity with her, as we do with my mother's Dutch mother. In any case, I have come to think of grief interrupted as a leitmotif of three generations of Couser family history.

～

This episode casts a long shadow over Dad's life and has powerful explanatory force for its overall shape. It helps to account for his attraction to Lena, who was older and a mother, and for his extraordinary empathy toward his niece Judy when she lost her mother at a tender age. Moreover, it helps explain his tendency toward depression and thus his alcoholism. His oral consumption of gin, straight from the bottle, may have gratified a need he didn't understand and couldn't articulate. His pattern of drinking in bed and mixing gin with milk may have returned him to the scene of a primal loss.

The traces of his trauma were no doubt bound up with his relationship with me as well, in ways I could not fathom. As I've admitted, for reasons of my own I withdrew from him in high school; my discovery of his alcoholism exacerbated that emotional detachment. My letter of 1969 may have been so painful for him because of the way it recalled that distancing and inadvertently reconfirmed it. In any case, I have come to believe that the departure of two significant others from his household in the mid-1960s, when Jane and I went off to college (coincidentally, but suggestively, an older sister and a younger brother), echoed his early loss of his siblings and opened a deeply repressed, acutely painful psychic wound. This is, of course, speculation, but it has grown out of my long pains-taking reconstruction of his life.

～

With this in mind, I find fresh significance in my birth announcement—that sweet greeting purportedly written by my two-year-old sister—but actually ghost-written by Dad.

> Dear Brother Tom,
>   In all the stir and excitement of your arrival into the solar system and the Couser family, I hope you will find time for this welcome from your sister Jane. A stupid hospital rule forbids it or I would come in to greet you myself. Daddy has told me wondrous tales about you, not all of it reliable, I'm afraid, especially the trailing clouds of glory part.

I read it now as an uncanny (because unconscious) imaginative re-creation of the shattered family of my father's Irish childhood. This memoir is my belated response to his letter welcoming me to the world.

～

Ultimately, my slow, unsystematic excavation of my father's life using his archive has enabled me to see his life through his eyes, or at least through his words, to see him as others saw him, or at least as they addressed him. To truly know a parent means acknowledging that he or she is not just—and perhaps not mainly—your parent. That recognition has been an important part of the work of this memoir for me. But writing it has also enabled me to reconcile myself to his life's sad end. In my narrative, I like to think that I have in some sense "saved" his life, at last.

Notes

2. SUBURBAN LIFE

1. Franz Kafka, *Dearest Father.* Trans., Hannah and Richard Stokes. (Richmond, UK: Oneworld Classics: 2008), 18.

7. MILL TOWN LAD

1. Sharon O'Brien, *The Family Silver: A Memoir of Depression and Inheritance* (Chicago: University of Chicago Press, 2004), 80.

11. MANLY LOVE

1. I draw in this section on E. Anthony Rotundo, "Romantic Friendship: Male Intimacy and Middle-class Youth in the Northern United States, 1800-1900." *Journal of Social History*, 23, no. 1 (1989), 1-25.

13. GEORGE SAYLOR

1. George Chauncey, *Gay New York: Gender, Urban Culture, and the Making of the Gay Male World, 1890-1930* (New York: Basic Books, 1994), 12-13.
2. Ibid., 14.
3. Ibid., 119-20.
4. Ibid., 1.
5. Ibid., 3.
6. Ibid., 4.
7. Ibid., 301.

www.ingramcontent.com/pod-product-compliance
Lightning Source LLC
Chambersburg PA
CBHW070241290326
41929CB00046B/2313